PROFESSIONAL DEVELOPMENT
IN HIGHER EDUCATION

PROFESSIONAL DEVELOPMENT IN HIGHER EDUCATION

A Theoretical Framework for
Action Research

Ortrun Zuber-Skerritt

**KOGAN
PAGE**

First published in 1992

Apart from any fair dealing for the purposes of research or private study, or criticism of review, as permitted under the Copyright, Designs and Patents Act, 1988, this publication may only be reproduced, stored or transmitted, in any form or by any means, with the prior permission in writing of the publishers, or in the case of reprographic reproduction in accordance with the terms of licences issued by the Copyright Licensing Agency. Enquiries concerning reproduction outside those terms should be sent to the publishers at the undermentioned address:

Kogan Page Limited
120 Pentonville Road
London N1 9JN

© Ortrun Zuber-Skerritt

British Library Cataloguing in Publication Data
A CIP record for this book is available from the British Library

ISBN 0 7494 0740 9

Printed and bound in Great Britain by
Biddles Ltd, Guildford

Cover design represents Ortrun Zuber-Skerritt's concept of Action Research based on an integration of various theories from three major traditions: Dialectic epistemology; personal construct psychology and critical action theory. Design by Teresa Jablonski.

Contents

v

List of tables

List of figures

List of abbreviations

AAU	National Academic Audit Unit
AVCC	Australian Vice Chancellor's Committee
CALAR	Centre for Action Learning and Action Research
CALT	Centre for the Advancement of Learning and Teaching
CEO	Chief Executive Officer
CRASP	Critical attitude, Research into teaching, Accountability, Self-evaluation, Professionalism
CVCP	Committee of Vice Chancellors and Principals
DPA	Decision Preference Analysis
DPHE	Diploma in the Practice of Higher Education
ERASMUS	European Action Scheme for Mobility of University Students
ESRC	Economic and Social Research Council
EUT	Excellence in University Teaching
FAUSA	Federation of Australian University Staff Associations
HDZ	Hochschuldidaktisches Zentrum
HE	Higher Education
HERDSA	Higher Education Research and Development Society of Australia
MAS	School of Modern Asian Studies
MED	Management Education and Development

MID	Measurement of Intellectual Development
MPhil	Master of Philosophy
MSc	Master of Science
PD	Professional Development
PhD	Doctor of Philosophy
PVC	Pro-Vice Chancellor
SAFARI	Success and Failure and Recent Innovation
TARGET	Teaching Appraisal by Repertory Grid Technique
TEVAL	Teaching Evaluation
TOTE	Test-Operate-Test-Exit
UK	United Kingdom
USA	United States of America
USDTU	University Staff Development and Training Unit
VC	Vice Chancellor
VSC	Video Self-Confrontation

Acknowledgements

I wish to thank Griffith University for granting me study leave and the opportunity to write this book. I am also grateful to the staff of the Universities' Staff Development and Training Unit of the Committee of Vice-Chancellors and Principals (CVCP/USDTU) in Britain for their hospitality and professional support during my study leave.

I wish to acknowledge the Commonwealth's support for this project in the form of a small grant from the Australian Research Council.

I wish to acknowledge and thank Susan Jarvis for proofreading the manuscript; Terry Wood and Teresa Jablonski for desk-top publishing and compiling the indexes; and the editors of my previously published papers (1990a, 1990b, 1990c) for their kind permission to reproduce parts of the material in Chapters 2, 5 and 10 of this book.

Finally, I appreciate the understanding and moral support of my husband Alan and my son Carsten.

Ortrun Zuber-Skerritt, 1992

Foreword

It is conventionally held that even in times of violent social change, universities serve to propose explanations for what is happening, rather than contribute to the happenings themselves. The role we academics are thus presumed to have assumed is one of generators of theory *about* action rather than practitioners of theories *in* action. This apparent reluctance to mix it in the 'real' world has us confined to our ivory towers, proffering advice that can only be of academic interest.

As Ortrun Zuber-Skerritt demonstrates in this vital publication, these images are now ripe for challenge. Researchers are increasingly involved across a wide range of domains in higher education, in situations where they are as active in changing things as they are in explaining the nature of those changes. Indeed, as this book submits, action researchers are illustrating an important new academic praxis—the generation of theory *through* practice.

Dr Zuber-Skerritt's book skilfully integrates the propositional theories of action developled by a host of other researchers with theories that she is developing through her own actions. That these actions include work in commercial organisations and bureaucracies as well as in institutions of higher education illustrates the relevence of this book to an extremely broad audience.

As action research becomes increasingly recognised as a useful and popular mode of human inquiry for managing choice in the face of change, the worth of this seminal publication will become increasingly obvious.

Richard Bawden

Professor and Dean
Faculty of Agriculture and Rural Development
University of Western Sydney, Hawkesbury

Introduction

The purpose and aims of this book

Professional development in higher education has often been criticised for lacking a sound theoretical framework. The present book is an attempt to fill this gap by building a theoretical model that integrates theory and practice, educational research and teaching in higher education (HE).

All too often educational research has relied on the philosophical assumptions and methodologies of the natural sciences by applying them to the study of learning and teaching behaviours and outcomes. More recently, a new paradigm of research has emerged in education and higher education — and in fact in the human and social sciences in general — which seems more appropriate for the improvement of learning, teaching and professional development.

The purpose of this book is to contribute to the establishment of this alternative paradigm in HE research and development. The aims are to explain how students and teachers in higher education come to know, and why experiential learning and collaborative enquiry are more effective for their continuing education or professional development than the mere technical application of theory to their learning or teaching practice.

To this end, the book explains the differences between the traditional and the alternative paradigms, their different epistemological assumptions and theories of learning, researching and teaching. The book also builds on certain aspects of various existing theories in order to develop an alternative model of learning, teaching and professional development in higher education.

1

Table 1 *The CRASP model of action research*

Action research is:

Critical (and self-critical) collaborative enquiry by
Reflective practitioners being
Accountable and making the results of their enquiry public,
Self-evaluating their practice and engaged in
Participative problem-solving and continuing professional development.

This model does not represent a 'grand' theory which would explain, predict and provide control over all aspects of higher education. Rather, it provides a theoretical framework, or meta-theory, which is developed by integrating various aspects of previously unrelated theories of learning with 'grounded' theories. These 'grounded' theories (Glaser and Strauss, 1967) are based on case studies and critical reflections of action researchers in one particular educational setting. Readers will then have to work out for themselves how the insights gained from this book may apply to their own situations and educational contexts.

The CRASP model

This model integrates educational theory and teaching practice through action research, which I define in the companion book (Zuber-Skerritt, 1992) as the acronym CRASP (see Table 1).

The two books are inter-related publications in that they are linked by the CRASP model. This model has been used for the case studies in the first book, entitled *Action Research in Higher Education — Examples and Reflections* (1991b), and it is explained in more detail at the theoretical level in the present volume. Thus, while the two books are perceived as a coherent whole, some people might only be interested in practical applications or theories of higher education improvement and therefore may wish to read only the first or the second volume.

Audience

Both books are aimed at an audience in higher education which consists mainly of educational researchers, staff developers or professional consultants, academics, administrators, counsellors and students who are interested in action research. However, the present volume is also of interest to anyone in industry and government who is seeking a theoretical base for improving their practice of learning, teaching, training and/or professional development through action research.

The companion book presents a series of case studies in developing student learning skills at the undergraduate and postgraduate levels as well as in professional development of teaching staff in higher education. These case studies demonstrate how teams of academics — in collaboration with their staff development colleagues — have:

- improved the practice of learning, teaching and professional development;
- advanced knowledge in higher education by generating 'grounded theory', research and publications; and
- documented excellent teaching.

The present book provides a theoretical and methodological framework for the practice of learning, teaching and professional development. It develops a model of higher education which is located in the alternative, non-positivist paradigm, based on theories of learning and knowing such as Reg Revans' Action Learning; Kurt Lewin's Action Research; Kolb's Experiential Learning; Kelly's Personal Construct Theory; Leontiev's Action Theory within Russian Critical Psychology; and Carr and Kemmis' Critical Education Science based on the Frankfurt School of Critical Theory.

The result is a model of professional development for teachers in higher education, again called CRASP, an acronym for *Critical* attitude, *Research* into teaching, *Accountability*, and *Self-Evaluation*, leading to *Professionalism*. However, this model and the theoretical framework developed in this book should not only be of interest to staff developers and teachers in higher education, but also to anyone engaged in the development of people and organisations in general.

The gap between educational theory and practice

There exists a vast amount of research literature on student learning and teaching methods, but educational theory has had relatively little impact on the practice of learning and teaching in higher education. Unlike secondary school teachers, most teachers in higher education — especially in universities — have not had any professional preparation or training for teaching. They normally do not read books or journals on higher education, because the issues raised and the discourse used (e.g. the terminology and jargon used in educational psychology) seem unfamiliar, alien, pretentious and irrelevant to their concerns. As Lucas (1990, 67) testifies:

3

Based on my experience in workshops I have conducted for department chairs and faculty at more than sixty college campuses over the past three years, most faculty are not familiar with this literature [i.e. the literature on adult learning and motivation or teaching pedagogy].

Frequently their first priority is research in their own disciplines, rather than teaching, because they see themselves as having more expertise, interest, time, tools, and rewards (in terms of tenure and promotion) for research than for developing their teaching (Seldin, 1985). So in general there is little incentive on the part of academics to spend more time and effort on improving their teaching than is absolutely necessary.

Recent pressures on teaching staff from students and governments have caused a crisis in higher education. As has been reported in the daily press and professional newsletters, students have demanded that institutions adapt their curricula, teaching and assessment methods to the changing needs of society and of students; meanwhile, funding bodies have demanded greater accountability and effectiveness in terms of costs, resources and the quality and relevance of teaching and research in higher education.

There have been national enquiries in response to these demands. For example, various reports and recommendations on staff development in higher education in Australia have included the Williams Report (1979); the AVCC Report by the Working Party on Staff Development (1981); Dawkin's White Paper (1989) and the Aulich Report (1990). In Britain there has been the Jarratt Report (1985); the CVCP Code of Practice on Academic Staff Training (1987); and the Universities' responses (Brown, 1989). In New Zealand the recent history of higher education has been shaped by the Hawke Report in 1988 and *Learning for Life: Two* in 1989 (Jones, 1991). In the United States, too, improving the quality of teaching has become a central issue, as reflected in the theme of the AAHE (American Association of Higher Education) for the past six years. But there have been criticisms of higher education as well (National Institute of Education, 1984; Newman, 1985; Boyer, 1987; Clark, 1987; Hirsch, 1987; Bloom, 1987). Rice and Austin (1987) indicate in their Council of Independent Colleges report that faculty morale is highest in institutions in which teaching and scholarship rather than research and publication are more highly valued.

Some critics say that nothing or little has changed and that progressive movements in higher education have failed in practice. When speculating on the reaction of many academics who are hostile and critical of the recommended changes, one might wonder whether some might feel threatened, some might resist change, or some might not know how to change; others might be ignorant of these developments. However, we do know that some changes have occurred. There are academics who have changed their approach and academics who want to improve their teaching. But it is not sufficient to require change and to offer recipes or cookbooks for alternative behaviour and strategies. What is needed is research into the processes of change in human attitude and behaviour.

My research and that of others suggests that it is not a question of knowing the ideal state of good teaching practice (and of following prescriptions of good practice), but that the problem is one of changing and improving the current practice of teaching in particular areas.

This book will argue that alternative patterns have to be explained and understood in theory, analysis and strategy, through self-discovery and personal involvement. This understanding of the changes in the theory of the self, of others, or of the world around us is more likely to be achieved at a reflexive learning level than at a mechanical, unself-conscious level.

The structure and content of the book

The book is structured in four main parts: the praxis in higher education (Part 1); the theory in higher education (Part 2); the integration of theory and practice (Part 3); and professional development in higher education (Part 4) (see the flowchart in Figure 1).

In trying to improve the practice of HE learning and teaching, one is exploring and experimenting with different techniques and approaches; but simultaneously, one is attempting to develop frameworks within which those more desirable practices are articulated and justified. This book demonstrates some of this dialectic of the development of theory and practice itself.

Part 1 provides the background for the theoretical framework of action research: first, by discussing the notion of practical reasoning, with reference to the development of my practice, initially at the specific level of cases (Chapter 1) related to the case studies in the companion book entitled *Action Research in Higher Education* (Zuber-Skerritt, 1992); and second, by discussing some basic assumptions about the connection between theory and practice which is perceived as a dialectical relationship rather than a dichotomy (Chapter 2).

Part 2 presents some of the theoretical bases of my views (Chapters 3–5), that is, developments in theories of knowledge, learning and teaching, or aspects thereof, which support an emerging

5

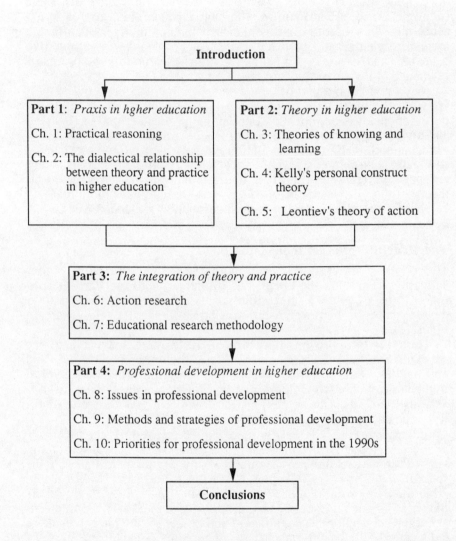

Figure 1   *The structure of this book*

view of improving learning and teaching in higher education, and which provide the foundation for the structure of my model of staff development and student learning, as developed in this book.

Starting with a discussion of behaviourist and cognitive theories of knowing and learning, which have advanced the theory of higher education but had little impact on its practice, I introduce the notion of holistic theories for the practical improvement of learning and teaching (Chapter 3).

While the first two theories are concerned with parts of the learner's system (e.g. behaviour, memory), the holistic theories consider the phenomenon of learning in the person as a whole. The other two chapters in this part discuss the learner as a personal scientist, based on Kelly's personal construct theory (Chapter 4) and the learner as an active, conscious agent in the learning process, based on cognitive and materialistic theories of action (Chapter 5). The learner may be:

1. a student developing his/her knowledge and learning skills;
2. an academic developing his/her professional knowledge and skills as a teacher; or
3. a staff developer trying to learn how to facilitate staff development and to assist academics in improving their professional competence as teachers.

Thus it is possible to develop a model of student learning, a model of academic activities and a model of staff development, all based on the above theories (see also Chapter 5).

Part 3 demonstrates the dialectical relationship between theory and practice in the discussion of action research, educational research methodology, and change and innovation in higher education. It discusses various ways in which educational problems can be researched by the academics themselves, in collaboration with their staff development colleagues, with the aim of improving learning and teaching in higher education.

Chapter 6 presents one of these possibilities: action research which has been applied to teacher training and in-service training in primary, secondary and further and technical education in the past, but rarely to higher education in a systematic way. Based on Lewin's (1952) and Kolb's (1984) models of experiential learning, and on Carr and Kemmis' (1986) action research as critical education science, I have developed the CRASP model of action research in higher education.

Chapter 7 explains the research paradigm which has guided my research and the research methods and techniques which I have used within this paradigm, in particular the case study methodology and the repertory grid technology.

Part 4 builds on the previous three parts by selectively discussing those issues, methods and strategies in professional development which are relevant to the theoretical framework and methodology generally, and particularly to the action research model developed in this book.

Chapter 8 discusses theories and practices of innovation and change which are pertinent to the improvement of learning and teaching (and particularly to professional development) in higher education. These are Argyris' theory-of-action (a personal model), Berg and Östergren's theory of innovation (a social model) and MacIntyre's dialectical approach (an interactionist model). Other issues are the role of professional consultants and models, focuses and policies for professional development.

Chapter 9 presents selected examples of methods and strategies in professional development which I have found appropriate and useful within the newly emerging paradigm of higher education research and development. This means professional development through:

- discussions in seminars and workshops;
- the Excellence in University Teaching Programme;
- distance education;
- peer consultancy;
- appraisal and self-appraisal;
- curriculum development;
- organisational development; and
- the development of professional consultants.

Chapter 10 as the final chapter looks into the future by discussing priorities for professional development in the 1990s. It argues that we in higher education have to develop alternative approaches, theories and methodologies, social technologies and strategies to develop, train and prepare students and staff for adapting to the rapid social, economic and technological changes of the future. Research and development in higher education will have to be focused — more than ever before — on change and innovation, new managerial and teaching/training competencies, action learning and action research, as well as assisting the university in:

- maintaining and constantly improving high quality teaching and research;
- meeting internal and external accountability;
- management development and training; and
- forging closer links with industry.

Conclusion

My conclusions in this book at the theoretical level are congruent with those arrived at independently at the practical level by my colleagues at Griffith University who participated in the action research projects discussed in the case studies in the companion book. That is, our conclusions are that *action research is the most effective method of professional development and of improving student skills in learning and researching.*

The last chapter in the companion book confirms these conclusions and it represents the link between the case studies in that book, *Action Research in Higher Education* (Zuber-Skerritt, 1992), and the theoretical framework for action research developed in this book.

Part 1

Praxis in higher education

The companion book, *Action Research in Higher Education* (Zuber-Skerritt, 1992) presents case studies of developments in learning and teaching at both the undergraduate and postgraduate levels, together with reflections on these case studies. This part is a brief discussion of praxis in higher education. Praxis is defined as reflective practice informed by theory.

The first introductory chapter is a brief outline of Schwab's (1969) distinction between technical and practical reasoning, with references to my case studies in the companion book on the one hand and to principles in the theoretical framework developed in this book on the other.

Chapter 2 is a discussion of the relationship between theory and practice perceived as dialectical rather than dichotomous. In other words, practice in higher education is not seen as non-theoretical, but as being informed by educational and personal theories; and educational theory is not considered to be non-practical, but rather as useful for the improvement of practice in higher education, if it is 'grounded' in practice. Both theory and practice are perceived as two sides of a coin handled by the active, 'reflective practitioner' as 'the personal scientist' and the 'critical education scientist' (explained in Part 2).

Part 1 therefore prepares the ground for Parts 2 and 3 (i.e. for those theories in higher education which integrate theory and practice, research and learning/teaching, reflection and concrete experience).

Chapter 1

Practical reasoning

Introduction

While it is common in any discipline to distinguish between two departments, that which deals with the principles or methods of the particular discipline (theory) and that which applies them (practice), this dichotomy in itself is problematic. Practice in higher education usually means the application of educational theory, but it may also be understood as the exercise of the teaching profession in higher education; the whole action or process of learning, teaching, and staff development; or the skills gained from this process and experience.

This book takes an integrated approach to theory and practice (i.e. to educational research and the practice of learning and teaching). It adopts a metatheoretical perspective on higher education concerning alternative modes of theorising, not only about the theory of higher education, but also about the practice and the relationship between theory and practice.

In this chapter I introduce Schwab's (1969) notion of technical and practical reasoning and its relevance to higher education. I then discuss a specific case of 'praxis' in higher education in relation to some theories and principles of learning and knowing (referred to in brackets and italics) which will be explained in more detail in subsequent chapters.

Technical and practical reasoning

Schwab (1969, 98) in his well-known paper 'The practical: a language for curriculum' distinguishes between the theoretic and the practical in curriculum, drawing upon Aristotle's distinction between technical and practical thinking or reasoning:

> By the 'practical' I do not mean the curbstone practicality of the mediocre administrator and the man on the street, for whom the practical means the easily achieved, familiar goals which can be reached by familiar means. I refer, rather, to a complex discipline, relatively unfamiliar to the academic and differing radically from the disciplines of the theoretic. It is the discipline concerned with choice and action, in contrast with the theoretic, which is concerned with knowledge.

Schwab (1969, 98) argues that the field of curriculum:

(a) is moribund because of its inveterate and unquestioned reliance on theory which is either inappropriate or inadequate to the tasks of solving the problems it was designed to attack;

(b) is in a crisis which is evident in the flight of its practitioners from the subject of the field; and

(c) can only be regenerated... if the bulk of curriculum energies are diverted from the theoretic to the practical, to the quasi-practical and to the eclectic. By 'eclectic' I mean the arts by which unsystematic, uneasy, but usable focus on a body of problems is effected among diverse theories, each relevant to the problems in a different way.

Schwab's advocacy of the practical in education is not totally new. As Kemmis and Fitzclarence (1986) point out, it is a call for a return to an old, venerable and still-living tradition of educational thought and action, in which the 'arts of the practical' (i.e. the arts of moral and political arguments) are more central to thinking about education than they are in the new 'progressive' natural science movement in education which arose towards the end of the last century and developed throughout this century.

Aristotle had already ranked practical above technical reasoning. Technical reason and action are guided by established theories, by following and applying rules, by employing means to attain given ends, and by evaluating the efficiency and effectiveness in those instrumental means–ends terms. In contrast, practical reason and action are essentially risky; they are guided by general and sometimes conflicting moral ideas about the good of humankind; and they involve wise judgement and moral decisions which to Aristotle were the main requirements for politicians and leaders of the state.

For higher education, this means that good teaching cannot be reduced to the technical application of educational theories, principles and rules, but that it involves not only constant practical judgement and decisions about alternative strategies to achieve given objectives, but also competitions and conflicts about which objectives and what kind of objectives should be pursued at any particular time. Practical reasoning requires the arts of wisdom and responsibility.

What are the requirements of the 'practical arts' and how can they be developed? Schwab (1969) describes four facets of the practical arts. The first begins with the requirement that existing institutions and practices must be altered piecemeal in small progressions, rather than being dismantled and replaced, so that the functioning of the whole remains coherent. This change, in turn, requires knowledge of the particular educational context, that is, empirical studies of educational action and reaction; new methods of empirical investigation, and a new class of educational researchers. A second facet of the practical is that it starts directly and deliberately from the diagnosis of problems and difficulties of the particular curriculum, not from aspirations imposed from outside the field. A third facet of the practical requires 'the anticipatory generation of alternatives' instead of waiting for the emergence of the problem itself. This means developing alternative solutions to identified curriculum problems. Finally, the practical requires a method of deliberation, a sensitive and sophisticated assessment of the behaviours, misbehaviours and non-behaviours of students.

To Schwab, a commitment to practical deliberation concretely means the establishment of new forums of communication for practical research in the field of curriculum (e.g. new journals, new forms of staff development and new kinds of research). Stenhouse (1975) takes Schwab's notion a stage further by giving examples of how to establish this new research tradition. His 'extended professionals' are individual teachers-as-researchers who take responsibility for appropriating curriculum research and development and for testing their theories in their own teaching practice. Kemmis and Fitzclarence (1986, 51) extend this notion of the profession as a source of critique of practitioners' own theory and practice by suggesting that the profession become an organised source of critique of institutionalised education and of the state's role in education:

> Moreover, critical curriculum theorising does not leave theorising to experts outside the schools, nor does it constrain curriculum theorising to the work of individual teachers and groups of teachers within schools; it offers forms of collaborative work by which teachers and other educationists across institutions can begin to form critical views of education which can challenge the educational assumptions and activities of the state, not only in theory (through having critical ideas) but also in practice (by

establishing forms of organisations which aim to change education — a practical politics of education).

The notion of practitioners as researchers is discussed in more detail in the companion book, and exemplified by the case studies there. In particular, the case in Chapter 6 of *Action Research in Higher Education* (Zuber-Skerritt, 1992) is an example of practical deliberation and critical curriculum theorising — or in other words, an example of praxis in higher education.

The case of praxis in higher education

In the remainder of this chapter, an attempt is made to explain the above case in terms of the main theories presented in the subsequent chapters of this present book. The aim is to show the relevance of these theories to practical and emancipatory action research for change and development in higher education. To begin with, the following is a brief summary of the case under consideration for the benefit of those who have not read, or who need to be reminded of the content of, the companion book.

The case is me, a senior consultant in higher education working with teaching staff in the School of Modern Asian Studies (MAS) at Griffith University on action research projects on developing student learning and researching skills. The first cycle in the action research spiral consists of:

*   *planning* strategies for helping undergraduate students become reflective, autonomous learners;
*   *acting* (i.e. implementing the strategic plan);
*   *observing* and evaluating the action using a variety of methods; and
*   *reflecting* on the results of the evaluation individually and as a team, in discussions and publications, leading to the identification of new areas of concern and further action research.

The second cycle in this case consists of similar activities and processes for helping Master by Coursework students learn how to develop their dissertation research and writing skills; and the third cycle focuses on action research into developing Honours students' research competencies, awareness of research paradigms and awareness of research effectiveness. Figure 2 (reprinted from the companion book) represents the three stages in the case with reference to publications arising from each cycle in the action research spiral.

The case can now be discussed in relation to the main theories included in this book, namely Kelly's (1955; 1963) personal construct

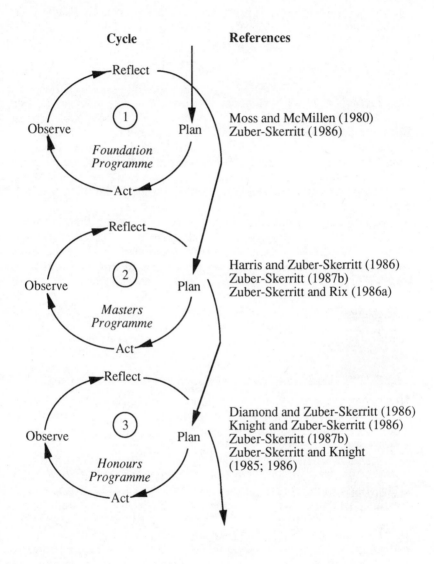

Figure 2   *The spiral of action research into developing student learning skills*

theory (Chapter 4), Leontiev's (1977) theory of action (Chapter 5), critical education science (Chapter 6) and the CRASP model (also Chapter 6).

The case in relation to Kelly's theory

Those people involved in the case were the convenors of the courses, the teaching teams, the students and myself as a teacher as well as an educational adviser. Each cycle has shown how each group of participants came to know and learn: students learnt to discover the processes of their learning and how they might influence them; staff learnt to discover the problems in their practice with students and how to alleviate them; I learnt to discern the processes by which students, staff and I might influence our own learning, understanding and any educational constraints.

All of us experienced Kelly's theory in this case: that we need not merely accept and apply theories, rules and principles to our tasks (of studying, teaching, administration) in a technical manner, but that we are 'personal scientists' *(capable of construing our own and others' experiences, of hypothesising, testing our hypotheses, and of anticipating and predicting future events which again have to be tested and submitted to critical reflection and self-reflection).* Kelly's repertory grid technique designed to elicit personal constructs and theories is explained in Chapter 7 of this book and applied in the case studies of Chapters 4 and 5 in the companion book.

The case in relation to Leontiev's theory

In Chapter 5 the implications of Leontiev's theory for higher education in general will be discussed. With reference to this particular case, Leontiev's subject–action–object model may be adapted as shown in Figure 3.

The 'action' in this case consists of the course review activities as action research (i.e. as the spiral of three cycles of planning, acting, observing and reflecting). The 'subject' in control of the action is the teaching staff themselves, in collaboration with the students in MAS and staff in the Centre for the Advancement of Learning and Teaching (CALT), all of whom have an influence on the 'object' (i.e. the outcomes of the reviews — the revised courses) and on changes made to the educational context in order to reduce those constraints which impede meaningful learning (e.g. changes to the tutorial system). These outcomes and changes, in turn, will have an impact on course reviews in MAS generally and specifically in these three courses, where the revised courses will be the starting point for any future review (i.e. for the next cycles of action research).

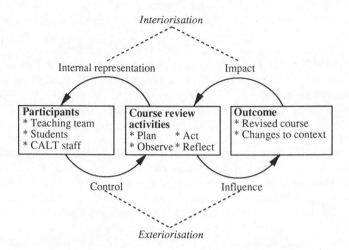

Figure 3   *The case of course reviews as action research (after Leontiev, 1977)*

The participants in this case have also been affected by the review activities. The interiorisation (and learning) process of the reflection of the action on the participants as personal scientists will be discussed in Chapter 5. It is important to note that the agents in this case are not only the representatives of the institution (e.g. the committees in Griffith University's course approval system and CALT), but all those who will be affected by the outcome of the action and subsequent decisions. Therefore, it is important that educational action research includes the perspectives of students as well as of teaching staff and that it is not conducted by outside researchers, but by the teachers themselves. The role of CALT staff is that of facilitators and critical friends who constantly remind the team of the institutional goals and constraints, even if these may be challenged by the participants. For an institution is not static, but dynamically changed in the process of critical debate by its members. Staff and students are not only shaped *by* the institution; they also *shape* the institution.

The case in relation to critical education science

I consider the third cycle in the action research of this case (see Figure 2), namely developing research skills in the MAS Honours Programme, as most successful and as 'emancipatory action research', because it fulfilled Carr and Kemmis' (1986, 127–8) five 'requirements that any approach to educational theory and research needs to accept'. First, knowledge was actively created, rather than being regarded as objective and as having a purely instrumental value; and educational issues were solved in theory *and* practice, rather than being seen as technical in nature *(rejection of positivist notions of rationality, objectivity and truth)*. Second, this action research was grounded in the interpretations of the teaching staff *(employing the interpretive categories of teachers)* and led to the teachers' consciousness which shaped their practice *(reality)*. Third, the practice in this course which had originally distorted teachers' consciousness of their ideological beliefs was critically examined, self-critically reflected and reviewed *(overcoming distorted self-understanding)*. Fourth, teachers recognised that some of the aims they were pursuing (or not pursuing) were not so much the result of conscious choice as of the constraints contained in the educational context *(identifying and overcoming those aspects of the existing social order which frustrate the pursuit of rational goals)*. Fifth, the teachers and I recognised through our publications that educational theory is practical *(in the sense that the question of its truth will be determined by the ways in which it relates to practice)* and that it must be oriented towards transforming the ways in which teachers see themselves and towards transforming the situations which hinder desirable educational goals to be achieved. Thus the results of action research in this case may be considered as critical education science.

The case in relation to the CRASP model

The CRASP model has already been mentioned in the introduction to this book and will be further explained in relation to higher education generally in Chapter 6. The specific case study of developments in learning and teaching confirmed the assumption of the model that action research by the academics themselves into their curriculum and into student learning had a direct and positive impact on their own teaching and professional development. Table 2 is a brief specification of each of the five requirements of action research in higher education using examples from the case.

Critical Attitude. The early examples of course evaluation in MAS (summarised in Figure 8 in Chapter 6 in the companion book) were not conducive to developing a critical attitude. The institution had an ideal model of what teaching should entail and tried to request staff to comply with that norm. However, the convenor and teaching team of course X were critical of the Education Committee's 'high-handed edict'. The other teams in cycles 1–3 of the case were critical of the status quo situation in which students were required to display

Table 2 *The case in relation to the CRASP model*

C	Critical attitude	Critique of status quo in practice and context.
R	Research into teaching	Identifying and solving problems in the curriculum and student learning through a spiral of action research cycles (plan–act–observe–reflect).
A	Accountability	Intrinsic and extrinsic: justifying the academic value of practice and publishing the theories and practices of the work and situation.
S	Self-evaluation	Self-reflection and self-evaluation as part of the teachers' research into their own teaching, inviting students and others to provide critical comments.
P	Professionalism	Professional development through action research; professionalism encompassing the above four requirements.

certain skills which were assessed but not taught. As a result, they were motivated to improve this situation by:

Research into Teaching. The teaching teams *planned* the strategic action (i.e. course reviews; workshops on student learning and research skills); they *acted* (conducted the reviews and workshops); *observed* the action and invited feedback from students and other participants; and they *reflected* on the observation data. As a result, they produced a report/paper. Apart from intrinsic satisfaction, this served as:

Accountability. There are three kinds of accountability, depending on whether the request comes externally from a government body, or internally from the institutional administration, or whether it is intrinsically valued by the staff as continuing self-evaluation. The early examples of course evaluation in which the data was collected by CALT staff were often concerned with accountability to the institution (and the teaching academics often paid mere lip service to the changes), rather than with a justification of the academic value of the course. In this case study, the teaching staff of course X, of the Foundation Course, the Masters and the Honours programmes were personally interested in and felt responsible for justifying the academic value of the course/component they were developing. The issue of accountability as bureaucratic accountability versus the justification of a programme/course is related to the issue of evaluation versus self-evaluation.

Self-evaluation. Justifying one's practice also means anticipating critique from others. This necessitates self critique, rigorous self-evaluation and self-reflection, all of which were practised in this case.

Professional Development. The above four requirements lead to professional development. Professional teachers in higher education are not expected to take and carry out orders from above in a technical manner, but to be *critical* in their examination of the implications for educational practices and conditions and to challenge the order if necessary. Professionals feel responsible for their actions and therefore *research* and revise their practice constantly so that they can justify it as intrinsic *accountability* after self-reflection and *self-evaluation*. The convenors and the teaching teams in this case have fulfilled the requirements of true *professionalism*.

Conclusion

This chapter has argued for a need for practical reasoning in higher education, involving choice, practical judgement and decisions, moral and political arguments, and the arts of wisdom and responsibility.

With reference to the case studies in the companion book, and foreshadowing the main theories in subsequent chapters of this book, I have reflected on a case of practical reasoning and 'praxis' in relation to Kelly's personal construct theory, Leontiev's action theory, critical education science, and the CRASP model. I have concluded that the action researchers in this case were personal scientists, shaped by and shaping the institution, and having fulfilled the requirements of emancipatory action research, of critical education science and of the CRASP model.

The next chapter argues that this critical, enquiring, professional attitude is necessary so that people are not only products (and victims) of their social environment, but also at the same time active producers of their own situations and work conditions. Finally, the chapter argues that theory and practice are not mutually exclusive, but dialectically related.

Chapter 2

The dialectical relationship between theory and practice in higher education

Introduction

Practice does not occur in a vacuum. It depends on the historical, social, political, economic and ideological context in which it takes place. The practice of learning and teaching in higher education equally depends on the whole educational context. Any attempts to improve learning and teaching must, therefore, take these issues into consideration.

Unlike structuralists, system theorists and functionalists, who view institutions as being governed by a static system of social relations which can be analysed and controlled to maintain the status quo, this book is based on different assumptions. It is based on action theory, the theory that human beings are 'knowledgeable and capable agents' (Giddens, 1982) whose creative actions are both bounded *and* enabled by the rules and resources or structures of the institution in which they work. Marx (1951, 225) argues that human agents both construct their social world and are in turn conditioned by it:

> ... men [sic!] make their own history, but they do not make it just as they please; they do not make it under circumstances chosen by

themselves, but under circumstances directly encountered, given and transmitted from the past.

This view of social transformation as an ongoing process has certain implications for higher education. It implies the importance of human responsibility in the non-functionalist, dialectical interaction between human agency and social constraints; it means a relative autonomy from institutional structures and, conversely, a relative dependence on those structures; it also implies the active participation of staff and students in the process of learning and teaching. Therefore, an action approach to higher education recognises, as Harmon (1981, 4) does, that:

> ... people are by nature active rather than passive, and social rather than atomistic. This means that people have a measure of autonomy in determining their actions, which are at the same time bound up in a social context.

In this interaction between human agency and the constraints of social structure, the human agents are not seen as automatons to be regulated by the system in a mechanistic way, but as having personal knowledge, values and attitudes and as being able to change and transform societies and organisations. For higher education, this means that staff and students are not totally subordinated to the rules and structures of their institution, but are able to bring about change. However, as Watkins (1985, 7-8) points out, they must first develop a suitable conceptual vision of the change as well as a sound knowledge of the existing conditions. Moreover,

> ... educational administrators should not only be aware of the dialectic interaction between actors and social structures but also be prepared to critique and reflect on the theoretical assumptions upon which present organisational structures are based. By placing theory and practice together as a totality of critique and reflection, educational administrators can avoid the one-dimensional stance that is the result of a solely technical view of education. The relationship of theory to practice is of essential importance in the comprehension of educational or any other organisations.

This relationship of theory to practice is discussed in more detail below.

Theory and practice

It has generally been assumed in industrial and post-industrial societies that theories are developed by theoreticians and applied by

The dialectical relationship between theory and practice

practitioners. With increasing specialisation and division of labour, there has been an acceptance of, and reliance on, technology and its application by technicians. For higher education, this means that the role of educational researchers has been to pursue truth, as in other disciplines, and to develop educational theories which can then be taken for granted and applied by academics to their teaching practice in a rather technical manner without much questioning or challenging of the researchers' assumptions or methods. Seen in this way, lecturers would adopt 'lecturing techniques' in order to improve their teaching and presentations. Similarly, students would adopt 'study techniques' to improve their learning. And both staff and students would use educational theory as educational 'technology' which might solve some superficial problems through the development of technical skills, but which could not solve more complex, existential problems at a very specific level. I shall argue in this section that the common assumptions made about theory and practice as two distinct and separate entities, about theory as being non-practical, and practice as being non-theoretical, are totally misguided. Instead, I take a view of theory and practice along the lines of Carr and Kemmis' (1986, 112–13) definition:

... the notion of 'theory' can be used in various ways. It can, for example, be used to refer to the products of theoretical enquiries like psychology or sociology and, when used in this way, it is usually presented in the form of general laws, causal explanations, and the like. On the other hand, it can refer to the general theoretical framework that structures the activities through which these theories are produced. Used in this sense, it denotes the underlying 'paradigm' in terms of which a particular theoretical enterprise is practised... 'theories' arise out of activities...

Now just as all theories are the product of some practical activity, so all practical activities are guided by some theory...

A 'practice', then, is not some kind of thoughtless behaviour which exists separately from 'theory' and to which theory can be 'applied'. Furthermore, all practices, like all observations, have 'theory' embedded in them and this is just as true for the practice of 'theoretical' pursuits as it is for those of 'practical' pursuits like teaching.

The first kind of theory may be referred to as 'grand theory', the second as 'grounded theory' (i.e. theory grounded in practice). This book is concerned with the latter, because learning, teaching and staff development in higher education are not purely theoretical and not purely practical activities; they are both, so the purpose of research and the research problems to be solved in higher education should therefore be practical as well as theoretical. Carr (1980) points out that to talk about 'the gap between theory and practice' and closing or bridging the gap is to misconstrue the relationship between theory and practice as a dichotomy. Rather, Carr (1980, 66) considers it to be a transformative relationship in which:

... theory transforms practice by transforming the ways in which practice is experienced and understood. The transition is not, therefore, from theory to practice as such, but rather from irrationality to rationality, from ignorance and habit to knowledge and reflection.

Reflective practitioners in higher education

Teachers in higher education come to know and theorise through knowing-in-action and reflecting on their practice. Schön (1983) refers to the 'reflective practitioners' who examine, reformulate and test their tacit knowledge and understandings of their practice. This tacit knowledge is embedded in practice. When trying to make sense of a practical problem, Schön's (1983, 50) reflective practitioner 'also reflects on the understandings which have been implicit in his [sic!] action, understandings which he surfaces, criticizes, restructures, and embodies in further action'. However, Smyth (1987) goes beyond Schön's reflective practitioners and develops a 'rationale for teachers' critical pedagogy'. Reflection *per se* is not sufficient; it has to be coupled with a self-critical and critical perspective of the teaching practice and its wider context.

The general purpose of higher education is to change students (and in staff development to change staff) in some desirable way. Practical problems cannot be resolved by pure theory (as theoretical problems can), but by adopting some course of action (i.e. by doing something). Problems in higher education usually arise when there is a mismatch between expectations about practical situations and the practical reality itself — in other words, when there is a gap between a teacher's theory and practice. Therefore, the criterion by which to assess research into higher education is not theoretical sophistication (e.g. grand theory, as in other sciences), but its ability to improve practice and its success in doing so. Put differently, research into higher education is valuable if it helps teachers (and their students) to improve their practice. This value claim can best be realised when theory is generated by, or in collaboration with, practitioners as 'personal theory' (Kelly, 1955; Polanyi, 1962). The evidence for this claim is furnished by the case studies in the companion book.

The dialectical relationship between theory and practice

Thus there is a dialectical relationship between theory arising from practice and practice being improved by theory. In critical theory this dialectic between theory and practice is called *praxis* (Habermas, 1974). In praxis, human beings are neither totally free subjects nor passive agents (Giddens, 1979). They are producers *and* products of social reality. Educational theory may be formed and developed from the concrete reality of educational practice with its socio-historical relations which exist and have evolved in society. Both theory and practice may be integrated by the teacher in higher education who is a 'reflective practitioner' (Schön, 1983) and a personal theorist or 'personal scientist' (Kelly, 1955), as will be discussed in Part 2. What Carr and Kemmis (1986, 124) claim for educational research in general is particularly appropriate for research in higher education:

> Indeed, if educational research is wholly committed to the investigation of educational problems, then it will be based on a realization that the only genuine source of educational theories and knowledge is the practical experiences out of which these problems are generated, and that the proper concern of educational research is with formulating theories that are grounded in the realities of educational practice.

Grounded theory

Glaser and Strauss (1967, 32) distinguish between two kinds of grounded theory, 'substantive' theory and 'formal' theory:

> By substantive theory we mean that developed for a substantive, or empirical area of... enquiry, such as... professional education... By formal theory, we mean that developed for a formal or conceptual area of... enquiry, such as... socialization or social mobility... substantive theory faithful to the empirical situation cannot... be formulated merely by applying a few ideas from an established formal theory to the substantive area.

Rather, relevant problems and hypotheses must be developed by induction from the 'raw data' of the substantive area study. It will then be possible to see whether any formal theories are useful for formulating and advancing adequate substantive theories. There are at least three implications for research into learning and teaching in higher education.

First, adequate 'substantive' theories in higher education cannot be produced by merely importing formal theories from other sciences; they must be grounded in, and generated from, the reality of learning–teaching situations. Second, the value and scientific status of research in higher education is determined by practice and its improvement (rather than practice being determined by theory). This means that research in higher education is scientific and useful only when it suggests improvements and when these suggestions are tested and confirmed by practical experiences. Third, the success of research in higher education is dependent on the active participation of practitioners in the research process and on the extent to which they develop an understanding of their own problems and practices. It is, therefore, inappropriate to treat staff and students in higher education as 'subjects' in the sense of objects for our scientific observations and to expect that they accept and apply our scientific solutions to their learning–teaching problems and practices. Rather, academics may become educational action researchers into their own teaching practices; and students may develop their own metalearning theories (i.e. they may learn to understand the processes as well as the content of their own learning). This idea is further developed in the companion book.

The role of educational theory

Apart from personally relevant knowledge, there is social knowledge which is not only constructed by individuals' concepts and ideas, but by historical, economic and material conditions (Chapter 5). These conditions, in turn, structure and affect people's perceptions and ideas. In higher education it is important to understand these ideological processes and to critically reveal them and their influences on staff and students' interpretations of reality. As mentioned earlier, one of the five requirements stated by Carr and Kemmis (1986, 129–30) as necessary for any approach to educational theory to accept is that: *educational theory is practical, in the sense that the questions of its educational status will be determined by ways in which it relates to practice.* Educational theory must be oriented towards assisting teachers in their understanding of their problems and practices, towards transforming the ways in which they see themselves and their situation, and towards transforming the situations which hinder teachers from achieving desirable educational goals which perpetuate ideological distortions and which impede rational and critical work in educational situations.

This latter transformation of situations and contexts is the most difficult to achieve. It has been the main concern of the Frankfurt School of critical theory which Carr and Kemmis (1986) have adopted for a critical education science. The Frankfurt group of philosophers and social scientists has, through its theoretical writings, articulated the views of a theory that aims to emancipate humans from the positivist 'dominion of thought' (e.g. that all practical problems are technical problems) through the understandings and actions of humans themselves. Kemmis and his associates at Deakin University have suggested and successfully carried out a practical solution of how to assist teachers in becoming critical, namely through emancipatory action research. This will be discussed further in Chapter 6.

Conclusion

This chapter has presented the problem of the supposed theory–practice dichotomy in higher education and my views that the separation of theory and practice is first a false dichotomy; second, that reintegration is necessary by reconstructing what counts as theory, as practice and as the relationship between them; and third, that an integration of educational theory and practice is not only desirable and necessary, but also possible, if teachers themselves are involved in 'action research' (i.e. research into their own teaching practice and into student learning).

In this chapter practice was conceived as praxis (i.e. in its dialectical relation to theory and in its socio-historical context). The next three chapters in Part 2 will present various aspects of theory in higher education that support the notion of action research.

Part 2

Theory in higher education

Before embarking on the question of how to bring about change and continuous development in staff and students in higher education, it is important to make explicit the epistemological and methodological assumptions underlying any strategic practice. The integrative, theoretical framework proposed here is not based on one unilateral, existing theory which could be applied to resolving the research questions of this book; rather, it is based on a dialectical integration of several domains of competing theories. For example, it is not based on behaviourism (and empiricism) or on cognitive psychology (and rationalism), or on induction or deduction as a methodological approach, but on some of the ideas from both the empirical and cognitive theories (as well as from other philosophies), using induction and deduction where appropriate. This dialectical approach would have been unacceptable in the past, not only to pure but also to applied scientists, since both groups, broadly speaking, based their work on an empiricist, deductivist epistemology. In recent years, however, a new paradigm has emerged in the social sciences as an alternative to the 'traditional' paradigm of scientific enquiry. It has now been more widely accepted that the study of humankind and of society requires different methodological foundations from those appropriate to the natural sciences (Burrell and Morgan, 1979).

Sociology became a new science and discipline in the last century when Auguste Comte derived his positivist principles from science. Although the term 'positivism' is used in a wide variety of meanings, it is usually understood to refer to a school of thought that is based on certain assumptions, the most important of which is what Kolakowski (1972, 11–12) calls 'the rule of phenomenalism'. This rule claims that valid knowledge can only be ascribed to that which is founded in 'reality' as apprehended by the senses and manifested in experience. In the social sciences, positivism is usually taken to contend that the aims, concepts and methods of the natural sciences are also applicable to enquiries in the social sciences, and that research strategies based on the logic and methodology of the natural sciences are equally applicable to educational research. For example, the hypothetico-deductive method argues that scientific enquiries start with hypotheses (e.g. in the form of general rules) which can then be refuted or verified by a comparison between their deductive consequences and the results of observation and experiments. Once hypotheses are verified by scientific methods, these sociological or educational laws — like the laws of physics — become established, 'objective' knowledge.

However, the history of science has shown that the positivist notions of knowledge, objectivity and truth are unrealistic, because many scientific theories have been questioned, refuted and replaced (e.g. Ptolomy's philosophy of the world was replaced by that of Copernicus, Keppler and Galileo; Newton's theory of gravitation was replaced by Einstein's theory). Moreover, it has been increasingly recognised that the human sciences require different methodologies from the natural sciences; that the nature, behaviour and mind of humankind constitute a complex whole which cannot be observed objectively or in parts by an outside researcher for at least two reasons: first, observations of individual or social behaviour are not neutral, objective or value free, but subjective interpretations dependent on the observer's theoretical framework and value system; second, the 'subjects' or persons who are the object of research have to participate in the research process (e.g. in the analysis and interpretation of the data) in order to make the results as objective as possible.

This point will be elaborated in Chapter 7, but what is important here for the theoretical background of this book is that the non-positivist research methodology used in this book is based on a new, emerging paradigm in the philosophy of science and of education which is considered to be more appropriate in higher education for at least three reasons. First, higher education is a human science and has to be approached differently from a natural science. Second, it is a large and complex network of interdisciplinarity. An educational problem has to be understood in its totality and approached by the knowledge, theories and skills from whatever disciplines are appropriate for solving the problem.

The third reason why a research approach different to the orthodox paradigm of science may be more appropriate in higher education is that the questions to be answered are very complex. For example, how do students and professionals learn? How do they acquire and use new knowledge? How important is the context in which they work? What motivates them to learn, etc.? Chalmers (1982, 166) argues that there is no single, timeless, universal criterion by which an area of knowledge, such as history, sociology or education, could be judged to be a science or not.

Each area of knowledge can be analyzed for what it is. That is, we can investigate what its aims are... and we can investigate the means used to accomplish those aims and the degree of success achieved.

Thus an area of knowledge, or a research project, can be assessed by evaluating the appropriateness of the methods used for attaining its aims. But these methods will in most cases be different from those required by positivists. On the contrary, the positivist, normative social science approach has been criticised (Cohen and Manion, 1980) mainly on two accounts: first, it ignores the profound differences between the natural and social sciences, and it does not take account of people's unique ability to construct theories about themselves and their world, to act upon these theories and to interpret their experiences. Second, it has been criticised for its technical perspective of the relationship between theory and practice (i.e. practice as the technical application of theory), and therefore because its findings may be trivial and irrelevant to those for whom they are intended (i.e. in the case of higher education, for teachers, administrators, counsellors, etc.).

The present book aims to be relevant to teachers, administrators and advisers in higher education. It takes account of people's unique and complex abilities to acquire knowledge (Chapter 3), to construct their personal theories (Chapter 4), and to act (i.e. to control and interpret their actions and experiences in the historical, ideological, cultural and social context of their educational practice in higher education) (Chapter 5). The book is based on a holistic view of humankind in which behaviour, thinking and acting are interrelated and interdependent.

In terms of research in higher education, this means that student learning, teaching and staff development can best be studied if all aspects of human nature (i.e. affective, cognitive, kinesthetic and inter-personal, social and ideological aspects) are considered simultaneously. All too often in the past, cognitive studies have neglected students' perceptions, feelings and motivations; behaviourist studies have ignored students' ability to think autonomously and to control their own learning; and both have emphasised learning, or the acquisition of knowledge, detached from the social context. This book — in accordance with the dialectical epistemology — suggests that people are existentially related to their social structure; their knowledge is a subjective interpretation of objective structures and is mediated through social processes. The taken-for-granted objective reality has to be subjectively realised before it has any meaning.

In brief, this book argues that higher education as a human science needs to establish itself in the new, alternative paradigm which has emerged in other human sciences and which already has a history and tradition of a substantial body of literature. Some of the key arguments for establishing an alternative approach to research in higher education are:

1. a critique of positivism itself, as mentioned above:

   (a) the debate over objectivity and empiricism (cf theory-ladenness of observation);
   (b) the fact-value distinction (cf value-ladenness of observation and personal construction of knowledge);
   (c) human action as intended, conscious and controlled action (rather than predicted behaviour) which cannot be understood from the outside;
   (d) the social and historical construction of theoretical knowledge in paradigms;
   (e) the difference between the human and the natural sciences;
   (f) the relationship between theory and practice;

2. the actors' interpretive categories of their practice and underlying assumptions as a basis for change;
3. culture, tradition, ideology and distorted perceptions.

The dialectical epistemology is explained by Esland (1971) in contrast to the traditional epistemology and is summarised in Table 3. These two epistemologies are the bases of psychological models: the traditional epistemology provides the foundation for the psychometric model or objective scientism (positivism, analytical philosophy and modern empiricism) and for the learning theory of behaviourist psychology; the dialectical epistemology provides the basis for cognitive psychology, personal construct psychology and critical psychology. These theories will be discussed in this part very briefly and only with reference to those aspects of learning and teaching in higher education which are preparing the ground and context for the major chapters on personal construct theory (Chapter 4) and action theories (Chapter 5). The two paradigms have developed historically;

they exist today side by side and must be taken into consideration by any educationalist who intends to work with and understand people from both sides in order to effect progressive change and reform in higher education. Theories of change will be discussed in Part 4 (Chapter 8). In this part we are mainly concerned with theories of learning and their underlying epistemologies.

Table 3 *The view of humankind in the traditional and dialectic epistomology (after Esland, 1971)*

Traditional epistemology	Dialectic epistemology
Humankind as	
Passive receiver of knowledge	Active seeker and negotiator of meaning
World-produced	World producer and social product
Having a static, analytic conception of knowledge	Being involved in an active construction of knowledge and experience
Believing in truth and validity of knowledge	Believing in changing forms and content knowledge, open to sociological revitalisation
Regarding teaching as the acquisition of skills and techniques to transfer knowledge from teacher to student	Regarding teaching as active knowledge and reflective understanding of curriculum pedagogy and evaluation

Chapter 3

Theories of knowing and learning

Introduction

Recent educational technology has undergone a change of emphasis in teaching and learning in higher education: from mass education through individualised instruction to group learning — or, in other terms, from dependent through independent to interdependent learning (Elton and Laurillard, 1979). Each of us, whether student or teacher, has an implicit model of the learning process which guides our behaviour as learner/teacher.

These models are based on underlying epistemologies which are intimately linked to general educational theories about the nature and development of humankind. Bruner (1960) sees instruction as an effort to assist or to shape growth and he regards any theory of instruction as a theory of how growth and development are encouraged. Thus, any teaching theory is intimately linked to an underlying view or model of the nature of the learner (e.g. as active or passive; emotional, cognitive or holistic; fixed or constantly developing; productive or reproductive, etc). In this book the view of the student and the academic as learners is based on Kelly's theory of the 'personal scientist', extended by Leontiev's theory of action theorists and Lewin's theory of action researchers.

Many theories of learning developed within psychology have been based on unexamined philosophical and epistemological assumptions, and many educationalists today are sceptical of the role of psychology in education and reject the discipline because it has not had a great impact on the practice of learning and teaching; on the contrary, many people think it has had a detrimental effect, mainly because of the orientation it took during the period of 'mechanistic behaviourism'.

This book does not enter a detailed discussion of behaviourist and cognitivist theories. Rather, it argues for the need for a more holistic and dialectical model of knowing and learning in which the learner is conceived as an active construer of knowledge through cycles of problem-solving. The process of problem-solving is taken to be a cognitive process of using conjectures and refutations (Popper, 1959; 1969) based on personally constructed theories (Kelly, 1955; Chapter 4) and a process of using action (Leontiev, 1977; Chapter 5) and experience (Kolb, 1984; Chapter 6) as the basis of observation and reflection (transformation or interiorisation) and critical self-reflection.

There is an enormous amount of research literature on theories of knowledge production and creation and of student learning pertaining to higher education. This brief chapter does not claim to cover their topics in depth or even reflect the main *pro* and *contra* arguments in the field; it merely functions as a preparatory chapter for the discussion of Kelly's personal construct theory (Chapter 4) and Leontiev's action theory (Chapter 5) to which they provide a background. Both Kelly (1955) and Leontiev (1977) developed their theories in reaction to behaviourism and in the tradition of cognitive psychology. Some of their main objections to behaviourism are outlined below, followed by some of the important characteristics of cognitive psychology relevant to their theories and to the improvement of learning and teaching in higher education.

Behaviourist theories

Behaviourist theorists believe in the scientific enquiry of human behaviour by methods of observation and experiment leading to 'laws' and derivative principles of learning and teaching. Based on the empiricists' view that only things publicly visible can count as observation, behaviourists do not look within the organism for explanation of behaviour. They observe external behaviour 'objectively', find variables of which behaviour is a function and establish laws. On the basis of these laws, they predict student responses to stimuli from outside (e.g. from the teacher or teaching material) for a particular goal, aim or objective. The learner is presented with a ready-made system and taught as many research findings as possible in a compressed way (i.e. optimum knowledge taught and learnt in minimum time).

Many behaviourist theorists have used experiments with animals for their research. For example, Skinner (1953) draws conclusions from his experiments with pigeons for the field of learning and behaviour control in education. His main concerns are techniques and methods of shaping behaviour and of maintaining behaviour in strength.

Gagné (1977) gives an account of the various versions of behaviourism, such as *associationism*, which considers learning as connecting separate elements in our experience to form 'associations'. But common to all these versions of the theory is the notion of the learner who responds to the impact of stimuli to him/her from without. In order to determine what learning is, Gagné (1977, 18) identifies the general types of human capabilities that are learned and the conditions of learning:

> Once these varieties of learning outcome have been identified, an account can be given of the conditions that govern the occurrence of learning and remembering. This leads to the description of the factors that determine learning, derived insofar as possible from available evidence in controlled experimentation. By this means it is possible to differentiate the sets of conditions that support the learning of different human capabilities.

'Controlled experimentation' and 'determination' or prediction of learning behaviour are central aims in the behaviourist school of thought. Gagné (1977) distinguishes five learning domains or skills:

1. *Motor skills*, or capabilities to perform practical tasks (e.g. using tools or instruments and pronouncing words). Motor skills require practice and repetition.
2. *Verbal information*, or knowledge such as facts, principles and generalisations required for learning across areas and for thinking in a general sense. Verbal knowledge is not learnt by repetition, but by understanding the meaningful context (cf Ausubel 1968).
3. *Intellectual skills* (e.g. concepts and rules that constitute the basic skills of the elementary curriculum). Learning intellectual skills requires prior learning of prerequisite skills.
4. *Cognitive strategies*, or internally organised skills governing the individual's behaviour in learning, remembering and thinking, and required for problem-solving.
5. *Attitudes* learnt not by practice but by means of the human model and 'vicarious reinforcement'.

These five categories of human skills are similar to Bloom's (1974) taxonomy of motor, cognitive and affective domains. They have been the basis for setting educational objectives in many higher education institutions all over the world for decades.

Gagné also believes that learning is hierarchical (i.e. the learner proceeds, step by step, from the easy to the more and more difficult, complex levels of learning). It follows that students must first master the knowledge and skills of one level before starting the next one. These principles of hierarchical learning and reinforcement of desired behaviour underlie the use of 'teaching machines' or 'programmed learning', 'mastery learning', Keller Plan, Personalised System of Instruction, Individualised Instruction, etc. Numerous studies in the 1960s and 1970s (e.g. Green, 1971; Kulik and Carmichael, 1974; Kulik et al., 1979) have shown the success of these programmes of individualised mastery learning compared with other teaching methods (i.e. measuring achievement in the form of examination results). This is an appropriate criterion for success within the traditional paradigm in which knowing and learning are defined as an accumulation of facts. This paradigm is still strongly represented by teachers in higher education, especially in those disciplines where factual knowledge is seen to be an essential part of professionalism (e.g. in medicine, law, accountancy and the natural sciences).

However, these behaviourist theories and strategies of learning and teaching have been criticised on two major counts. The first is a criticism of associationist theories, coming originally from the Gestalt psychologists who believe that we do not understand a new experience through the summation of reflexes or other individual elements, but that, from the outset, we try to see it as a whole, a pattern (*Gestalt*). The second major criticism considers behaviourist theories as being mechanistic and inappropriate to developing critical and creative thinking. The many critiques of behaviourism are succinctly summarised by Novak's (1981) argument:

> Ignoring or negating the internal world of people misses the essence of their personhood, flattens human reality and leads to educational practices which are mechanistic and lacking in respect for the basic integrity of the person.

Skinner himself (1975, 38) admits this when he says:

> It is true that the techniques which are emerging from the experimental study of learning are not designed to 'develop the mind' or to further some vague 'understanding' of mathematical 'relationships'.

As a result of such criticism, we have seen the emergence of other theories in cognitive psychology, constructivist psychology, critical psychology and action science. It might have been this challenge to behaviourism, combined with a favourable climate and an abundance of research funds in the 1960s and 1970s, that gave birth to a great number of theories which did justice to the internal world of the person.

But before turning to some of these theories, it should be pointed out in defence of behaviourism that behaviour is *one* criterion by which to know and judge people. Another criterion, for example, is *action*. The difference between behaviourist and action theories is that the former conceive student behaviour as a response to a stimulus controlled by the teacher or the system, whereas the latter see action consciously and intentionally controlled by the agent (i.e. the learner) him/herself. But in higher education we need an understanding of both. In order to guide people to conscious action, it may be necessary to make them observe their conditioned responses and unconscious behaviour first (e.g. through video self-confrontation), to gradually raise their awareness of their present and of alternative behaviours and to encourage them to try out alternatives, so that they may finally control their actions consciously. Critics of behaviourism seem to have overlooked this point and focused on the shortcomings of the stimulus–response theory applied to people and on its failure to consider the human mind of *homo sapiens*.

Cognitive theories

As a response to behaviourism, cognitive theories emerged; in turn, these were supplemented by more holistic theories, such as personal construct theory and action theories. Cognitive psychology focuses on the human mind: its memory, cognitive structures, and processes of information storage and retrieval. These concepts are briefly introduced in this section, because they are relevant to, and used in, the discussion of personal construct theory (Chapter 5) and action theories (Chapter 6). However, no attempt is made to survey the research literature in cognitive psychology or to evaluate the various theoretical positions. The terminology of memory, cognitive structures and information processing is merely explained in general operational terms.

The human memory

The human memory can be differentiated into sensory information storage system, short-term memory and long-term memory (Norman, 1976). The sensory information storage system is a representation of experiences of the world as they are received by the sensory system. This picture of the world lasts only one-tenth to half a second. The short-term memory does not retain a complete image of the events but retains the immediate interpretation of those events. The capacity of the short-term memory is very limited, but a small amount of material can be retained indefinitely by rehearsal (i.e. by repeating the material). The long-term memory has a large capacity. It is most important and most complex. Millions or billions of items are stored in the long-term memory, but the difficulties stem mainly from one source: retrieval. Lindsay and Norman (1975) compare the long-term memory with libraries and computer-based systems. The difficulty is not to store huge amounts of information, but to be able to retrieve selected pieces of data on request. The retrieval strategies of the long-term memory are similar to those of problem-solving processes.

Cognitive structures

Cognitive structures are generally defined as knowledge stored in an organised way. For example, when solving a task or problem, we use the knowledge which is structured and organised in our memory; and we select only those things which are related to the task or needed for solving the problem. Ausubel (1968) views the storage of information in the brain as highly organised. There are linkages formed between various older and newer elements, leading to a conceptual hierarchy in which minor elements of knowledge are subsumed under larger, more general, more inclusive concepts. Thus the individual's representations of sensory experience are structured in a framework of hierarchically organised concepts.

The development of cognitive structures is seen differently by behaviourist and cognitive psychologists. On the one hand, behaviourists believe that the development consists of an accumulation of knowledge which enters our brain via the senses; and we learn to solve new problems by learning new behaviours which are accumulated in our memory and called upon when needed. On the other hand, cognitive psychologists maintain that some knowledge is inherited and that existing knowledge is continuously changed by the individual in order to master the problems of our environment. Like Ausubel, Bruner (1960) believes that learning is more effective if the memory stores general structures or overarching concepts which can be applied to many similar problems than if it adds another stimulus to a previous association. Thus cognitive structures are partly inherited (i.e. initial capital through environment and culture) and partly developed or learnt.

Processes of information storage and retrieval

Unlike behaviourists, whose focus of enquiry is mainly the outcome of learning (the end product), cognitive theorists focus on the process of knowing and learning. For example, Bruner (1960, 490) regards cognition and knowing as a process, not a product. He believes that we acquire knowledge by three almost simultaneous processes:

1. acquisition of new information or the replacement of old knowledge;
2. transformation of information in a new situation; and
3. evaluation or appraisal of the manner in which the information has been used.

Bruner (1975, 108–9) believes that the acquisition of knowledge is an active process within the framework of cognitive structures as a system of representation. This psychological frame of reference enables the learner 'to go beyond the information given':

> Let me suggest that, in general, material that is organized in terms of a person's own interests and cognitive structures is material that has the best chance of being accessible in memory. That is to say, it is more likely to be placed along routes that are connected to one's own ways of intellectual travel. It is my hunch that it is only through the exercise of problem solving and the effort of discovery that one learns the working heuristic of discovery; and, the more one has practised, the more likely one is to generalize what one has learned into a style of problem solving or enquiry that serves for any kind of task one may encounter - or almost any kind of task.

Ausubel (1963; 1968), too, believes that our brain acquires information in a retrievable form and takes in new concepts under a pre-existing hierarchical structure. Like Bruner, Ausubel (1975, 93) argues that new material is acquired more easily and retained better if it is related to the learner's previous knowledge and concepts:

> Existing cognitive structure is the principal factor influencing meaningful learning and retention. Since logically meaningful material is always, and can only be, learned in relation to a previously learned background of relevant concepts, principles and information which make possible the emergence of new meanings and enhance their retention, it is evident that the substantive and organizational properties of this background crucially affect both the accuracy and the clarity of these emerging new meanings and their immediate and long-term retrievability.

In general, it might be true to say that researchers in both behaviourist and cognitive psychology approach the learner from outside as objectively as possible. The learners, although called 'subjects', are the *object* of research and do not actively participate in the research process. They have no influence on the researcher's analysis and interpretation of the research data. Although this issue will be discussed in more detail in the methodological chapter (Chapter 7), it has some bearing on the theories of learning. More holistic theories which have emerged from phenomenological research (i.e. research from the student's perspective as well as from the researcher's view) should be briefly mentioned in this context.

Holistic theories

Holistic theories do not consider parts of the learner's system (e.g. behaviour, memory, speech acts, etc.) but the phenomena of learning in the person as a whole; they describe the phenomena as they appear in the person's consciousness. The research emphasises phenomenological differences which different learners bring to their approaches to learning. It is concerned with the descriptive charting of those phenomena without a commitment to the further step of phenomenological reduction. This kind of research is therefore described by the terms phenomenology and phenomenography. For further explanation and discussion of these terms, see Marton (1981, 1986) and Marton and Ramsden (1988).

Apart from personal construct psychology, which will be discussed in Chapter 4, and action science, which will be dealt with in Chapters 5 and 6, the study of learning from the student's point of view has received increased attention by educational researchers in the past two or three decades (e.g. Pask, 1976; Fullan, 1982; Marton, Hounsell and Entwistle, 1984; Entwistle and Ramsden, 1983; Gibbs, Morgan and Taylor, 1982; Taylor, 1986; Bowden, 1986). As Marton (1975, 136) puts it: 'We believe that it is precisely the content of man's (sic!) view of the world around him that is the proper subject of research on learning and thinking.'

Approaches to learning

Through in-depth interviews with students, the following main approaches to learning have been identified and classified:

1. the 'surface' approach versus the 'deep-meaning' approach, or 'verbal' and 'non-verbal' learning (Marton, 1975; 1984), depending whether the learner tries to memorise a written or spoken discourse or whether he/she tries to go beyond it towards the meaning and message the discourse is intended to communicate;
2. 'serialist' versus 'holistic' approaches and accompanying styles of 'operation' versus 'comprehension' learning respectively (Pask, 1976);

3. 'reproducing' versus 'personal meaning' versus the 'achieving' approach (Entwistle, 1981; Entwistle and Ramsden, 1983). The reproducing style of learning is similar to the verbal/operation learning of the surface/serialist approach and is associated with extrinsic motivation, fear of failure, anxiety and syllabus-boundedness. 'Personal meaning' is associated with intrinsic motivation, a preference for autonomy and a deep approach to learning. 'Achieving' is associated with hope for success and a willingness to adopt any method (e.g. reproducing or meaning approach) leading to success. Danial (1975, 90) believes:

> Efficient learning must be versatile, combining both types. The pure operation learner can only climb vertically on the domain map without being able to transfer his understanding to other areas, whereas the pure comprehension learner is a cursory globetrotter who sees analogies everywhere but is unable to employ any concept in a practical way.

Research has demonstrated that students remember new information more easily when they understand the concept which forms the basis for the detail (e.g. Marton and Säljö, 1984) and when they can link the new concept to their existing knowledge (Ausubel, 1963) — in other words, when their learning is meaningful.

Laurillard (1984) has found that students may change their approach to learning and problem-solving depending on their perceptions of the task, their previous experience, and their perceptions of the teacher's expectations and marking. Bowden et al. (1987) also conclude from their research that departmental approaches to (language) teaching have a strong correlation and impact on the students' approaches to learning. Therefore, departments and teachers in higher education should attempt to encourage and facilitate meaningful learning, even when they aim at their students' acquisition of merely factual knowledge, especially when their students are mature adults.

Andragogy

Knowles (1985) coined the term andragogy for the science of adult learning as opposed to pedagogy, the science of child learning. The difference between the two is that adults are self-directed learners, with a rich life experience and therefore a rich resource for learning from each other in groups. They usually want to learn for a purpose (e.g. to perform a task, to solve a problem, or to live in a more satisfyir way), not for the sake of learning *per se*.

Therefore, adult learning theories and learning contracts (Knowles, 1986; Tompkins and McGraw, 1988) are most appropriate in higher education. Candy (1991) provides a comprehensive survey and analysis of the concept of self-direction for life-long learning based on constructivism. Constructivism is a branch of philosophy dealing with personal systems of meaning (i.e. with how people make sense of their worlds and create personal construct systems which guide them throughout their lives) (cf Chapter 4 in this book). Keys are presented to promoting and developing student autonomy (e.g. by Boud, 1981) and self-direction in learning in higher education (by Candy, 1991; Baird, 1988; Brookfield, 1985; and Knowles, 1975) as well as self-organised learning environments for personal growth and organisational effectiveness (by Harri-Augstein and Thomas, 1991).

It is also interesting in this context to note the work of Belenky et al (1986) who, on the basis of interviews with women, have identified five adult cognitive developmental stages unique to women: silence, received knowledge, subjective knowledge, procedural knowledge and constructed knowledge. Oja and Smulyan (1989, 106) illustrate this development in their analysis of a case.

Their work is also of general interest to the topic of this present book, because they focus on the investigation of adult development and group processes in collaborative action research. Action research to them has three main goals: staff development (of high school teachers), improved school practice and the modification and elaboration of theories and learning. These goals and outcomes of theirs in America are the same as those of Baird's (1988) and mine in Australia, although we were completely unaware of each other's work until 1991 and had come to similar conclusions totally independently of each other — they on the basis of action research with teachers and student teachers in high schools, and I through work with students and teachers in higher education. We also have in common a belief that the difference between pedagogy and andragogy is not qualitative, but quantitative. In other words, our research and experience have led us to conclude that high quality education is not linked *a priori* to the level of education (whether primary, secondary or higher), but to the development of intellectual independence. Intellectual independence can be achieved through certain processes (e.g. reflection, metacognition, collaboration, group processes) and methods (e.g. collaborative action research).

Mumford's (1990) work is based on that of Knowles (1985; 1986) and Kolb (1984), but with reference to the individual and learning opportunities of managers. Figure 4 shows the multidimensional

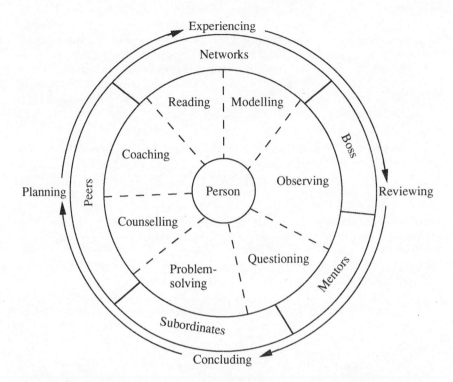

Figure 4   *Interaction in learning (Mumford, 1990, 19)*

process of learning which is individual as well as social and job related. Learning from experience can be powerful but also inefficient, unless it is followed up by formal and systematic opportunities to conceptualise the effect of this experience. On the other hand, formal training and development, especially in management and higher education, have been criticised for being too abstract and irrelevant to the participants' practical work. Therefore the revitalisation of action learning seems to be the answer for the 1990s.

Action learning

Revans' (1984, 16) equation for learning is: $L = P + Q$ (i.e. learning equals programmed knowledge plus questioning insight):

> P is the concern of the traditional academy; Q is the field of action learning... On the whole, however, programmed knowledge, P, already set out in books or known to expert authorities, is quite

insufficient for keeping on top of a world like ours today, racked by change of every kind. Programmed knowledge must not only be expanded: it must be supplemented by questioning insight, the capacity to identify useful and fresh lines of enquiry. This we may denote by Q, so that learning means not only supplementing P but developing Q as well. It is arguable which is more important in 1984; the evidence is that a surfeit of P inhibits Q, and that experts, loaded with P, are the greatest menace to adaptation to change by questioning, Q.

According to Revans (1982; 1984), action learning is a process by which groups of people (whether managers, academics, teachers, students or 'learners' generally) work on real issues or problems, carrying real responsibility in real conditions. The solutions they come up with may require changes to be made in the organisation, and they often pose challenges to senior management, but the benefits are great because people actually own their own problems and their own solutions. Revans (1991a; 1991b) sums up his work and illustrates it with examples of action learning in various organisations, such as coal mines, hospitals and manufacturing companies.

Apart from approaches to learning, adult learning theories and the philosophy of action learning, another important consideration in a holistic approach to learning is the difference in individual learning styles.

Learning styles

On the basis of the phenomenological research mentioned above, learning style questionnaires and study habits inventories have been designed (e.g. by Entwistle and Ramsden, 1983; Kolb, 1984). In management education and development, similar instruments are aimed to identify learning styles, task preferences and managerial preferences and underlying values. Since these latter inventories are not as well known to educationalists as the former, they are briefly outlined here, because they may usefully be applied to higher education.

Honey and Mumford (1986) have adapted Kolb's learning styles inventory by using simpler language: 'activist', 'pragmatist', 'reflector' and 'theorist'. They also give checklist advice on how to improve each style, how to make the best use of one's learning style and how to choose learning activities to suit one's style.

Kable (1988) has designed a decision preference analysis (DPA) which measures people's personal (psychological and motivational) preferences somewhere between highly quantitative and highly qualitative tasks. People's achievements and satisfaction can be increased by changing the task to suit the person. For example, a student might change from a quantitative subject or course (e.g. accountancy, economics, natural sciences) to a qualitative one (history, literature, social sciences) or vice versa. An awareness of different preferences is also important in professional development (e.g. job satisfaction, career-path planning, personnel decisions and team building).

Margerison and McCann (1990) have designed an index for team management profiles which has also been used with Heads and Deans in higher education. Managers can be provided each with a profile of their role preferences which they discuss as a group in order to form or lead a 'winning team'.

Learning defined as conceptual change may also be influenced by people's values and world views, because people's attitudes and values underlie and guide their intentions and goals, which in turn influence their commitment and perseverance. A tool by which values and world views can be identified is the Hall–Tonna inventory of values (Hall, 1986; Hall et al., 1990; Chippendale and Colins, 1991).

These examples might suffice to show that people's styles of learning and performing differ from individual to individual. However, Ramsden's (1985) research has shown that there is not any *one* learning approach, style or orientation which is, of itself, the best or most desirable; what *is* desirable is that the learner controls the quality of his/her learning by selecting the appropriate strategies for matching personal goals and talents with the nature and demands of the learning task.

Therefore, in teaching and professional development, we can no longer assume that everyone should learn and be treated in the same way. The above examples also show that awareness-raising for these individual differences in learning is important for increased personal satisfaction and job performance.

Metalearning

It might be appropriate in this context to mention another kind of educational research which investigates the influence a student's understanding of learning has on the student's learning of some matter. It is assumed that learning is more effective if the student not only tries to learn the subject matter directly, but also if he/she knows something of the processes by which effective learning occurs. The term 'metalearning' was coined to describe this kind of learning. Baird (1988, 145–6) states:

Metacognition refers to the *knowledge, awareness*, and *control* of one's own learning. It subsumes various aspects of intellectual competence and performance, such as conceptions of the nature of teaching and learning (metacognitive knowledge), perceptions of the nature, purpose, and progress of current learning (awareness), and the decisions made and behaviours exhibited during learning (control)... Adequate metacognition means that 'self-direction' or 'responsibility and control' of learning is considered, informed, and purposeful. Improving learning is a process of intellectual development towards enhanced metacognition.

Related to metacognition, there is a growing literature dealing with reflection in and on action or learning (Schön, 1983; Boud et al., 1985; Mezirow, 1990), reflective judgement and critical thinking (Schmidt and Davison, 1983; Brabeck, 1983; King et al., 1990; Winter, 1989; Kitchener and King, 1990). They all imply — impicitly or explicitly — that metacognition, reflective judgement and critical thinking skills can be developed.

Some techniques, such as 'concept mapping' and 'vee technique' (Novak and Gowin, 1984; Gowin, 1981), 'learning conversations' (Thomas and Harri-Augstein, 1982; Harri-Augstein and Thomas, 1979; 1991) and the 'repertory grid technique' (Kelly, 1955; Shaw, 1980; 1984), have resulted from research on metacognition. Apart from developing metalearning and critical thinking, another related educational concern is the development of dialectical thinking.

Holistic dialectical thinking

Holistic thinking is a method which can be learnt and applied to all walks of life. The concept of holistic thinking is based on the principle of the dialectic. The dialectic is often described in the Hegelian sense (i.e. as the opposition of a 'thesis' against its 'antithesis' with a reconciliation of both in a new 'synthesis'). The thesis represents an original tendency; the antithesis is its opposing tendency; and the synthesis is constituted by their unification in a new movement. This formula seems mechanistic. However, dialectical thinking, according to Carr and Kemmis (1986, 36–7) is:

> ... an open and questioning form of thinking which demands reflection back and forth between elements like *part* and *whole, knowledge* and *action, process* and *product, subject* and *object...* In the process, contradictions may be discovered, ... new constructive thinking and new constructive action are required to transcend the contradictory state of affairs... In the dialectical approach, the elements are regarded as mutually constitutive, not separate and distinct. Contradiction can thus be distinguished from paradox: to speak of a contradiction is to imply that a new resolution can be achieved, while to speak of a paradox is to

suggest that two incompatible ideas remain inertly opposed to one another.

There have been several different definitions of dialectical reasoning in the history of philosophy. For example, in ancient Greek philosophy, Socrates understood it as a search for knowledge by a method of question and answer. In German philosophy, Kant (1724–1804) referred to dialectical logic (the logic of reasoning) as distinct from analytic logic (the logic of understanding); Hegel's (1770–1831) conception of the dialectic (thesis–antithesis–synthesis) was revised by Marx (1818–1883) to found it on materialist premises. Since Marx, dialectical reasoning has aimed to overcome simple dualism, such as the conceptual separation of theory versus practice, individual versus society, etc., by adopting the principle of the unity of opposites. According to Kemmis and Fitzclarence (1986, 55):

... dialectical reasoning attempts to understand the dynamic, interactive, mutually-constitutive relationships between theory and practice, seeing both theory and practice as socially constructed and historically developed, rather than seeing either as exclusively determining the other. And similarly, dialectical reasoning is employed in studying how schooling is shaped by the state *and* how the state is shaped by schooling as one whole set of problems, not as a one-way determination in either direction (schooling determines the nature of the state, or the state determines the nature of schooling).

This idea of the dialectical relationship between schooling and state, between higher education institutions and government, deliberate action and educational context, is taken up in the discussion of Leontiev's model of action (Chapter 5).

The following is an example of how an understanding of dialectical reasoning can be developed. At the University of Technology in Aachen (West Germany) a series of seminars on 'Holistic Thinking' has been offered by its Hochschuldidaktisches Zentrum (HDZ, i.e. Centre for Research and Development). The course designer, Job (1986), believes that the ancient Chinese philosophy of 'Yin and Yang' was based on the same principles of context, contradiction and change as in dialectical reasoning. It might be worthwhile to explain Job's ideas regarding these principles in more detail. Since holistic, dialectical thinking is one of the most important educational principles leading to understanding and social responsibility, I shall summarise Job's ideas as follows:

Context. It has become more and more difficult for staff and students in higher education to see the context of their daily work (i.e.

to have a holistic view of the relationships and interrelationships of subjects). There are three obvious reasons why it is difficult for staff and students to grasp the context of their work. The first is the division of labour and increasing specialisation in manual activities, as well as in scientific research, which has led to the emergence of more and more disciplines. When teaching students the results of scientific research, we as teachers in higher education should provide the context for these results — within the disciplines and beyond — but we seldom do. Usually, students are confronted with a huge quantity of facts from various disciplines. But if scientists themselves are unable to see the connections between their own and other disciplines, students are even less likely to succeed. The second reason is the development of technical and scientific terminologies which have occurred in parallel to the development of scientific disciplines. Each discipline has its own professional esoteric language, the advantage of which is that the experts can communicate fast with colleagues in their own field. The disadvantage is that the communication between scientists (e.g. psychologists, philosophers, engineers, lawyers, etc.), as well as an outside control of scientific projects, has become more and more difficult. (We might note that this is also a reason, mentioned earlier in this book, why teaching academics are not inclined to read educational or psychological research findings and why there is a gap between educational theory and practice.) The third reason relates to the fact that many researchers focus on analysis only with the aim of going into a matter more deeply in order to one day understand it fully and to control it. This pattern of thinking can be compared with spectacles. Spectacles can be useful, but only if one owns more than one pair. Many researchers use one pair only: those of analysis. But analysis and synthesis belong together like theory and practice for a coherent view of the world.

Contradictions. Job (1986) suggests that we should develop in students this coherent view of the world based on their experiences as students. The first step is to make them aware that everything has two sides, like the two sides of a coin. This dialectical contradiction means that the two sides belong together like Yin and Yang (e.g. passivity and activity), that is, they are mutually constitutive, not separate or exclusive of each other. There are 'inner' and 'outer contradictions'. Inner contradictions occur within a system or process. For example, within a human being, there is the contradiction between feelings and reasoning. Outer contradictions occur between two systems or processes. For example, in the case of an effective academic losing his/her job because of redundancy or government cuts, the outer contradiction refers to the relationship between a human being and society. We are all part of society and influenced by it. Society consists of individuals and is influenced and shaped by them. This inter-relationship is in constant tension and contradiction, sometimes hardly noticeable, sometimes explosive.

Change. The idea that 'everything changes' negates all static and deterministic thinking. It focuses on thinking as a process, change, action. Change occurs in a dialectical process of thesis, antithesis and synthesis. For example, Job (1986) refers to Heisenberg and others who believe in progress and change in thinking through the simultaneous study of two different philosophies (e.g. occidental and oriental philosophies). After studying the logics of the West (thesis) and the dialectics of the East (antithesis), and arguing with and on both sides of the contradiction, he arrives at a synthesis which is neither one nor the other side, but it is something new. Both sides have contributed to it, and parts of both have flown into the new theory.

Another reference to holistic, dialectical thinking is provided in Perry's developmental theory based on his study with Harvard students. Perry (1970; 1981) focuses on students' intellectual and ethical development and identifies a qualitative change in students' thinking from dualistic thinking to relativistic reasoning and on to commitment.

Perry's theory of intellectual and ethical development in college students has recently become increasingly important in higher education in terms of learning/teaching issues (Boyer, 1987; Belenky et al., 1986; Commons et al. 1989; 1990), outcomes assessment (Astin, 1991; Baxter Magolda, 1987) and a phenomenological approach to educational research, because Perry used unstructured interviews. From the qualitative analysis of these longitudinal interviews emerged what came to be known the 'Perry model'.

Perry's model constitutes a nine-position (or stage) progression of thought from dualism (a black and white view of the world) to contextual relativism (a world of shades of grey in which one makes meaning by making judgements). There has been an increasing interest in extending the model to assessment and instrumentation research with the aim of measuring education outcomes.

The best-known instruments are the MID or 'Measurement of Intellectual Development' (Moore, 1988) and the MER or 'Measure of Epistemological Reflection' (Baxter Magolda and Porterfield, 1988) based on Gibbs and Widaman's (1982) work. Both of these instruments are 'production-task' measures based on students' semi-structured essays in which they generate their own responses as compared to reacting to given materials (as in comprehension and recognition-task measures). The problem with these instruments is that they attempt to measure and standardise the phenomena of cognitive and ethical development, which are extremely complex and individually different. Another problem is that they require trained raters for scoring purposes, and the training process is too lengthy for normal educators. More research and development is needed to make a greater impact on the practice of higher education.

Conclusion

Basically, behaviourist theories relate to human behaviour and achievement in response to stimuli from outside, while cognitive theories focus on the cognitive structures, operations and processes which occur within the human mind. Behaviourists are interested in *how much* students learn, whereas cognitivists ask *how* students learn. Both unconscious behaviour and cognitive, conscious processes of information handling (or of knowledge creation and use) occur in learning, teaching and staff development in higher education. Therefore, behaviourist and cognitive theories need not be seen unilaterally and as exclusive of each other (as they are by many educational researchers) but dialectically and as complementing each other.

Holistic theories are the result of a phenomenological approach to researching student learning. This means that the researcher does not focus on one part or on a single aspect of the learner, but he/she studies the learner as a holistic person (i.e. the motor, cognitive, affective and inter-personal domains). The theories emerge from the perspective of the student, rather than from that of the researcher.

From the vast number of theories of knowing and learning, only those that relate to my later discussion of improving learning, teaching and staff development in higher education have been briefly introduced in this chapter. Some examples of metalearning and inventories on individual learning styles, task and role preferences illustrate the usefulness of this research for practice in higher education.

The principles of adult learning lead to a revitalisation of action learning which is a basic concept in action research to be discussed further in Chapter 6.

Dialectical, holistic thinking is a method that can be learnt. It is based on the principles of context, contradiction and change. It might be clearer to consider these three key concepts of holistic thinking in contrast:

* thinking in context ←—→ isolated thinking
* thinking in contradictions ←—→ unilateral, dogmatic thinking
* thinking in processes of change ←—→ static, deterministic thinking.

It is an important task of higher education to develop holistic dialectical thinking (in context and contradictions) in order to bring about continuous change and progress. The aim is to overcome a 'black and white' view of the world (i.e. a dualistic view that the world consists of logical contradictions which exclude each other, such as good *or* bad). Instead, dialectical contradictions (e.g. good *and* bad), which stipulate and permeate each other, are a driving force providing change and reform. Perry (1970; 1981) has shown that this change from dualistic thinking to dialectical, relativistic reasoning is developmental and can be promoted.

The disadvantages for an institution of promoting holistic thinking might be that it takes more time and effort in the short run; it requires co-operation, patience and perseverance; and it might lead to temporary insecurity because old, familiar and favourite cognitive structures and actions have to be dismissed. But the advantages outweigh the disadvantages, because holistic thinking prevents single-mindedness and immunises against the 'hidden persuaders' (e.g. in politics, advertising); it enables a more grounded point of view; and it might spare frustrations through a more realistic view of things. In brief, it facilitates change and reform.

The learner is not merely a passive consumer of accumulated knowledge, but an active producer and reproducer of knowledge and theory. This idea is developed further in the next chapter on personal construct theory, in which the learner is conceived as a 'personal scientist'.

Chapter 4

Kelly's personal construct theory

Introduction

The theoretical framework of this book is mainly based on Kelly's personal construct theory, extended by action theory (Chapter 5) and resulting in action research (Chapter 6). As pointed out before, the previous chapter had a preparatory role in this theoretical framework, preparing the ground for the discussion in the chapters to follow.

Kelly (1955) published his theory as a potential alternative to both the dominant behaviourism and the various psychoanalytical theories of the time. But it is only in the last two decades that the climate has been conducive to a discussion and appraisal of his theory, due to the emergence of cognitive theories and an increased emphasis on constructivism in philosophy, psychology, sociology and education. While both behaviourist and cognitive theorists analyse parts of the learner and individual aspects of learning (e.g. behaviour, memory, cognitive structures, information processing, motivation), personal construct psychology focuses on the complete, purposeful person as an active and creative agent in his/her own right, not simply as a responder to stimuli.

Kelly's epistemological assumptions are that there is no objective knowledge of reality, but that reality can only be known through our constructions, which are subject to constant revision; we do not have direct access to an interpretation-free reality. We can only make assumptions (hypotheses) about what reality is and then test how useful or useless these assumptions are. Kelly's theory begins with and centres around the person as a 'personal scientist' and as an active knowing subject whose ultimate aim is to predict and control events. Kelly proposes that every person is a scientist not only by disposition but also by right; and that every person is an incipient experimenter and by daily necessity a fellow psychologist.

Kelly has been criticised for the use of the term 'man' in his model. In order to avoid sexist language in this book, 'man' has been rendered 'humankind'. Fransella (1980, 258) suggests that this 'as if' model is proposed at such a high level of abstraction that a separate model of 'woman as scientist' becomes obsolete. Shaw (1980) uses the term 'personal scientist' to describe Kelly's view of the person as an active knowing subject. This book uses 'humankind', 'personal scientist' or '(wo)man' interchangeably.

This chapter gives an exposition and critical appraisal of Kelly's theory and then discusses the implications of his theory to learning and teaching in higher education.

Kelly's theory

Kelly's epistemological position is 'constructive alternativism', that is, the assumption that our present constructs or interpretations of the universe are subject to revision or replacement. This means that people understand themselves and their environment, and anticipate future events, by constructing tentative models or personal theories and by evaluating these theories against personal criteria as to whether the prediction and control of events (based upon the models) have been successful or not. All theories are hypotheses created by people; they may be valid at any particular time, but may suddenly be invalid in some unforeseeable respect and replaced by a better theory. According to Kelly (1963, 8–9):

> Man looks at his world through transparent patterns or templets [sic!] which he creates and then attempts to fit over the realities of which the world is composed. The fit is not always very good. Yet without such patterns the world appears to be such an undifferentiated homogeneity that man is unable to make any sense out of it. Even a poor fit is more helpful to him than nothing at all.
>
> Let us give the name constructs to these patterns that are tentatively tried on for size. They are ways of construing the world. They are what enables man, and lower animals too, to chart a course of behaviour, explicitly formulated, or implicitly acted out, verbally expressed or utterly inarticulate, consistent with

other courses of behaviour or inconsistent with them, intellectually reasoned or vegetatively sensed.

Kelly also believes that people construe reality in an infinite number of different ways. Although he does not deny the importance of childhood experiences or present environmental constraints, he suggests that it is more important to explore people's thinking about their present situation (i.e. their current hypotheses structure). He believes that people need not be trapped by their early experiences or be impotent in the face of present environmental constraints, but that change can occur if they see their personal theories as open to refutation and not as 'objective truth'.

For example, Kelly (1963, 15) writes about his core metaphysical commitment: 'No one needs to paint himself into a corner: no one needs to be completely hemmed in by circumstances; no one needs to be a victim of his biography'.

On the basis of his epistemology, Kelly has developed his theory in terms of a fundamental postulate elaborated by eleven corollaries. The fundamental postulate — or basic assumption — and those corollaries (i.e. eight out of eleven) which have implications for higher education are summarised below. Corollaries are propositions which amplify the system; the system in Kelly's case is the psychology of personal constructs.

Kelly's fundamental postulate

A person's processes are psychologically channellized by the ways in which he anticipates events (Kelly, 1963, 46). Kelly believes that science and theory building are not the prerogative of scientists, theorists or researchers, but that every human being is a 'personal scientist' and capable of creating theory at various levels. Personal scientists are engaged in a process of observation, interpretation, prediction and control. They erect for themselves a representational model of the world which guides their behaviour and action. This model is constantly tested, modified or replaced in order to allow better predictions and control in the future. These activities are symptomatic of both scientific theorising and daily explorations of life around rival hypotheses. Personal scientists are engaged in the anticipation of events with a view to the prediction and control of events. Kelly (1955, 72) describes the progressive evolution of our construction system through the invalidation of our anticipation of events:

> ... the successive relevation of events invites the person to place new constructions upon them whenever something unexpected happens... The constructions one places on events are working

hypotheses, which are about to be put to the test of experience. As one's anticipations or hypotheses are successively revised in the light of the unfolding sequence of events, the construction system undergoes a progressive evolution.

To sum up, Kelly's fundamental postulate states that people's behaviour in the present is determined by the way they anticipate events in the future through the use of personal constructs in order to forecast events (theory building) or to evaluate previous forecasts and their validity or efficiency (theory testing). This process of knowledge creation and constant review of one's knowledge is applicable to the researcher and to the learner in the formal education system, as well as to people in everyday life. The only difference is the level of theorisation and abstraction, as discussed below (in the modulation corollary).

The organisation corollary

Each person characteristically evolves, for his convenience in anticipating events, a construction system embracing ordinal relationships between constructs (Kelly, 1963, 56). Kelly believes that constructs do not exist in isolation but are hierarchically ordered in subordinate or superordinate positions within the individual construction system. The 'construction system' refers to the whole-person system. The term 'evolves' emphasises that this organisation is not a static entity, but in a constant state of motion and open to change.

The individuality corollary

Persons differ from each other in their construction of events (Kelly, 1963, 55). Each person's construct system is unique. Constructs can differ in their position, focus, range or permeability within the hierarchical framework, and in the strength of their relationships with other parts of the system. Kelly's idea of encouraging clients to articulate at least a part of their individual constructions is important in higher education. For example, a student's articulation allows the teacher to have some understanding of the personal models the learner is using to impose meaning on the world; and the process of articulation may help the learner to clarify thoughts and reflect on potential avenues for change. To Kelly, the first explanation is vital for an effective consultation or teaching situation. Therefore his next proposition is also of importance to higher education.

The sociality corollary

To the extent that one person construes the construction process of another, he may play a role in a social process involving the other person (Kelly, 1963, 95). In the higher education context this means that the process of communication will be inadequate unless the teacher has some understanding of the student's personal constructs about the domain within which he/she wishes to converse, and unless the student has some understanding of the teacher's constructs. Teachers, for example, need not have the same or similar construct systems as their students, but they must be able to subsume and understand their students' construct systems in order to 'interact' with them rather than 'act' and teach them. Kelly even admits the possibility of shared areas of personal meaning in the following proposition.

The commonality corollary

To the extent that one person employs a construction of experience which is similar to that employed by another, his psychological processes are psychologically similar to those of the other person (Kelly, 1963, 90). Kelly suggests that people — despite their individuality — may be similar to others because they attribute approximately the same meaning to events and thus share their culture or tacit theory of the world. People who are similar in the way they think, act, construe their experience and anticipate or predict other people's behaviour and expectations form a cultural group. Kelly (1963, 93) defines culture not in the traditional sense, as 'persons grouped according to similarities in their upbringing and in their environment', but as 'similarity in what members of the group expect of each other'. However, he approaches problems of cultural similarity and the commonality of behaviour mainly from the point of view of the individual person. He stresses the personal nature of meaning and elevates the personal scientist to the central focus of enquiry.

Three further corollaries are relevant to education generally, and to conceptual change particularly: modulation, fragmentation and choice.

The modulation corollary

The variation in a person's construction system is limited by the permeability of the constructs within whose range of convenience the variants lie (Kelly, 1963, 77). 'Permeability' in Kelly's terms means a degree of openness to change, the potential to countenance new features. Kelly (1970a, 19) describes it as a construct's 'capacity to be used as a referent for novel events and to accept new subordinate constructions within its range of convenience'. The variants are those constructs which replace each other and which lie within the range of convenience of a permeable regnant construct. If some parts of a person's construct system are impermeable, those parts will resist change. Fransella (1980, 246) explains the resistance to change with what Kelly calls 'hostility':

> ... we can resist change and refuse to accept the invalidation for what it is. We thereby show hostility. As personal or psychological scientist, as psychotherapist or teacher, as worker or boss, as parent or child, we often 'make' the events support our predictions. One reason for this refusal to accept the invalidatory evidence could be that to acknowledge this reality staring us in the face would require personal change of such enormity that we could not contemplate it. It is too threatening.

Kelly believes that conceptual development is an evolutionary process. Conceptual structures are groups of constructs which are independently organised substructures. These substructures are hierarchically organised at progressively higher levels of abstraction. The substructures are also functionally differentiated so that the 'range of convenience' of an individual's construct system is enhanced. This means that some features or events which are viewed as inappropriate or not applicable by a construct or substructure (i.e. which are viewed as neutral or lying outside 'the range of convenience') may be viewed as adequate or appropriate by other constructs or substructures on the basis of different functions. These differing substructures are hierarchically integrated in a person's construct system. The hierarchical integration enables the individual to make a wider range of cross-references than would be possible within a very differentiated system. It is therefore an essential aspect of conceptual development or, in Bruner's (1977) terms, the development of intelligence.

The fragmentation corollary

A person may successively employ a variety of construction subsystems which are inferentially incompatible with each other (Kelly, 1963, 83). Some people can tolerate more incompatibility than others, depending on the permeability of their superordinating constructs. Although good cognitive functioning requires integration through the deployment of superordinate constructs, inconsistency or 'fragmentation' and differentiation can be of advantage as well. For example, when testing out new constructs or hypotheses, the constructive alternativist can employ old, incompatible constructs. Kelly (1970b, 258) sees this ability as a useful feature of human thought:

The nice thing about hypotheses is that you don't have to believe them. This, I think, is a key to the genius of scientific method. It permits you to be inconsistent with what you know long enough to see what will happen. Children do that. What is wonderful about the language of hypothesis is its refreshing ability to free the scientist from the entangling consistencies of adulthood. For a few precious moments he can think again like a child, and, like a child, learn from his experience...

Fragmentation and modulation corollaries suggest how a person uses a variety of differing subsystems which are semi-independent, but at some point, they are subsumed by some superordinate construct. That is, we have a number of constructions, each specific to a task or domain and separate and fragmented from one another, but at some level we can join them together. As mentioned before, the hierarchical integration enables us to see relations and to make cross-references, an essential feature of conceptual development and change.

The choice corollary

A person chooses for himself that alternative in a dichotomized construct through which he anticipates the greater possibility for the extension and definition of his system (Kelly, 1963, 64). This proposition is particularly relevant to the higher education context, because it embodies the *intentionality* of personal change. It is the individual's cognitive and conscious activity, rather than his/her response to an external stimulus, which brings about personal, conceptual development and change. A person makes his/her choice of a dichotomous construct (e.g. security versus adventure) in such a way as to enhance his/her anticipation of events. For example, whether his/her choice is for constricted certainty (and a clear definition of his/her system) or for broadened understanding (and an extension of the predictive range of his/her system) depends not on mere intellectual insight or a single issue, but on a complex of issues. In any case, his/her decision is essentially elaborative, so that we may refer to an 'elaborative choice'.

Critical appraisal of Kelly's theory

Common charges levelled against Kelly's theory are that it is first too 'mentalistic', and second too 'individualistic'. The first argument, even by some of those who admire the theory (e.g. Bruner, 1956), claims that Kelly's description of construct systems deals only with the 'rational' aspect of the person, merely describing his/her 'thinking', not 'feeling'. But these dualists see the dichotomy of reason versus passion, cognition versus emotion, whereas Kelly considers the complete person. He avoids this dualism by focusing on certain constructs (e.g. anxiety, hostility, guilt, threat, fear, aggressiveness) which he defines as aspects of construct systems in a state of change. From the position of personal construct theory, Bannister (1970) argues that much of traditional psychology has achieved a rather inadequate statement of its subject because it has declined to use the idea of a person. Instead, psychologists have studied behaviour or the mind or emotion. As pointed out earlier (Chapter 3), behaviour can be an important criterion in the study and evaluation of learning and teaching in higher education, but only if seen in a holistic manner, as Bannister and Fransella (1986, 31) argue:

> But instead of trying to treat behaviour in its own right, personal construct theory argues that behaviour must be related to the person who behaves. What people do, they do to some purpose and they not only behave but intend to indicate something by their behaviour.

Behaviour is seen not as a reaction but as a proposition, not as the answer but as the question. As Kelly (1970a) has pointed out, behaviour is an experiment and in behaving we are asking a question of our world — a person's behaviour will make little ultimate sense to us unless we understand the question which they are asking. Behaviour, like words (referred to by psychologists as verbal behaviour), has *meaning* — and changing, elaborating and negotiated meaning at that.

The second line of criticism refers to Kelly's focus on the individual person, rather than on his/her interaction with others (Holland, 1970). Although Kelly does include the social process (sociality corollary) and the commonality of thinking (commonality corollary) in his framework, he stresses the personal nature of meaning and focuses on the personal scientist as the centre of enquiry. This is the reason why this book extends Kelly's theory with a more interactionist theory of action (Chapter 5), because learning and teaching in higher education are not only activities conducted by individuals, but also group processes.

One of Kelly's (1955, 24) design specifications for a theory of personality is that it should be fertile in creating new ideas: 'It should lead to the formulation of hypotheses; it should provoke experiments; and it should inspire invention'. Judged by this criterion, Kelly's personal construct theory has been successful in that it has stimulated a great deal of innovative research in educational psychology. It is hoped that it will also inspire more research in higher education.

Implications of Kelly's theory for higher education

There are a number of implications for higher education. Kelly's theory bridges the gap between traditional theorists on the one hand and practitioners on the other. The conflict between theorists and practitioners can be solved by the personal scientists. Everyone is a personal scientist: students, teachers, counsellors and administrators. But they will only adopt those of the theories we might want them to learn which are permeable to their construction system (modulation), which they choose and intend to integrate into their system (elaborative choice), and which are related to their representational model of the world and the way they anticipate events (fundamental postulate). Therefore, it is important to know students' construct systems (i.e. their existing knowledge) (cf Bruner, 1975; Ausubel, 1975) before teaching them new knowledge or theories and before selecting appropriate teaching content, materials and methods. Teachers in higher education, too, are personal scientists, able to construe their own and their students' experiences, to hypothesise, to test their hypotheses and to anticipate or predict future events. They may be guided by educational researchers, but essentially they are capable of doing action research into their own teaching experience. Just as students are able to acquire knowledge of a subject, staff can acquire knowledge in educational theory by starting from their personal knowledge and extending it by a continuous process of formulating hypotheses, testing them, confirming or rejecting them, and starting anew. Even if their hypotheses turn out to be wrong, they have learnt something.

As a psychotherapist, Kelly suggests the encouragement of clients to articulate their theories or world views and to recognise these theories as current hypotheses open to refutation and invalidation. Clients have to be guided to acknowledge that it is they themselves who construct their own world views and that they should also accept the responsibility for change. This has implications for higher education. Although Kelly himself has written little about the learner in the educational context, Pope and Keen (1981) have adapted his ideas to student learning and teaching. If the learners (whether as students or as teachers) are encouraged to articulate their world views and to open their minds to refutation and potential alternatives, they will learn that our 'ways of seeing' reality are not static, but open and subject to change.

Kelly realises from his own experience (e.g. with critics of his theory) that people may be very resistant and hostile to accepting refutation and invalidation of their personal constructions. They may feel threatened and insecure if their constructions of 'the world as it really is' are contradicted; and they may be reluctant to experiment with alternative models. He describes this feeling as 'anxiety' which may act as a barrier to conceptual change and freedom from personal prisons. This is an important insight into the problem of people's change, whether it be in student learning or staff development.

Kelly (1970b, 2) recognises this challenge of constructive alternativism:

> ... a person who spends a great deal of his time hoarding facts is not likely to be happy at the prospect of seeing them converted into rubbish. He is more likely to want them bound and preserved, a memorial to his personal achievement. A scientist, for example, who thinks this way, and especially a psychologist who does so, depends on his facts to furnish the ultimate proof of his propositions. With these shining nuggets of truth in his grasp it seems unnecessary for him to take responsibility for the conclusion he claims they thrust upon him. To suggest to him at this point that further human reconstruction can completely alter the appearance of the precious fragments he has accumulated, as well as direction of their arguments, is to threaten his scientific conclusions, his philosophical position, and even his moral security. No wonder, then, that, in the eyes of such a conservatively minded person, our assumption that all facts are subject — are wholly subject — to alternative constructions looms up as culpably subjective and dangerously subversive to the scientific establishment.

This insight is of importance to any educationalist who is concerned with conceptual change, a notion to be discussed in Chapter 8.

Conclusion

Kelly's fundamental postulate and his corollaries give a picture of the person/learner as a 'personal scientist, with a hierarchical construction system (organisation) which is personally unique (individuality) and which can be explored by him/herself as well as by others (sociality). Apart from their individuality, a group of people may be similar in terms of their construction of experience (commonality). The development of intelligence or conceptual change depends on the permeability of a person's constructs (modulation) and on the balance between hierarchical integration and consistency of differing constructs on the one hand and their differentiation and inconsistency (fragmentation) on the other.

Kelly's constructive alternativism has implications for higher education in that it challenges conventional views held by those academics, administrators and students who resist to experiment with alternative models and consequently to change their 'nuggets of truth' (i.e. their scientific conclusions, philosophical positions or their moral security). Similarly, Leontiev's theory of action, to be discussed in the next chapter, might be threatening to those conventional teachers and learners in higher education who believe in the transmission model of knowledge (from expert to novice), rather than in an action model of self-directed, self-organised and consciously controlled knowledge creation and learning.

If learning is the active, creative, rational, emotional, intentional and pragmatic construction of reality (Kelly), students are not to be seen as the passive receivers of knowledge but the active constructors (or self-instructors) and interpreters of their experiences. Academics need not merely apply theory, constructed by educational researchers, to their practice, but they can be action researchers themselves, as shall be explored further in Chapter 6. It is in this way that knowledge and theory become personalised, relevant to and fully integrated into educational practice.

The theoretical framework developed so far is based on the new, emerging, dialectic epistemology (cf Table 3). My general criticism of behaviourist and cognitive theories is not that they are wrong, but that they regard thinking/learning as an isolated process rather than as embedded in the general context and organisation of human action, including practical activities, self-reflection, emotional and other effective processes. Kelly allows for emotions and feelings to enter and influence the construction process within the individual, but he does not fully explain the relationship between the external (objective) and the internal (subjective) conditions of human action. This relationship between subjective and objective conditions exists in and through action and is therefore not static, but dynamic. The development of a dynamic model which is of practical value to higher education is the subject matter of the next chapter.

Chapter 5

Leontiev's theory of action

Introduction

Like cognitive theories and Kelly's personal construct theory, theories of action have evolved as a critical reaction to behaviourism and empiricism. In the behaviourist theories, knowing and learning behaviour are described, explained and predicted as responses to certain stimuli, but processes of conscious planning, action and decision are not the central focus of enquiry; at the most, cognition and consciousness are additional side-effects observed in the change of behaviour. In contrast, action theories regard cognition and conscious action as essential factors in human behaviour. They assume that mental processes, such as reasoning, problem-solving or decision making, as well as motor procedures, are dependent components of the macro unit 'action'. However, it should be pointed out that the terms 'action' and 'activity' are sometimes used synonymously and sometimes with distinctly different meanings. The confusion in the literature is probably due to the fact that many action theories have been translated differently into English from German (e.g. Holzkamp, Lenk, Hacker, Volpert) and from Russian (Leontiev, Galperin, Vygotskij, Zincenko). In this book 'action' is to be understood as the superordinate concept of the state or process of acting or doing; 'activity' as a specific action, deed or a sphere of actions (e.g. learning/teaching activities); and 'operation' as a process of a practical or mechanical nature in some form of work or production (*Macquarie Dictionary*).

In many disciplines (e.g. Psychology, Sociology, Linguistics) recent discussions have emphasised action as an integrative concept. The background to the vast numbers of different action theories varies and can only be sketched out briefly here. The main ideas of action theory in cognitive psychology are outlined below and are followed by a description of Leontiev's theory of action which is then applied to provide the structure for a theoretical model of action in learning, teaching and staff development. After a critical appraisal, some implications of these models are discussed for higher education.

Cognitive theories of action

The main characteristics of cognitive theories generally have been outlined in Chapter 3. Basically, these theories are subject-oriented (e.g. studying cognitive structures and processes) and/or object-oriented (e.g. task- or problem-oriented). The relationship is seen to be static, rather than dynamic. This might be one of the reasons why academics have been unwilling to accept psychological research as being relevant to their teaching practice, in which subjective and objective conditions do not appear in isolation, but are integrally interrelated through the learning–teaching activity. The following example from Seeger and Bromme (1979, 465) might illustrate the point.

> The teacher's assessment of students and the students' actual abilities are not independent of each other. The teacher's decisions in terms of a student's ability are at the same time developmental conditions for the student's ability and are, therefore, again constitutive for the teacher's judgements and decisions. In a similar way, the students' actual abilities are dependent on the teacher's evaluation. [My translation]

It becomes evident that the reduction of cognitive theories to subject orientation (i.e. a focus on cognitive aspects of information processing) or to object orientation (i.e. an emphasis on aspects of problems and tasks) is not sufficient for a system description and an explanation of teaching as an action. For it is the teacher's action that constitutes the interplay between students' and the teacher's abilities and students' and the teacher's expectations. Therefore, the concept of 'action' is a necessary category, not only for the description of empirical events, but also for theory building. The above example has shown that there is a dynamic relationship between subjective and objective conditions and that this dynamic relationship is produced by action. This theorem could be related to Piaget (1977, 30) who sees the role of action as a necessary element in the conceptualisation of thinking:

> The figurative aspects of the cognitive functions, though obviously useful and necessary to the knowledge of states, are incapable of accounting for thought, because by themselves they cannot succeed in assimilating the transformations of reality. The reason is that knowledge is not a static copy of reality. *To know an object* is not to furnish a simple copy of it: it *is to act on it so as to transform it* and grasp within these transformations the mechanism by which they are produced. To know, therefore, is to produce the object dynamically; but to reproduce it is necessary to know how to produce, and this is why knowledge derives from the entire action, not merely from its figurative aspects. [My emphasis]

This theoretical transformation of action in the subject or person has been called 'interiorisation' or 'interior representation' (Galperin, 1967; Leontiev, 1977), 'active reflection' (Kolb, 1984), 'inner model' or 'operative image' (Britchcin, 1982). It is an area which has not been sufficiently researched in higher education, but which is of central importance to learning and teaching. Piaget (1977, 31) gives us some cues in his formulations of the subject–object problem:

> The subjects S and the objects O are therefore indissociable, and it is from this indissociable interaction S $\longleftrightarrow$ O that *action, the source of knowledge,* originates. The point of departure of this knowledge, therefore, is neither S nor O but the interaction proper to the action itself. It is from this dialectic interaction $\longleftrightarrow$ that the object is bit by bit discovered in its objective properties by a 'decentration' which frees knowledge of its subjective illusions. It is from this same interaction $\longleftrightarrow$ that the subject, by discovering and conquering the object, organizes his actions into a coherent system that constitutes the operations of his intelligence and his thought. [My emphasis]

Holzkamp (1984) explains the origin of this whole process phylogenetically by saying that the qualitative leap in the human development from a biological animal to a conscious being occurred at the stage when human beings started to reflect on their actions and became conscious that they reproduced themselves and their abilities and recognised themselves in the products of their actions. These ideas will be expanded in the next sub-chapter on Leontiev's materialistic psychology, from which Holzkamp has developed his critical psychology. Both, in turn, are based on Marxist–Leninist philosophy; but only those aspects of theory will be discussed which are relevant to 'action'. For action is the missing link in the subject–

object interaction; it is 'the source of knowledge' and must be at the very heart of, and of vital importance to, an emerging theory of higher education.

Miller et al. (1960) were among the first to present the hierarchical-sequential organisation of action in their TOTE (Test–Operate–Test–Exit) Unit. The main idea is that behaviour can be recalled; that on the basis of this process of recall, a comparison takes place with the aims of the action; and as a result, that the action is continued, changed or terminated. Thus there is a strong emphasis on consciousness which is based on a view of a person as a naive or intuitive action theorist. Unlike other creatures, human beings have the capacity of consciousness, conceptualisation, generalisation, abstraction, and theorisation.

Whether consciously or unconsciously, Kagan (1984) and Perlberg (1984) have applied this theory of recall, consciousness, developmental action and change to higher education in their models of student learning and staff development through 'interpersonal process recall' (IPR) and 'video self-confrontation' (VSC) respectively.

Behaviourist psychologists (e.g. Skinner, Gagné, Bloom) believe in the hierarchical-sequential organisation of human behaviour too, but they regard this structure as common to all people. In contrast, cognitive psychologists (e.g. Lindsay and Norman, Bruner, Ausubel) believe that although the basic structure of memory and the machinery for manipulating, reorganising, interpreting and recalling information is similar in all people, the memory products are not necessarily the same. They depend on a person's experience and on differences in the environment. For example, Lindsay and Norman (1975) view the structure of memory as a system which learns through an active interaction with its environment, rather than a passive build up of stimulus–response connections.

Although cognitive structures belong to a very complex and hierarchically organised system, they appear sequentially in action. They are developed through processes of internal representation or reflection of external situations in the mind. But these processes are not passive: the acting person selects and evaluates external events before integrating them. Through these active processes, the external real world is refracted by the individual's mental constitution (i.e. the personal construct system) before being reflected in his or her cognitive system. The external events or activities which are transformed and internally reflected and integrated in a person's mind are not restricted to mental activities, but include material ones as well, as the next sub-chapter will show.

Materialistic theories of action

Leontiev (1977), in his theory of activity, consciousness and personality, emphasises even more strongly than Western cognitive psychologists that human action is determined by social conditions. Leontiev and his followers (e.g. Holzkamp, Galperin, Rubinstein, Seeger, Bromme, Heger) believe that human abilities are not only self-developed, but also passed on from generation to generation as historically derived knowledge. Their key concept of 'material action' (i.e. action with concrete matters) is of central importance to their theory.

Galperin (1967, 374) whose educational interest led him to focus on mental activities, developed his so-called 'interiorisation theory', which in essence says 'that mental activities (or thinking) are the result of a transformation of external, material activities to interior representation and active reflection (i.e. to the form of perceptions, ideas and concepts)'. [My translation]

Starting from this strong determinism (i.e. a dependency of inner activities on exterior activities) and starting from a hierarchy of these internal, mental activities, Galperin (1967, 388) differentiates between certain progressive stages in this internalisation process which are characterised by increasing abstraction; language is an important constituent of interiorisation.

Rubinstein (1973) has formulated the principle of the unity of cognition and action which Leontiev (1977) has developed further by emphasising the importance of concrete, material action for solving the problem of the relationship between subject and object. According to Stadler and Seeger (1981, 206), this concrete, materialistic action is characterised as being: holistic; co-operative/social; a system having its own structure (i.e. action is not mere 'reaction'); and perceived as 'the manifestation of life provided by mental reflection and having the material function to orient the subject in the concrete world' (my translation).

Like Piaget, Leontiev sees the interaction of subject and object through action and recognises the importance of action as a theoretical category, but he also considers action as a promising non-cognitive conceptualisation of cognitive–psychological problems. Since the following is a fundamental statement, it is reproduced in the original German as well as my translation (Leontiev, 1977, 44–5):

> Die Übergänge Subjekt–Tätigkeit–Gegenstand bilden gewisser-massen einen Kreis. Es mag daher unerheblich erscheinen, welches Glied als das erste genommen wird. Doch das ist keineswegs so. Der Kreis öffnet sich, er öffnet sich in der

praktisch sinnlichen Tätigkeit. In direkter Berührung mit der gegenständlichen Realität und sich dieser Realität unterordnend, wird die Tätigkeit verändert, bereichert. In dieser bereicherten Form eben kristallisiert sie sich im Produkt. Die realisierte Tätigkeit ist reicher, wahrer als das sie antizipierende Bewusstsein. Dem Subjekt jedoch wird der Beitrag seiner Tätigkeit nicht bewusst, wodurch der Anschein erweckt wird, als sei das Bewusstein Grundlage der Tätigkeit.

The transitions of subject–action–object to a certain extent form a circle. Therefore, it may seem irrelevant which element comes first. But this is not at all so. The circle breaks open in the practical physical (or material) action. The action is changed and enhanced by a direct communication with the concrete (materialistic) reality and submitting to this reality. In this enhanced form it is crystallised in the product. The realised action is more enhanced and correct than the consciousness by which it was anticipated. However, the subject is not aware of the contribution made by his/her action so that it appears as if the consciousness were the basis of action. [My translation]

The diagram in Figure 5 represents Leontiev's subject–action–object schema (adapted from Seeger and Bromme, 1979, 467). The terminology 'subject–action–object' is not used in the common sense, but (with reference to the German translation of 'Subjekt–Tätigkeit–Objekt') in the meaning of the English grammar usage of 'subject–activity–object', where the subject is the agent; the activity refers to the action; and the object is that which the agent creates or acts upon. In this sense, the interaction between the subject and the object can be seen in two fundamental processes and in four components. There are two fundamental processes which Piaget calls 'accommodation' and 'assimilation', and which Galperin names 'exteriorisation' and 'interiorisation'. The four components are:

1. the conscious and intentional control of the action by the subject $(S \rightarrow A)$;
2. the influence through the action on the object $(A \rightarrow O)$;
3. the impact of the object on the action $(O \rightarrow A)$; and
4. the active reflection or internal representation of the action in the subject $(A \rightarrow S)$.

This model may be applied to all kinds of everyday activity as well as to an analysis of learning, teaching, research and staff development.

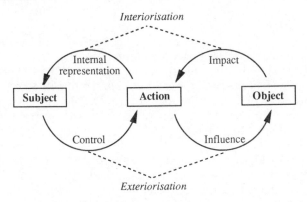

Exteriorisation

Figure 5   *Subject–action–object schema (after Leontiev, 1977)*

But before doing so, the following operational definitions are restated in terms of learning and teaching in higher education: subject, action, object.

The *subject* is the holistic person and his/her consciousness, including intentions, motivations, cognitive aspects (e.g. thoughts, ideas, concepts) as well as effective aspects (e.g. emotions, feelings, anxiety). The subject might be students, academics, administrators, counsellors or staff developers

The *action* may refer to any aspect of learning, teaching or other professional activities. Whether the action is practical (exterior) or mental (interior), its aim is to be reflected, refracted or transformed in the subject's consciousness together with the product of action (the object) which is to be reproduced in the subject's consciousness.

The *object* refers to a task, problem or to that which is produced (e.g. learnt or taught) by the subject (e.g. students or staff) through action (e.g. learning or teaching). It includes all given factors within the context and system of an institution (e.g. the curriculum — content, structure, assessment system), the philosophy of the institution, its conditions, requirements, regulations, etc., as well as outside the institution (e.g. the country's economic and political situation, government cuts, etc.).

The dynamics in this subject–action–object schema can be explained in simple terms. The subject consciously plans and controls a course of action or activity in his/her consciousness based on existing knowledge, hypotheses, intuitive theories and past experiences. During and after the implementation of the action, the action is interiorised in the subject's mind as 'refracted', personal, new or modified knowledge integrated in the hierarchy of his/her existing knowledge system. This knowledge is personal, because it has been refracted by the subject's own active reflection on, and evaluation of, the action. Thus staff and students are both the creators and the products of the social situations in which they teach and learn. Freire (1970, 27) describes the process as 'conscientisation' or social change: 'the process in which people, not as recipients, but as knowing subjects, achieve a deepening awareness both of the sociohistorical reality which shapes their lives and of their capacity to transform that reality'.

The action, on the one hand, is limited and influenced by the object (i.e. by the demands and requirements of the task or of the institution); on the other, it may influence and change the object (task and/or context) and produce new conditions for future actions.

A model of student learning

Heger (1986) was among the first to apply Leontiev's theory to higher education and to develop a model for the analysis of student learning, of teaching, and of evaluating a staff development programme. Within this framework, Brandt and Sell (1986) have adopted this model to the three strands of studying in higher education:

1. The *subject*: being a student: the subjective elements of studying (i.e. the student as a person);
2. The *object*: context of studying: the objective elements of studying (i.e. the institution);
3. The *action*: actions of studying: the student's actions under the influence of personality traits and external demands (e.g. study strategies).

The actions of studying:

• are controlled by the student (e.g. on the basis of his/her personality traits — motivation, anxieties, abilities and competencies, satisfaction, etc.);
• are internally represented in the person of the student, as a basis for action;
• influence the institutional context of studying (e.g. the students can influence the institution through individual or group criticism or through the students' union);
• are under the impact of this institutional context (e.g. the student has to respond to the demands or expectations of the institution, especially to its assessment requirements).

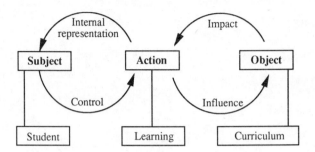

Figure 6 *A model of student learning (after Leontiev, 1977)*

Brandt and Sell have used this model as a structure for their particular courses on study skills, on oral and written communication, co-operation, group dynamics and problem-solving. These courses are voluntary and conducted by their centre for students of all faculties, but primarily of engineering. However, it would be of greater advantage if the academics themselves (rather than educationalists) conducted such courses, so that both the content and the process of knowing and learning would be integral parts of a student's academic programme. Such a model could be explained in simple terms as in Figure 6.

A model of academic activities

The same basic model of action may be applied to a teacher's main activities and responsibilities in higher education: research, teaching, administration and community services. Figures 7 and 8 are adaptations of Heger's diagrams from the German higher education system to the Australian one.

The different aspects of the academics' action in Figure 7 can be associated with the appropriate aspects of the object. The diagram is self-explanatory: every reader will be able to tell a story and arrive at his/her own interpretation. However, with particular reference to the teaching activity it should be pointed out that the teaching matter (the object side) is predominantly ideational or symbolic, and its aims and products (also the object side) are to be found in the production of ideational, regulative structures in students' minds. So there is a close connection between the object side of the teaching activity and the subject side of student learning. This linkage in the model must be taken into consideration, not only in an analysis of learning–teaching activities, but of communication in general. The point will become clearer in the next sub-chapter, in which the same model will be

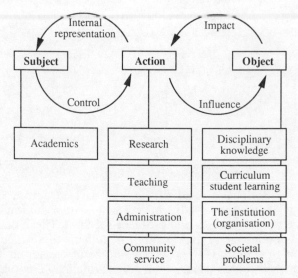

Figure 7   *A model of academic staff activities (after Heger, 1986, 65)*

applied to staff development (i.e. to the communication between academics on the one hand and educational advisers or staff developers on the other).

A model of staff development

For the purpose of applying Leontiev's model to staff development, the term staff development is simply defined as the professional development of teachers in higher education with the advice and assistance of educational advisers called staff developers. A more differentiated explanation of this topic will be given in Part 3.

Figure 8 is an extension of Leontiev's basic model and an adaptation of Heger's (1986, 68) evaluation model. It is an overlap of two subject–action–object schemata for there are two sets of subjects with differentiated intentions and tasks which are partly congruent in staff development activities.

The three double strands can be described as follows:

1. The *subject* is represented by academics from two groups: the teaching staff (Subject 1) and the staff developers (Subject 2). People in both categories may be employed full or part time as outside experts on a short-term contract, as general or academic

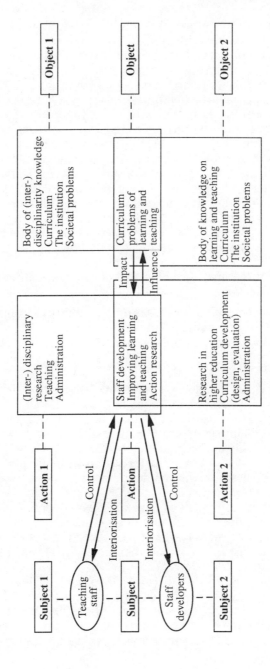

Figure 8 *A model of staff development (after Heger, 1986, 68)*

staff on a fixed term appointment, or as academics in a special department/unit/centre in continual employment.

2. The *action* consists of an overlap of two fields of action: the activities of teaching staff (Action 1), such as teaching, (inter)disciplinary research and administration; and those of the staff developers or educational advisers (Action 2), such as research in higher education, curriculum design and evaluation/review, administration, etc. Where these two fields of action overlap, there is a possibility of joint action, such as staff development, improving learning and teaching, or action research.

3. The *object*, too, consists of an overlap of two objects: the object of the teaching staff (Object 1), which includes (inter)disciplinary tasks or problems, the curriculum, the institution and societal problems; and the object of staff developers (Object 2), including problems of learning, teaching, curriculum, the institution and society. The overlap of the two objects shows the mutual object or tasks in staff development at which all activities are aimed: problems of learning, teaching and curriculum within the context of higher education.

Before considering the practical implications of Leontiev's theory for learning, teaching and staff development in higher education, a brief critical appraisal seems appropriate.

Critical appraisal

Both personal construct theory and materialistic action theory share a central epistemological assumption: that human beings are subjects capable of cognitive construction, reflection and interpretation; they are reflexive individuals generating and testing their hypotheses and applying them by way of example to their consciously controlled actions. Human actions are not perceived as absolute phenomena, but as constituted by descriptions and interpretations. As Lenk (1978) puts it, 'actions are interpretation constructs'. Both theories take an 'internal perspective', that is, the agents themselves (as personal scientists) interpret the meaning of their actions. This is in contrast to most behaviourist and cognitive theorists who take an 'external perspective', that is, the action is observed and interpreted by an outside observer. This new internal perspective has led to a new methodology in educational research which will be discussed in Chapter 7. However, action theory methodology (just as other methodologies critical of the external-aspect research) has not been able to find a methodological rationale which, on the one hand, includes the complexity and historicism of the social science subject, but which, on the other hand, is also capable of specifying factors and conditions which are the main determinators of the processes under investigation.

As Kelly has been criticised for his emphasis on individualism, so have Leontiev and Galperin for over-emphasising the adaptation of the human mind to social conditions and for leaving too little space for the creative development of the individual (e.g. Rubinstein, 1962, 19). But leaving this ideological debate aside, the concept of the central importance of action for human cognition and for the creation of knowledge is a useful one in both Leontiev's and Galperin's materialistic theories of action.

To Leontiev, social conditions are more important than individual conditions, a view which is to be explained by the political–historical and ideological tradition in Russia at the time. Western social scientists in recent times have tended to emphasise the individual's rights and needs in a democratic society. The position taken in this book is not to see the relationship of the individual to society as a dichotomy, but as a dialectical relationship between them.

For higher education, this means that staff and students are both enabled and restricted by their environment and its cultural and socio-historical tradition; they have the ability of seeing the need for changing any conditions that might hinder learning and critical thinking; and they have the responsibility of searching for alternatives to bring about this change. They are not total victims of their environment, but active problem solvers and responsible citizens. Therefore, it is an important role of higher education to prepare students for this task and develop holistic, critical, dialectical thinking, as discussed in Chapter 3. Other implications of Leontiev's theory for higher education are discussed in the next sub-chapter.

Implications for higher education

There are implications of action theory for learning by both students and staff. First, which are the principles that can be drawn for student learning?

Student learning

There are at least four important principles of learning and teaching (i.e. teaching to be understood as the facilitation of learning) which we may derive from Leontiev's materialistic theory of action. The first is that the action of learning should be as concrete and practical as possible in the early stages of studying a new area of knowledge in order to facilitate internal representation. Gradually the action may become more and more abstract as the interiorisation process and the consciousness develop progressively in the student.

The second principle is that the degree of consciousness and conceptualisation depends on the extent to which actions — whether practical/concrete or mental/abstract actions — are interiorised in the learner. Important constituents of interiorisation are language, communication with others and active reflection. It should be emphasised that 'interiorisation' is not only meant as a mirror-effect of the action of learning on the learner but also as the student's own effective reaction to and reflective thinking about the content and processes of learning. Mere internalisation of action (i.e. storage of information or events and accumulating them in one's memory) is only the lowest level of thinking. In order to reach Galperin's (1967, 388) higher levels of abstraction, generalisations and theory, thinking must become progressively active, reflective, critical, self-critical and creative. An instrument to reach more and more advanced levels of theory is language in both oral and written forms. This means that one can theorise better through discussions with others and through writing a report or paper than just through thinking on one's own.

The third principle of learning and teaching derived from Leontiev's theory of action is that students' existing knowledge and skills should be utilised in action learning. Action learning (e.g. by doing, experiencing, participating through discussion, problem-solving, project work, etc.) and metalearning (e.g. reflecting on the processes of learning, evaluating, etc.) are possible because of students' previous experience and existing knowledge in most areas of learning. Their minds are not '*tabulae rasae*, but full of life experiences which should be used as a base of, and link to, the new knowledge and skills to be learnt' (cf Bruner, 1975; Ausubel, 1975).

The fourth principle relates to the dialectical relationship between institutional requirements and students' needs in a fast-changing world. On the one hand, active learning and metalearning may influence the curriculum and assessment system, or students' conditions generally (see Figure 6, the 'influence' arrow), through open discussions between staff and students, through students' evaluation of courses and of teaching and through students' representation on committees, etc. On the other hand, institutional conditions, requirements, expectations and rules have a great impact on learning (the 'impact' arrow). They may even restrict or prevent active learning. For example, an assessment system with 100 per cent end-of-semester/term examinations is likely to encourage rote learning (surface approach) and to discourage active learning (deep-meaning approach). It follows that an institution which is a critical and self-critical community of 'personal scientists' in Kelly's terms provides the ideal environment for continuously negotiating the right balance between institutional requirements and students' needs in a constantly changing society. This means, with reference to Figure 6, that the strength of the 'influence' and 'impact' arrows would be about equal, whereas in the present higher education climate, the 'impact' arrow is considerably stronger; in some traditional departments the 'influence' arrow is almost non-existent. This principle is important not only with regard to student learning, but also to staff action and learning. There are other implications of Leontiev's theory for staff learning.

Academic staff learning

Academic staff understand themselves systematically as learners in their research in their own field. Usually they have learnt the foundations of their discipline and developed research skills, and they are eager to continue to learn through solving new research problems and to advance knowledge in their field. The rewards are extrinsic as well as intrinsic: personal satisfaction, publications, patents, royalties, awards, honours, tenure, promotion, etc.

The question is: how do staff learn about their teaching? In general, learning about teaching in universities is not as self-evident, systematic and rewarding as learning through (inter)disciplinary research. This issue is further developed in Chapter 8. Here it is of interest to indicate how the theoretical models based on Leontiev's action theory can throw light on the theory and practice (or the praxis) of staff learning.

With reference to Figure 7, learning is the interaction of the subject (i.e. the academic staff) with the object (i.e. knowledge, tasks, problems, etc.) through action (i.e. research and teaching). In research as well as in teaching, staff are concerned with specific, concrete, material, tangible actions which have to be also considered in the context of their practice (e.g. the imparted values and the traditions from which they come). In the same way as staff learn about their discipline through doing research, they can learn about problems of student learning and of curriculum development through their teaching praxis and critical reflection on their praxis.

With reference to Figure 8, teaching staff and staff developers may collaborate in areas where their objects overlap (i.e. in areas of the curriculum and problems of learning and teaching) through joint actions of improving learning and teaching and staff development activities such as action research. Action research is the subject of the next chapter.

Conclusion

It has been possible to present Leontiev's model of action and its derivatives (i.e. the models of learning, academic activities and of staff development) in a brief, concise manner, because the main concepts and principles had been introduced and discussed in previous chapters. The theoretical framework on which this model of higher education is built, and the model itself, have been developed gradually and dialectically from traditional and alternative epistemologies, from behavioural and cognitive theories, from the idea of holistic, dialectical thinking, through to Kelly's personal construct theory and finally, to action theories. Leontiev's subject–action–object model may serve as a theoretical framework in higher education for learning, teaching and staff development, all of which are conceived as conscious, active and ongoing processes of learning and knowing. But how can this model of learning, teaching and staff development, or any other educational theory, be put into practice? The issue of the relation between the results of research and effective action based upon it in higher education practice is an important one. In the past there has been a gap between educational theory and practice in higher education. More recently, attempts have been made to bridge this gap through staff development. One of these possibilities for integrating theory and practice — action research — will be treated in more detail in the next chapter, because it has not been sufficiently explained and developed at the higher education level. Chapter 6 contains a discussion of the theoretical base and the main arguments for action research in higher education, whereas action research strategies and examples are given in the companion book entitled *Action Research in Higher Education* (Zuber-Skerritt, 1992).

Part 3

The integration of theory and practice

The aim of this part is to extend the discussion of the praxis of higher education (outlined in Part 1) in more detail. By this I mean the practice of learning and teaching in its dialectical relationship to educational theory and in its cultural and educational context. In other words, praxis is understood as the dialectical relationship between theory arising from practice and practice being improved by theory. This book presents a metatheoretical perspective on higher education concerning alternative modes of theorising about the theory and praxis of learning and teaching in higher education.

Part 1 discussed the notions of practice and praxis in higher education and explained why theorising should not be totally left to outside experts; why good teaching cannot be reduced to the technical application of educational theory; and why it requires constant practical reasoning involving judgements, decisions, responsibility and wisdom. Schwab's (1969) notion of the 'practical' was introduced, suggesting gradual, not radical, change through curricular problem identification and solution primarily conducted by the practitioners themselves, not by outside researchers. Schwab concludes that the practical requires new forums of communication, new methods of deliberation, new kinds of educational researchers and new forms of staff development, but he does not specify in detail how these new requirements can be met in the praxis of higher education.

This book aims to fill this gap by discussing a new form of staff development, namely through academic course development, and in particular through collaborative enquiry into the practice of learning and teaching. Schwab's proposed new educational researchers are suggested to be action researchers (i.e. 'teachers as researchers') not only individual teachers and groups of teachers, but also teachers' organisations involved in practical politics of higher education.

Part 1 also discussed the interaction between human agency and the constraints of social structure. In praxis, people are producers as well as products of social reality. In order to improve the praxis of learning and teaching in higher education, educational research must be concerned with formulating 'grounded' theory (i.e. theory generated from the reality of higher education practice and learning–teaching experiences). The value of educational research must be judged by the extent to which:

1. it improves practice;
2. teachers participate and develop an understanding of their own problems and practices; and
3. it assists them in transforming situations which impede educationally desirable, rational and critical work in educational situations.

Part 2 discussed the theory in higher education and the dialectical integration of several competing theories (Chapter 3). It was argued that higher education as a human science needs to establish itself in the new, alternative, non-positivist, epistemological paradigm, based on a holistic view of humankind in which behaviour, thinking and acting are interrelated and interdependent. Part 2 also took account of the unique and complex abilities of learners to acquire knowledge through problem-solving, to construct their personal theories (Chapter 4), and to act and interpret their actions and experiences in the socio-historical, cultural and ideological context of their educational practice (Chapter 5).

Part 3 will discuss ways of integrating theory and practice in higher education, first by presenting the theory and development of action research (Chapter 6) based on:

1. Lewin's field theory;
2. experiential learning theory;
3. critical education science; and
4. the newly developed CRASP model in higher education.

This new kind of professional development through action research requires a new educational methodology discussed in Chapter 7 which is also the methodology used in this book, based on:

1. a new paradigm of research in higher education;

2. using new research methods;
3. case study methodology; and
4. the repertory grid technology.

Part 3 starts with Chapter 6, which discusses action research as a new form of educational research, a new kind of professional development through academic course development, a new method of improving the practice of learning and teaching, and simultaneously of advancing knowledge in higher education. In other words, action research is suggested as a methodology that seems appropriate to meet Schwab's requirements of the 'practical' discussed in Chapter 1.

Chapter 6

Action research

Introduction

The aim of this chapter is not to present techniques of action research or a step-by-step approach to its planning process and research procedures. This has effectively been achieved before in the *Action Research Guidebook* by Bennett and Oliver (1988) and in *The Action Research Planner* by Kemmis and McTaggart (1982; 1988) respectively. Rather, this chapter aims to provide an explanation and development of the theoretical concept.

Action research has been suggested as an appropriate and effective way to integrate educational research and teaching practice (Rudduck, 1985; Baird, 1988; Altrichter, 1988; Orteza y Miranda, 1988; Altrichter et al., 1989; Oja and Smulyan, 1989; Zuber-Skerritt, 1991a; 1992). The ideas and theoretical frameworks provided by Lewin (1948), Kolb (1984) and Carr and Kemmis (1986) have been successfully applied by 'teachers as researchers' at the primary and secondary levels and in (pre- and in-service) teacher education in various countries. For example, in 1989 the following action researchers presented their work at the annual meeting of the American Educational Research Association in San Francisco: Wasley and McElliott, Noffke, Sockett, SooHoo, Pine and Keane from the USA; McKernan from Ireland; Rudduck and Elliott from the UK; and Baird from Australia. In the same year, the books by Oja and Smulyan (USA), Winter (UK) and Altrichter et al. (Austria) on collaborative action research by teachers and teacher educators appeared, as well as many articles in various journals of teacher education (e.g. by Ward and Forrester, Argyris and Schön, Walton and Gaffney, Fergus and Wilson, and Whitehead, to mention only a few). What they all have in common is the main message that action research is an effective way of professional development for teachers and of improving the practice of learning and teaching.

However, there is a dearth of literature on action research in higher education which demonstrates that academics in subject areas other than teacher education can also advance and improve learning and teaching and achieve professionalism as teachers. It is one of the aims of this book to explore the feasibility and appropriateness of action research by academics in higher education, as a means to improve learning, teaching and professional development and to advance knowledge in higher education.

Action research is based on the fundamental concepts of action learning, adult learning and holistic, dialectical thinking as outlined in Chapter 3, and on the principles of experiential learning and critical thinking as discussed in this chapter.

The term action research has been defined in many different ways, but there are unifying theories that underlie the various types of action research. The main ideas of these theories will be discussed in this chapter. The operational definition of action research used in this book is *research by higher education teachers themselves into their own teaching practice and into student learning* (with the aim of improving their practice or changing their social environment) or briefly, 'the teacher as researcher' (Stenhouse, 1975), the 'personal scientist' (Kelly, 1955), and the critical, 'reflective practitioner' (Schön, 1983). This definition is in line with the CRASP model of action research listed in Table 1 in the 'Introduction' of this book and with the working definition generated by the participants of the 'International Symposium on Action Research in Higher Education, Government and Industry' (Zuber-Skerritt, 1991a, 8).

I have consciously and deliberately not made a distinction, but included Batchler and Maxwell's (1987) notion of 'action evaluation' and Argyris and Schön's (1989) concept of 'action science' in my definition of action research. This means that action research, like action evaluation, is, in Batchler and Maxwell's (1987, 70) terms:

> a process in which the 'practitioners' are included as evaluators, which features collaborative planning and data-gathering, self-reflection and responsiveness, and which embodies a substantial element of professional development. 'Ownership' of the evaluation is vested in the 'practitioners'.

Like action science, action research as I understand it must meet the standards of appropriate rigour without sacrificing relevance. Therefore, it is logical to prepare action researchers in higher education to meet such expectations by developing the necessary collaborative research skills in the same way as Knudson (1988) has suggested for teachers and student teachers. The methods of systematic, rigorous research will be discussed in Chapter 7. Here it suffices to point out that my definition of action research includes the methodology of action science.

In the light of the theories outlined in this book so far, we may assume that teachers in higher education are personal scientists (Kelly, 1955) with a critical, self-critical, dialectical thinking attitude who control the action (learning, research, teaching) consciously, with the action also having an imprint on their cognitive and affective systems. Similarly, the action may influence the object (i.e. the 'objects' of teaching and the teaching context), but the object has also an impact on the action (e.g. it may shape, restrict or enhance the action).

This model of the action researcher is useful in higher education, because it explains the need for an ongoing, continuous, cyclical process of 'coming to know' and of improving practice, and thus of integrating theory and practice. In this chapter the model will be extended and further discussed in the light of complementary theories: Lewin's field theory, Kolb's experiential learning theory, and Carr and Kemmis' model of action research as critical education science. Each of these sub-chapters contains some critical appraisal and implications for learning and teaching in higher education.

Lewin's theory

Kurt Lewin coined the term 'action research' and the phrase 'There is nothing so practical as a good theory'. This quotation symbolises his commitment to integrating theory and practice, enquiry and social problem-solving. The main purpose of his life, according to his biographer (Marrow, 1969, xi), was 'to seek deeper explanations of why people behave as they do and to discover how they may learn to behave better'. His concern for social problems in the 1940s, especially the fight of the Jews and other minority groups for democratic equality of rights and opportunities, led him to focus on the analysis of the nature and causes of social conflicts and the search for approaches, strategies and techniques capable of preventing or resolving them.

The theories and methods Lewin developed to investigate social change are relevant to higher education, for higher education is in itself a social process. Lewin talks about a 'general atmosphere' which is the background for all specific situations. Therefore, any research study of learning–teaching situations, processes or changes may benefit from Lewin's holistic, phenomenological approach to research as 'action research'. For example, student behaviour (e.g. withdrawal or deferral of enrolment) and staff attitudes (e.g. towards lecturing, mass education) may be influenced by cuts in funding and the general economic crisis in a country; therefore educational attitudes and behaviours should not be studied as separate variables — they have to be considered in context. Or, as Lewin (1948, 17) puts it:

> If one wants to understand the interrelationship between the parts and properties of a situation, the possibility of their coexistence, and its possible effects upon its various parts, ... it is necessary to analyze the situation. But this analysis must be a 'gestalt-theoretical' one, because the social situation, like the psychological situation, is a dynamic whole. It means that a change of one of its parts implies a change of the other parts.

Lewin was influenced by the German tradition of Gestalt psychology. *Gestalt* means an organised configuration or pattern of experiences or acts (as distinct from the separate experiences or acts). Gestalt psychology suggests that experiences do not occur through the summation of reflexes or other individual elements (as described by behaviourist psychology), but through configurations or *Gestalten* which operate individually or interact mutually.

Three particular aspects of Lewin's work which are of special relevance to higher education are his field theory, experiential phenomenology and action research.

Field theory

Field theory is a human science in contrast to a natural science. De Rivera (1976, 4) points out that Lewin's field theory should not be considered as a closed system of completed conceptualisations which could be applied to a range of problems, but rather as a way of looking at events determined by contemporary structures and forces: 'He viewed field "theory" more as an approach to conceptualization, the beginning of a set of concepts that could be used to represent fundamental psychological processes and reality.' Lewin (1952, 45) himself defines the term: 'Field theory is probably best characterized as a method: namely, a method of analyzing causal relations and of building scientific constructs'.

'Field' is Lewin's fundamental construct. The field in individual psychology is the 'life space' of the individual which consists of the person and the psychological environment. Applied to higher education, the life space of staff and students consists of the staff and students themselves and their environment as it exists for them. Lewin believes that it is the scientist's task to develop constructs and techniques of observation and measurement which are adequate to characterise the properties of any given life space at any given time; and to state the laws which govern the changes of these properties. The scientist's methodology might even have to go beyond what is accepted traditionally as 'scientific'. Cartwright (1952, xv) quotes Lewin's reference to Cassirer's philosophy of science:

> To proceed beyond the limitations of a given level of knowledge the researcher, as a rule, has to break down methodological taboos which condemn as 'unscientific' or 'illogical' the very models or concepts which later on prove to be basic for the next major progress.

Experiential phenomenology

The methodology which Lewin and his Berlin Group developed was in contrast to the method of statistical experimentation at that time. They used relatively few subjects and observed them as fully as possible with all the phenomena around them. They called it 'experiential phenomenology', which is particularly appropriate to the study of any aspect in higher education (e.g. student learning from the students' perspective or staff development from the staff perspective). The term is explained by Koffka, a member of Lewin's Berlin Group (quoted in De Rivera, 1976, 13):

> A good description of a phenomenon may by itself rule out a number of theories and indicate definite features which a true theory must possess. We call this kind of observation 'phenomenology', a word which has several meanings which must not be confused with ours. For us phenomenology means as naive and full a description of direct experience as possible.

Phenomenology will be discussed further in Chapter 7, but it is relevant in this chapter of action research, because it is a method of observing behaviour, experience and action. Lewin is often referred to as a behaviourist but, as De Rivera (1976, 14) points out:

> ... his behaviourism is grounded in the phenomenological enterprise of understanding, rather than the pragmatic enterprise of prediction and control. Consequently, Lewin and his students carefully attend to the meaning which the situation has for each subject and make a close observation and careful description of the details of the psychological processes that are involved.

People's behaviours are determined by their situation (or life space), but not totally; we also influence the meaning of our situation by our intentions. To Lewin, behaviour is a result of tensions and forces in the life space. But, with reference to Kelly and Leontiev, I suggest that the person is also an actor who is responsible for the very organisation that then determines the forces upon him/her. So Lewin's 'life space' may also be seen as the result of a person's organisation. This complementary perspective may be more appropriate in higher education: although there is a set of objective conditions that determine human behaviour, the perspective of persons as actors, as much as persons who are acted upon, stresses our responsibility in determining the meaning of our life in the world. Carr and Kemmis (1986, 161) refer to Marx's critique of the old materialist (i.e. empiricist) doctrine of determinism that views human beings as the products of circumstances and upbringing and which 'forgets that it is men that change circumstances and that the educator must himself be educated'. They also refer to Marx's conception of 'practice' as the dialectical process of changing circumstances and simultaneously of changing people and their activity. Matthews (1980, 86) comments on Marx's achievement in transcending the old into the new version of materialism:

> Specifically, it was historical materialism; a materialism which saw practice or conscious human activity as mediating between mind and matter; between subject and object. It was something which by its mediation altered both society and nature. Consciousness arises out of and is shaped by practice, and in turn is judged in and by practice.

This is the crucial argument in Marx's epistemology which Leontiev and his followers have adopted and which Carr and Kemmis (1986, 162) use in their theory of educational research as a critical educational science and in their discussion of the contribution of this kind of research to the improvement of education:

> Clearly, a critical educational science requires that teachers become researchers into their own practices, understandings and situations. While there is a role for 'critical friends' (i.e. educational researchers who remain outside the educational context) in helping teachers and others involved in education to conduct critical research, the primary work of educational research must be participatory research by those whose practices constitute education. [Parentheses added]

The idea that practitioners can gain insight into a process by creating a change and then observe its variable effects was introduced and frequently repeated throughout Lewin's work (Marrow, 1969, 235).

To return to Lewin's notion of the dialectical relationship between a person's intentions and 'life space', there are certain conclusions we may draw. While our behaviour may be determined by our situation, it is also true that we can make choices which determine the meaning of our situation (see Kelly's choice corollary). We may choose to take responsibility to assert our own meaning and accept the consequences, or we may passively allow someone else to determine the meaning of our situation for us.

There are clear implications for students and staff in higher education. For example, students have the choice of becoming independent, autonomous learners responsible for their own learning or of depending on their teachers to tell them what and how to learn. Staff have the choice of being actively involved in the evaluation of their performance and curricula or of relying on external reviews and implementing the curricula based on the theories and decisions of 'experts' in curriculum development. But, in most cases, there is a dialectical relationship between intentional, strategic action, personal responsibility, involvement and self-direction on the one hand, and certain constraints within an institutional framework on the other. Although Lewin does not refer to curriculum development in particular, some of his ideas on action research can be applied to higher education.

Action research

Action research, to Lewin (1948, 201–16), aims to improve inter-group relations. Lewin (1948, 202–3) defines the nature of action research:

> The research needed for social practice can best be characterized as research for social management or social engineering. It is a type of action research, a comparative research on the conditions and effects of various forms of social action, and research leading to social action. Research that produces nothing but books will not suffice.

> It should be noted that Lewin's use of terms, such as social management and social engineering, reflects his compromise in the direction of a determinist, managerial and technicist kind of theory and a concession to that language, characteristic of his age and its faith in science and technology.

> Apart from the aims and content, the research methods and the planning process of action research are of interest to higher education

research. Lewin (1948, 204–5) states that two types of scientific research are needed in combination for any field of action: the knowledge of general laws (i.e. 'if so' propositions dealing with the relation between possible results) as a guidance for the achievement of certain objectives under certain conditions, and a scientific fact-finding called diagnosis which must be 'complemented by experimental comparative studies of the effectiveness of various techniques of change'.

Lewin (1948, 205–6) describes the process of planning action research as follows: starting with a general idea to reach a certain objective, the idea must be examined carefully by fact-finding about the situation. This will lead to an 'overall plan' of how to reach the objective and to a decision in regard to the first step of action. The second step is to execute the first step of the overall plan followed by certain fact-findings. The fact-finding or reconnaissance has four functions:

1. to evaluate the action in regard to the expectations;
2. to give the planners the chance to learn and to gather new general insights;
3. to serve as a basis for correctly planning the next step; and
4. to serve as a basis for modifying the overall plan.

The third step again consists of a circle of planning, executing, and reconnaissance or fact-finding, this time in order to evaluate the second step, to prepare a rational basis for planning the fourth step and maybe to modify the overall plan again. Thus action research proceeds in a spiral of steps. Each step is composed of a cycle of planning, action and fact-finding about the results of the action.

The action research process is a problem-solving process. Lewin, like Kelly, regards the process of research (scientific as well as action research) and knowledge creation as identical to the process of learning and problem-solving in everyday situations. This ongoing, active process starts with a problem and its analysis through a conceptualisation of the known facts or events, followed by the planning and implementation of an action programme. The action researchers, then, critically evaluate and review these activities in order to either confirm the tentative hypothesis or plan of action; if it proves to be wrong, they identify the new problem and continue a new cycle of research.

Lewin's research led him to believe that learning is best facilitated in an open environment where researchers and practitioners discuss the data in feedback sessions and where there is a dialectical tension and conflict between immediate, concrete experience and analytic detachment. His own evaluation of action research suggests that a close integration of action, training and research holds promising possibilities for higher education learning, teaching and staff development. For example, Lewin (1948, 210–11) says:

> I have been deeply impressed with the tremendous pedagogical effect which these evaluation meetings, designed for the purpose of scientific recording, had on the training process. The atmosphere of (relaxed) objectivity, the readiness by the faculty to discuss openly their mistakes, far from endangering their position, seemed to lead to an enhancement of appreciation... The training of large numbers of social scientists who can handle scientific problems but are also equipped for the delicate task of building productive, hard-hitting teams with practitioners is a prerequisite for progress in social science as well as in social management for intergroup relations.

After Lewin there was a decline of action research in the 1950s and 1960s. However, there has been a resurgence of recent interest in educational action research, mainly in Britain, America, Australia,Europe and in developing countries such as India, Colombia, Malaysia and Thailand. For further reference to a comparative history and analysis of educational action research in its social context see Noffke (1989), who identifies central aspects and themes. Areas of focus include: democracy, social engineering and social change; research for re-education; curriculum studies and the science of education; growing up in educational practice; the method of science; depoliticising action research; in-service and professional development; persistent themes in action research; and understanding action research today. The strongest theme identified by Noffke in educational action research is the idea of the teacher as researcher. Other themes are the knowledge–practice gap; issues of race, class and gender; demographic changes in the school population; and school-based alternative models for curriculum development.

Critical appraisal

Some issues and criticisms have arisen from action research projects based on Lewin's theory. For example, Cohen and Manion (1980) report on problems experienced in two major British projects: the Humanities Curriculum Project and the Keele Integrated Studies Project. Although these projects permitted action research by teachers, they are not outstanding examples of action research compared with, for instance, the Ford Teaching Project. The difficulties in the former two projects arose mainly from problems of communication between teachers and researchers — for example, from the way the project was perceived or misperceived by the teachers in the experimental schools, from complaints from the teachers about the research team's jargon and lack of specific advice, and from the research team's discontent with the low priority given by teachers to feedback and consultation. However, it is unlikely that the problem would have been solved even if the favourable conditions suggested by Cohen and Manion (1980, 188) were put into practice:

... a willingness on the part of the teachers to admit limitations and to make themselves familiar with the basic techniques of research; the provision of opportunities to invent; the encouragement of new ideas; the provision of time for experimentation; a mutual trust of those involved; and a knowledge on the part of the participants of the fundamentals of group processes.

These conditions are not easily achieved in actual practice, even if teachers agree to them at the espoused level. What is needed is a different condition which will then facilitate the above and other favourable conditions: it is essential that the teachers themselves are the initiators of the research problem(s) which they are personally and professionally interested in solving and that they are actively involved in each step of the research process, including the writing of the report or research paper. The role of the educational researcher is not to design and control the research project and to treat the teachers as 'subjects' providing feedback for their own research purposes and interests, but to act as facilitators of learning and research, as educational advisers, resource persons and equal members of a co-operative team of action researchers, each of whom is a personal scientist. The educational adviser must familiarise him/herself with the educational context and fully understand the teachers' problem areas. In this way, the responsibility for and ownership of the research project is shared equally between teachers and advisers; the positive contributions of both can be maximised and the constraints of each on the other are kept to a minimum.

Figure 9 is a diagrammatic representation of Lewin's model of action research and laboratory training as a four-stage cycle of experiential learning designed by Kolb (1984, 21). Immediate concrete experience is the basis for observations and reflection. These observations are assimilated into a 'theory' which is tested and from which new implications or hypotheses for action can be deduced. These implications or hypotheses then serve as guides in acting to create new experiences.

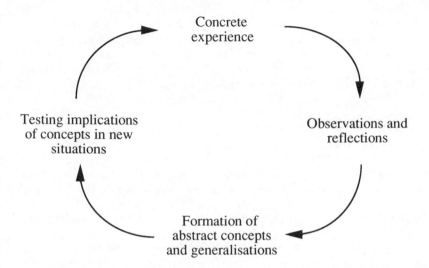

Figure 9   *The Lewinian experiential learning model (Kolb, 1984, 21)*

Kolb emphasises two aspects of this learning model as noteworthy. The first is that the focal point for learning is the 'here-and-now' concrete experience validating and testing abstract concepts; this immediate personal experience can be shared with others fully, concretely, and abstractly. The second important aspect of the Lewinian model, according to Kolb (1984, 22) is that action research and laboratory training are based on feedback processes which generate valid information 'to assess deviations from desired goals. This information feedback provides the basis for a continuous process of goal-directed action and evaluation of the consequences of that action.' Action research is a process of experiential learning. Kolb's theory which is partly based on Lewin's model will be the subject matter of the next sub-chapter.

Action research as experiential learning

Experiential learning consists of various approaches and practices that use the first-hand experience of the learner as a major source of knowing and learning. It involves the whole person in the learning process, not only his/her intellect, but also emotions, feelings, values and interpersonal aspects. In recent years there has been a growing awareness, acceptance and use of experiential learning, but there have been critics and sceptics too. Some see experiential learning as faddish and gimmicky, more concerned with process and technique than content and substance. This may well be true if it is used as a technique without guiding theory and principles. For this reason, Kolb (1984) has developed a comprehensive theory which offers the foundation for an approach to education and learning as a lifelong process and which is soundly based in intellectual traditions of philosophy and cognitive and social psychology.

Kolb's experiential learning theory

Kolb's experiential learning theory provides a link between theory and practice, between abstract generalisations and concrete experiences, between the affective and cognitive domains. It pursues a framework for examining and strengthening the critical linkages among education, work and personal development as shown in Figure 10.

Therefore, this model is particularly useful for higher education, not only for student learning, but also for staff development through action research. Kolb (1984, 11) refers to Argyris and Schön in this respect:

> They maintain that learning from experience is essential for individual and organizational effectiveness and that this learning can occur only in situations where personal values and organizational norms support action based on valid information, free and informed choice, and internal commitment.

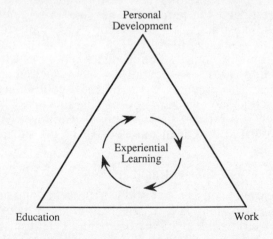

Figure 10 *Experiential learning as the process that links education, work and personal development (Kolb, 1984, 4)*

Kolb (1984) describes the process of experiential learning and proposes a model based on three major traditions: Dewey (1938) from the philosophical perspective of pragmatism, Lewin (1952) from the phenomenological perspective and Piaget (1970), the developmental psychologist and genetic epistemologist, from the rationalist perspective. Lewin's phenomenology has been outlined above. Before presenting Dewey's and Piaget's models, other related schools of thought which have influenced Kolb's theory should be mentioned.

First, there are the therapeutic psychologies (e.g. Carl Jung's psychoanalysis, Carl Roger's humanist, client-centred therapy, Fritz Perls' Gestalt therapy and Abraham Maslow's self-actualisation psychology). Kolb (1984, 15) mentions two major contributions this group has made to experiential learning:

First is the concept of adaptation, ... that healthy adaptation requires the effective integration of cognitive and affective processes... The second contribution of the therapeutic psychologies is the conception of socio-emotional development throughout the life cycle.

It is these socio-emotional development schemes, together with the cognitive development models, that provide a holistic framework for describing the process of adult development. The second school of thought that has contributed to experiential learning theory are the radical educators: Ivan Illich (1972), who criticises Western education and advocates the 'deschooling' of society; Paulo Freire (1972), who suggests that the present education system be changed by instilling 'critical consciousness' in people and actively to explore the personal, experiential meaning of concepts through discussion. Both argue that: 'the educational system is primarily an agency of social control, a control that is ultimately oppressive and conservative of the capitalist system of class discrimination' (Kolb, 1984, 16).

What links these approaches is a dialectical conception of education and higher education, not only between abstract concepts and subjective personal experience, but also between the conservative priority on maintenance of social order and the revolutionary value of individual freedom and expression.

Kolb emphasises the central role that experiential learning theory plays in the learning process. This differentiates this theory from cognitive theories (that focus on the acquisition, manipulation, and recall of abstract symbols) and from behaviourist learning theories (that deny subjective experience and consciousness in the learning process). However, Kolb (1984, 21) does not propose to pose experiential learning theory as a third alternative to behaviourist and cognitive theories, but rather to suggest 'a holistic integrative perspective on learning that combines experience, perception, cognition, and behaviour'.

Dewey's model of learning

Dewey's model of learning, which has influenced Kolb, is very similar to Lewin's theory, but Dewey explains more explicitly how learning transforms the impulses and feelings of concrete experience into higher order purposeful action. Figure 11 shows Kolb's representation of Dewey's model of experiential learning.

This is again a four-stage cycle of:

1. the impulse of experience;
2. observation of surrounding conditions;
3. knowledge of similar situations in the past; and
4. judgement based on observation and knowledge.

Like Lewin, Dewey considers learning as a dialectical process which integrates experience and concepts, observation and action. Kolb (1984, 22) explains:

> The impulse of experience gives ideas their moving force, and ideas give direction to impulse. Postponement of immediate action is essential for observation and judgement to intervene, and action is essential for achievement of purpose. It is through the integration of these opposing but symbiotically related processes that sophisticated, mature purpose develops from blind impulse.

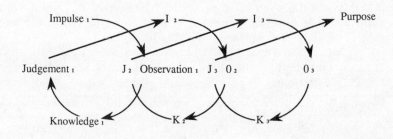

Figure 11 *Dewey's model of experiential learning (Kolb, 1984, 23)*

Piaget's model of learning and cognitive development

This is the third intellectual pillar on which Kolb's theory is built. Piaget (1970) assumes that the dimensions of experience and concept, of reflection and action, form the basic continua for the development of adult thought. In Piaget's terms, learning results from a balanced tension between two processes: the process of *accommodation* of concepts or schemas to experience in the world and the process of *assimilation* of events and experiences from the world into existing concepts and schemas. Kolb (1984, 23) explains:

> When accommodation processes dominate assimilation, we have imitation — the molding of oneself to environmental contours or constraints. When assimilation dominates over accommodation, we have play — the imposition of one's concept and images without regard to environmental realities. The process of cognitive growth from concrete to abstract and from active to reflective is based on this continual transaction between assimilation and accommodation, occurring in successive stages, each of which incorporates what has gone before into a new, higher level of cognitive functioning.

The four major stages of cognitive growth identified by Piaget's work refer to children from birth to about the age of 14–16 and are therefore not of direct interest to higher education. However, Kolb has incorporated Piaget's developmental continua into his model of adult learning (i.e. the development from a concrete phenomenological view of the world to an abstract constructionist view, from an active, egocentric view to a reflective, internalised mode of knowing).

Figure 12 represents Kolb's structural dimensions underlying the process of experiential learning and the resulting knowledge forms. There are two basic structural dimensions of the learning process: the prehension dimension and the transformation dimension. The first includes two dialectically opposed modes of grasping experience, one through direct apprehension of immediate concrete experience, the other through indirect comprehension of symbolic representation of experience. The second structural dimension of the learning process includes two dialectically opposed modes of transforming experience, one through intentional reflection, the other through extentional action.

This model is in agreement with Piaget's theory, except in one important point: Kolb (1984, 60) maintains 'that apprehension and comprehension as prehension processes, and intention and extension as transformation processes, are equipotent contributions to the learning process'.

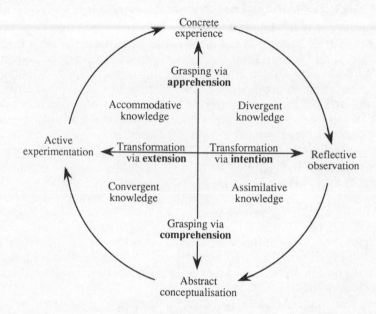

Figure 12 *Kolb's model of experiential learning (Kolb, 1984, 42)*

To Piaget, comprehension and intention are superior processes. His view has been the dominant one in Western education, in particular in higher education. It would be a great progress and advancement in higher education if Kolb's view were accepted in theory and practice — that is, the view that extensional action and direct apprehension of immediate concrete experience can equally lead to knowledge, just as intentional reflection and indirect comprehension of experience can. If higher education teachers themselves experience through action research that they can gain and advance knowledge about learning and teaching through experiential learning processes, it is more likely that they will adopt Kolb's theory implicitly or explicitly and facilitate experiential learning for their students in their courses and programmes of study. How this action research can be facilitated for higher education teachers and conducted by them is demonstrated in the companion book (Zuber-Skerritt, 1992).

Kolb's definition of learning

Kolb's characteristics of learning have been derived mainly from Lewin's, Dewey's and Piaget's models of the learning process discussed above. Kolb (1984, 25–38) has developed the following six propositions which are shared by these three major traditions of experiential learning.

1. *Learning is best conceived as a process, not in terms of outcomes.* This principle reminds us of Bruner's (1960, 72) view: 'knowing is a process, not a product'. It could be criticised as being undialectical and not in line with Kolb's overall theoretical framework. Obviously, a process of learning will lead to an outcome; and outcomes of learning are the result of a process. So the principle should read: 'learning is a process as well as an outcome'. But since learning had been conceived mainly in terms of outcomes rather than as a process in the past, Kolb probably fell into the trap of making too blunt a distinction when trying to emphasise the importance of the process more strongly. For he continues to explain that, although we cannot totally abandon the assessment system in higher education (because we have to award degrees and keep certain standards), a shift from a preoccupation with tests and examinations to a greater attention to the process of learning is likely to produce more personalised and lasting knowledge than mere accumulation of abstract knowledge, which is easily forgotten after the examinations.

2. *Learning is a continuous process grounded in experience.* A teacher's task is not only to implant new ideas in the learners (as if they were blank minds), but also to dispose of or modify old ones. Despite other fundamental differences, this principle reminds us of Ausubel's theory (1963) of meaningful learning and retention if new information is related to previous concepts. In action research, teachers start with their existing knowledge and experience and build up and create knowledge from that vantage point.

3. *The process of learning requires the resolution of conflicts between dialectically opposed modes of adaptation to the world.* These dialectics are:

   (a) for Lewin: the conflict between concrete experience and abstract concepts, between observation and action;
   (b) for Dewey: between the impulse that gives ideas their 'moving force' and reason that gives desire its direction; and
   (c) for Piaget: between accommodation of ideas to the external world and assimilation of experience into existing conceptual structures.

We could add many more examples, but instead refer back to Chapter 3 with regard to holistic dialectical thinking, which is also relevant to the next principle.

4. *Learning is a holistic process of adaptation to the world.* Learning is not a partial functioning, such as cognition or perception, but it involves the integrated functioning of the total organism, such as thinking, feeling, perceiving and behaving. Lewin, Dewey and Piaget have taken the scientific method as their model for the learning process. Kolb (1984) has combined not only the experiential learning cycle and a model of the scientific enquiry process (Kolb, 1978), but also the models of the problem-solving process, the decision making process, and the creative process.

This is an excellent example of holistic thinking, integrating the findings from different specialised areas into a single general adaptive model. This kind of holistic thinking is needed in this day and age more urgently than ever, otherwise the high achievements of the analytical–empirical sciences and technologies may destroy us suddenly (e.g. nuclear power) or gradually (e.g. pollution). In this respect, higher education has an important role to play in advocating holistic thinking across disciplines.

5. *Learning involves transactions between the person and the environment.* Educational research has been criticised to be essentially decontextualised and lacking ecological validity. For example, behaviourist theories emphasise how the environment shapes behaviour with little regard for how behaviour shapes the environment. Piaget's work can also be criticised for its failure to take account of environmental and cultural circumstances. The position of Kolb's (1984, 36) experiential theory is:

> ... that personal characteristics, environmental influences, and behaviour all operate in reciprocal determination, each factor influencing the others in an interlocking fashion. The concept of reciprocally determined transaction between person and learning environment is central to the laboratory-training method of experiential learning.

As well as the above principles of experiential learning, this principle in particular is complementary to Leontiev's subject–action–object model. In action research the problem to be solved has to be considered within the educational context of the particular institution/department.

6. *Learning is the process of creating knowledge.* If we want to understand learning, we must have an understanding of the nature of knowledge and the processes by which this knowledge is

created. Kolb distinguishes social and personal knowledge. Social knowledge is the civilised objective accumulation of previous human cultural experience (cf Dewey) or the historically developed cultural knowledge (cf Leontiev). Personal knowledge is the accumulation of the individual person's subjective life experience (cf Dewey) or his/her construct system developed through abstractions of personal experiences (cf Kelly). In higher education learning, teaching and staff development it is important to realise that 'knowledge is the result of the transaction between social knowledge and personal knowledge' (Kolb, 1984, 36).

From the above six characteristics of the experiential learning process Kolb (1984, 38) offers a working definition of learning: *learning is the process whereby knowledge is created through the transformation of experience.* This definition emphasises several critical aspects of the learning process as viewed from the experiential perspective. First, there is an emphasis on the process of adaptation and learning as opposed to content or outcomes. The second aspect is that knowledge is a transformation process, being continuously created and recreated, not an independent entity to be acquired or transmitted. Third, learning transforms experience in both its objective and subjective forms. Finally, to understand learning, we must understand the nature of knowledge, and vice versa.

This definition of learning is used in this book at all levels (i.e. for student learning; for staff learning how to teach in order best to facilitate student learning; for personal development; and for educational advisers learning how best to facilitate learning for students, for staff and for self-development).

Boud and Pascoe's extensions of Kolb's model

Boud and Pascoe (1978, 2) point out that experience does not necessarily lead to meaningful learning; that experience without reflection, generalisation, hypothesis formation and testing does not result in learning.

This model makes it clear how individuals can sabotage their own learning. Generalisations may be drawn too hastily or from a limited base of knowledge; experience may fade from memory without reflection; observations may be influenced by expectations; and generalisations may be inadequately tested.

Boud and Pascoe have extended Kolb's model to include an experiential teaching model developed by Burch and Miller (1977). The diagram in Figure 13 shows the relationship between stages of the Kolb model of learning and phases of the Burch and Miller model of teaching.

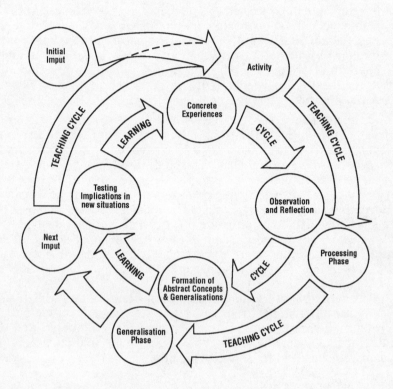

Figure 13 *An experiential learning and teaching model (Boud and Pascoe, 1978, 5)*

The inner circle represents Kolb's learning model, the outer circle Burch and Miller's teaching model. The former model has been explained above. The latter is again a four-phase cycle: of input phase, activity phase, processing phase and generalisation phase. The aim of the input phase is to structure the learning activity (e.g. by guidelines, directions, time limits). Thus a general framework is established in which the students work through the activity according to the guidelines. The teacher's role is that of a monitor and time keeper. In the processing phase, the students, with the help of their teacher, examine the activity in respect to those particular aspects which are personally important. For example, they might be asked to express (orally or in writing), and to reflect on, the thoughts and feelings that have been stimulated by the activity and to discuss the activity and their experience of it in small groups. The aim of the generalisation phase is to move beyond the single concrete experience towards generalisations based on their own as well as the group's reactions. These generalisations may be tentative principles or plans for the future. The teacher's main function is to raise students' awareness, to encourage them to share this new awareness, and to test it against other students' views, against their own past experiences, or against any other criteria that might be appropriate. The result may be hypotheses for improvement or alternatives that could be tested through subsequent activities. The next input phase starts a new cycle of the teaching process, which may arise from the previous generalisations to be tested or a new alternative to be tried. It is important that the teaching process takes the learner through all four stages of the learning model, if it is to be successful; and that the students *themselves* experience, observe, reflect, form abstract concepts and test the implications in new situations. However, as Boud and Pascoe (1978, 6) point out:

> This is not to advocate that *everything* to be learned must somehow be drawn from the direct experience of the learner. To do so would ignore the rich store of existing knowledge and would devalue the worth of accumulated experience of our society. Properly managed an experiential approach will put the learner into the role of an active inquirer, investigator and problem-solver.

Boud and Pascoe (1978, 61–3) and Boud (1989) have extended Kolb's model further by constructing a three-dimensional model. These three dimensions are what they consider the most important characteristics of experiential education:

1. the involvement of each individual student as a holistic person (i.e. not just his/her cognition, but expectations, desires, affects or emotions as well);
2. the correspondence of the learning activity to real world problems (i.e. the degree to which learning tasks simulate activities outside the institution); and
3. learner control over the learning experience. A low level of learner control over decision making in his/her learning programme exists in the traditional course in which staff unilaterally take all decisions about course aims, objectives, content, methods of learning and assessment. A high level of

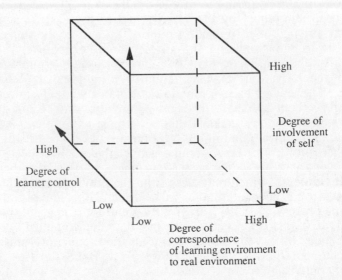

Figure 14 *Dimensions of experiential education (Boud and Pascoe, 1978, 63)*

learner control can be found in those courses in which the above decisions are taken jointly by staff and students (e.g. in independent study programmes).

Figure 14 represents these three characteristics as though they were dimensions.

Both these extensions of Kolb's model by Boud and Pascoe can be applied to action research and staff (self-) development. In Figure 14, traditional educational research by outside experts can be located in the space close to the point of intersection of the three axes (i.e. low), while action research by the practitioners themselves would be placed in the opposite corner of the cube (i.e. high), constituting a high degree of involvement and of correspondence of the research activity to the real problem in their educational practice, and a high degree of autonomy or control on the part of the academic staff over specifying, testing, evaluating and reflecting upon their aim-oriented, intentional actions. In Figure 13, the inner circle refers to the process of learning that takes place in the team during the action research project. It is the very essence of action research. The outer circle refers not only to the staff developer's activities, but also to the teachers' subsequent teaching activities which result from the knowledge and experience gained from action research. This teaching process is a mirror or model of the learning process. Teachers facilitate the same learning process which they themselves have experienced.

However, experiential learning is only part of the concept of action research as defined in this book. Being critical is another important aspect which will be discussed in the next sub-chapter.

Action research as critical education science

Kemmis and his associates at Deakin University have developed an action research programme in teacher education (pre- and in-service) which is based in a theoretical framework consisting of Lewin's field theory combined with Habermas' critical theory. What both these intellectual traditions have in common is their rejection of positivism and 'scienticism' (i.e. the belief that science through its scientific methods can construct objective knowledge of reality, of 'the world as it really is', and that scientists can be detached observers of objective facts). They also reject the claim by scientists that this kind of knowledge, which is just one kind among others, is the only valid and legitimate one. Both Lewin and Habermas maintain that knowledge in the social sciences must be practical. This means theory must improve practice in order to be valid and useful. The methods used must be phenomenological and interpretative in order to be able to fully understand a social situation or problem. But Habermas (1978) goes one step further. For him, *Verstehen* (i.e. mere understanding of phenomena) is insufficient in social science. He argues that the method required is that of *critique* (i.e. relentless criticism of all existing conditions). Kemmis and his associates have taken up this line of argument for action research. To them the quintessence of action research is the group process of deliberation (i.e. the process of rational reflection generating a critique of the social milieu in which the group operates). Grundy and Kemmis (1982, 84) define educational action research as:

> ... a term used to describe a family of activities in curriculum development, professional development, school improvement programmes and system planning and policy development. These activities have in common the identification of strategies of planned action which are implemented, and then systematically submitted to observation, reflection and change. Participants in the action being considered are integrally involved in all of these activities.

In this definition the Lewinian concept of the spiral of cycles of planning, acting, observing and reflecting is preserved, as well as the notion of 'participation' and improvement through change, all of which are essential features in the action research process. New in this definition is the notion of strategic action. This means an action is strategic when it is consciously and deliberately undertaken, rather than on the basis of custom, habit, unreflective perception or hearsay. It is what Leontiev calls the conscious and intentional control of the action. Unlike mere behaviour, strategic action is constructed. It is retrospectively guided by planning and its rationale, but it is also flexible and open to change in the light of circumstances (e.g. political and material constraints — cf the impact of Leontiev's object on the action). It requires practical judgement, recognition of extenuating circumstances and instant decisions. Grundy and Kemmis (1982, 85) conclude:

> ... (a) behaviour, regarded as such, might be retrospectively explained by reference to theoretical or empirical propositions, but it cannot be justified by appeal to these propositions; (b) theoretical principles can inform but cannot justify practical action; (c) practical action must be justified by reference to the practical judgement of the practitioner as well as the circumstances and determinants which constrain action.

Thus the knowledge which justifies practical action is not just the knowledge of principles, but also a kind of personal knowledge which is recognised in, and rationally developed through, action research. It is neither 'subjective' nor 'objective' knowledge, but 'personal knowledge' as defined by Polanyi (1962, 300):

> Insofar as the personal submits to requirements acknowledged by itself as independent of itself, it is not subjective; but insofar as it is an action guided by individual passions, it is not objective either. It transcends the disjunction between subjective and objective.

Personal knowledge is acquired through rational reflection on experience. It is judged by the criterion of authenticity. This means personal knowledge is authentic when it arises out of one's own rational reflection on one's strategic action, rather than through rules, principles or theories.

Kemmis and his associates (Grundy and Kemmis, 1982; Kemmis and McTaggart, 1988; Carr and Kemmis, 1986) see the four fundamental moments of action research linked dynamically in a cycle: to plan, to act, to observe and to reflect. The main benefits of action research are the improvement of practice, the improvement of the understanding of practice by its practitioners, and the improvement of the situation in which the practice takes place. In order to achieve the full potential of these gains, a single loop of action research (or 'arrested' action research) is not sufficient. What is needed is an organised process of learning or the 'organisation of enlightenment' in critical communities (Habermas, 1978), that is, the use of a spiral of action research cycles by the learning community of action researchers. The main features of this kind of action research are: participation and collaboration; action-orientation; critical function; and a spiral of cycles of planning, acting, observing and reflecting. Let us now consider the four moments of action research in more detail.

The four moments of action research

To do action research means (Kemmis and McTaggart, 1982, 7):

- to develop a *plan* of action to improve what is already happening;
- to *act* to implement the plan;
- to *observe* the effects of action in the context in which it occurs; and
- to *reflect* on these effects as a basis for further planning, subsequent action and so on, through a succession of cycles (cf Figure 2).

The *plan* is constructed action, it is forward looking and thus prospective to action. Since all social action is somewhat unpredictable, the overall plan must be flexible in order to cope with unforeseen effects or constraints.

Action is deliberate, controlled, aim-oriented, but also backward-looking to planning for its rationale, and thus retrospectively guided by planning. Practice means ideas-in-action.

Observation has the function of documenting the action process, the effects of intended and unintended action, the circumstances of and constraints on action and the way these affect action. The purpose of observation is to provide the basis for critical self-reflection and, thus, it is prospective. Like the action itself, observation plans must be flexible in order to record the unexpectable.

Reflection is retrospective because it recalls action as it has been recorded in observation. Discussion among the participants, and practical as well as theoretical discourse, can aid reflection, leading to the reconstruction of the meaning of the social situation and to the construction of the revised plan.

The four moments of an action research cycle are summarised by Kemmis and McTaggart (1982, 10) in a table which I have transformed into the diagram in Figure 15 in order to show the dynamic and cyclic character of the constructive and reconstructive relationships.

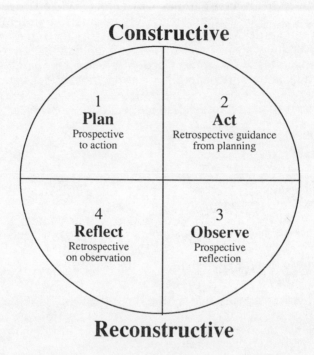

Figure 15   *The moments of action research (after Kemmis and McTaggart, 1982, 10)*

These four aspects are not to be understood as static steps, but as dynamic moments in the action research spiral of planning, acting, observing and reflecting, similar to Kolb's cycles of concrete experience, reflective observation, abstract conceptualisation and active experimentation (cf Figure 12). In the action research model (cf Figure 15), the aim is to bring together the two dimensions: discourse and practice on the one hand and construction and reconstruction on the other; similarly, in the experiential learning model (cf Figure 12), the aim is to integrate the two dimensions: comprehension and apprehension on the one hand and transformation via intention and transformation via extension on the other. Emerging propositions which can be checked against practice will gradually develop into a critical education theory including considerations of such matters as how students learn and how the message systems in higher education (e.g. curriculum, institutional organisation, teaching and learning activities, and assessment practices) create meanings for students.

Types of action research

As mentioned above, action research in Australia, led by Kemmis and his associates, has been influenced by Lewin's principle of the action research spiral and by Habermas' dialectical approach of critical theory, as outlined above. One of the major aims of critical education science is to change 'practice' (habitual or customary action) into 'praxis' (informed, committed action) through critical and self-critical reflection which help practitioners to emancipate themselves from the often unseen constraints of habit, custom, precedent, coercion and ideology (Carr and Kemmis, 1986, 192).

However, action research should not be confused with field (or applied) research. The latter can be carried out by educational researchers without the practitioners' full participation, responsibility and commitment to self-critical reflection, to social criticism and to change in educational practice. Carr and Kemmis (1983, 173–7) differentiate between three kinds of action research: *technical, practical* and *emancipatory action research*.

The aim of *technical action research* is to improve the effectiveness of educational practice judged by the educational researcher's standards. The practitioners are co-opted and depend greatly upon the researcher as a facilitator.

Practical action research, in addition to effectiveness, aims at the practitioners' understanding and professional development. The educational researcher's role is Socratic and to encourage practical deliberation and self-reflection on the part of the action researchers.

Emancipatory action research has the same objectives as practical action research, but also aims at a critical response to organisational constraints. The educational researcher's role is that of a moderator who ensures that conditions are established and maintained which are necessary for the 'organisation of enlightenment'. The main features of the three types of action research are summarised in Table 1 of the companion book.

Technical action research is the least powerful and emancipatory action research is the ideal. According to Carr and Kemmis (1983, 177) only the latter is true action research:

> Indeed, only emancipatory action research can unequivocally fulfil the three minimal requirements for action research... : having strategic action as its subject matter; proceeding through the spiral of planning, acting, observing and reflecting; and involving

participation and collaboration in all phases of the research activity.

From my experiences I suggest that the three types of action research are developmental stages, and that it is quite legitimate to start with technical action research and gradually to proceed to the higher levels, as long as one is aware of the full range of possibilities and of the ultimate aims. These include the improvement of practice in a systematic way of planning, acting, observing and reflecting; and, if warranted, making changes to the environment, context and conditions in which that practice takes place, especially if the conditions impede desirable improvements, effective practices and innovative developments.

Examples of such developments from the beginning stages of technical and practical action research to the planning of action research for institutional reform are the books by Nixon (1981), Hustler et al. (1986) and Altrichter et al. (1989). These books present case studies and essays describing teacher-based research. As Wilhelmer concluded (in Altrichter et al., 1989, 197–8), action research by teachers can be successful and enjoyable

- in professional development for teachers;
- as an instrument of internal school reform and curriculum development;
- in teacher education and teaching practice; and
- for the advancement of knowledge in education from the grass roots by reflective practitioners.

In my own view and experience, the same applies to action research in higher education.

Action research in higher education: the CRASP model

Action research has been generally successful in social work, industry, business, and in primary, secondary and further education. How feasible is it at the higher education level?

There are at least five reasons why action research in higher education, too, might lead to a better understanding and improvement of learning, teaching and staff development, as well as to a more critical reflection on an institution's 'status quo' operations and on its role and function in society. These five reasons, summarised in the acronym CRASP, are:

- *C*ritical attitude;
- *R*esearch into teaching;
- *A*ccountability;

- *Self-evaluation*; and
- **P**rofessionalism as teachers.

Critical attitude

The development of *critical* thinking in students is one of the major goals of higher education. That means teachers must be masters of critical thinking themselves. The development of critical practice of academics and their critical reflection is one of the salient features of action research. In fact, *critique* (in the Habermas sense) of all social practice, not only in the educational context, but also in the wider social context of a community, state or nation, is an important role and function of higher education.

Research into teaching

Research into teaching, as discussed earlier, is not only possible for higher education teachers as personal scientists and reflective practitioners, but it is also likely to have a more powerful effect on the improvement of learning, teaching and staff development than research produced by educational theorists. It appears that educational research has not had a great impact on the practice of teaching and learning in higher education. There is a lack of communication between academics (here referred to as practitioners) and educational researchers. One might speculate why academics, whose responsibility includes teaching students, rarely read books and journal articles on learning–teaching theories. When they do, they often find the material irrelevant or the language (jargon) incomprehensible. Normally they would not have been formally introduced to this literature in a degree programme or diploma of teacher education as a preparation for their profession, as primary and secondary school teachers have. It has been argued in this book that the division between educational theory by researchers on the one hand and educational practice of higher education teachers on the other has resulted in ineffectiveness or estrangement of theory and practice.

The underlying assumptions for this separation of theory and practical application are based implicitly on a kind of behaviourism that regards students as respondents to a teacher's stimuli, and teachers as technicians applying certain techniques of transmitting knowledge and skills to students, and putting into practice the ideas and research findings developed by educational theorists. Although these assumptions have resiliently survived in higher education, they are in contradiction to the goals of higher education, especially the major goal of developing critical and self-critical thinking. It is unreasonable, therefore, to expect higher education teachers to apply and translate theories (developed by educational researchers) into their practice uncritically and technocratically.

Action research integrates theory and practice. This means action research by practitioners into their own teaching practice seems to be more appropriate than educational research conducted by theorists and applied by practitioners. Action researchers' teaching practice might be informed by theory, but not be bound totally by the normative prescriptions of high-level and often abstract theories. Instead, they may arrive at an educational theory and knowledge appropriate to their own situation through reflection or a certain kind of criticism directly tied to their practice.

For example, higher education teachers could critically analyse one major problem they share with other colleagues, plan a strategy of action, implement and evaluate the action programme and reflect on the results, analyse them for further action and proceed to a continuation of another cycle in the action research spiral until a satisfactory solution has been found. Some concrete examples are presented in the companion book, examples which have culminated in action research reports or journal articles contributing not only to the participants' development and to the advancement of knowledge in higher education, but also, in a sense, to their institution's accountability.

Accountability

Accountability of higher education institutions to society (i.e. to the taxpayer and the funding government), has become more and more pressing in recent years, as higher education has become a focus of public attention and debate. Whatever changes will be necessary in the future because of cuts in government funding, reviews and revisions of higher education curricula are best carried out by the academics themselves on the basis of their own action research, rather than on academic policies and curriculum decisions imposed upon them by the government or the institution's central administration. Action research by academics into their own curricula could contribute to safeguarding autonomy and to avoiding excessive government control of higher education. The reports and publications resulting from emancipatory action research could form part of the institution's, department's or school's ongoing responsibility to provide accountability for the effectiveness of its teaching programmes. To date, responses by the higher education institutions have been defensive and slow, but it has been recognised by staff associations and vice-chancellors' committees in many countries that self-evaluation is preferable to evaluation from outside.

Self-evaluation

Self-evaluation of teaching performance, of individual courses and of whole programmes by the practitioners themselves, individually as well as in teams, is at the very heart of action research. It is the machine by which the goal can be reached (i.e. the improvement of practice, the improvement of understanding practice by the practitioners — individually and collaboratively — and the improvement of the situation in which the action takes place).

Apart from the need for accountability and the preference of self-evaluation over outside evaluation, there is another rationale and incentive for academic staff to engage in action research, namely the satisfaction and reward which publications resulting from action research will bring. Although the institution's criteria for promotion and tenure include research, teaching and administration, research seems to have been the primary decisive criterion in actual practice — at least this has been the perception by many faculty staff. Hence there is more incentive for staff to put a greater effort into research than into teaching and curriculum development.

More recently, the governments in various countries have released 'White Papers' and come to agreements with the committees of vice-chancellors and principals and with faculty staff associations or unions to increase the effectiveness and efficiency in higher education through policies of staff development and appraisal.

Since 1989 Britain has been leading in new government initiatives, such as the 'Enterprise in Higher Education' projects of the National Training Agency, the establishment of the Committee of Vice-Chancellors and Principals' Universities' Staff Development and Training Unit (CVCP/USDTU) in 1989 and the CVCP Academic Audit Unit in 1990.

In Australia and other countries as well, efforts have been made to emphasise the importance of teaching (Aulich Report, 1990) and to include the teaching criterion for promotion more consciously and systematically in promotion and tenure decisions. Much more remains to be done, but there is a new and growing awareness by academics that the quality of teaching will be taken increasingly into consideration as more sophisticated procedures for evaluation are developed.

What is needed now is a review by each individual institution of its reward structure and policies on staff development, promotion and tenure to such an effect that equal weighting is given to the quality of teaching and research, not only in written statements, but also in actual practice. As a result, there might be a change in academic culture (i.e. in the academics' shared beliefs and perceptions of teaching as a profession). Increasingly, then, there will be an incentive for staff to invest as much effort in teaching and course administration as in research. However, teaching and research need not necessarily be isolated activities. Action research is an ideal procedure for linking and integrating theory and practice. Research and teaching can be married to the advantage of both and of the academic.

Professionalism

Last but not least, action research can contribute to the professionalism of higher education teachers. In the last few years, there has been a growing professional awareness among higher education teachers who normally have not had any formal training (as primary and secondary school teachers have), but who are willing to seek ways of better understanding and mastering their work. Some of these ways and methods of professional development will be discussed further in Chapter 9. But the point to be stressed here is: to become truly professional, academics must aim at the highest quality of learning and teaching; they must be involved in educational research and theory on which to base their practice; and they should participate in decisions about the broader context in which they operate. Instead of leaving these decisions and the formulation of their educational, theoretical framework to outside experts and educational researchers, they can be active participants in the process; and they will be changed in this process from uncritical technocrats to critical and self-critical action researchers into teaching and student learning in higher education.

To sum up, the CRASP model of this book assumes that action research by academics into their curricula and into student learning will have a direct and positive impact on the quality of their own teaching and professional development. It seems to be particularly appropriate to the goals of higher education in recent years (i.e. being *critical*; integrating *research* and *teaching*; meeting the requirements of *accountability* to the outside world through reports and publications; *self-evaluation* rather than outside control; and *professionalism* of academics as teachers in higher education).

Interpretations of the CRASP model

The CRASP model may be interpreted in many ways. Three examples are given below: interpretations with reference to:

1. cybernetics;
2. Leontiev's theory; and
3. critical education science.

First, with reference to cybernetics, Brandt (1984, 38) structures action into an aim-oriented analysis of the situation; generation of an action plan; and controlled action. This structure may also be applied to the CRASP model of action research presented in Figure 16, with the addition of and emphasis on reflection upon the controlled action and self-evaluation of one's own practice.

As teachers or staff developers, we have developed a certain *critical attitude* which enables us to analyse a situation. On the one hand, we develop our own constructs, intrinsic values and aims of learning and teaching. On the other hand, we are influenced by the constraints of a wider context which require from us *accountability* for what we are doing. This accountability provides us with external values for our actions. So we do research into our practices (i.e. *research into teaching* or into academic development). In the process of this research, we go through cycles of learning, as discussed before (e.g. see Kolb's cycle in Figure 12 or the action research cycles in Figures 2 and 15). We reflect on this process and undergo a *self-evaluation* of our achievements, measured against the aims we started from. ·The cycle is closed and might be repeated. If this whole process is successful, we have developed our *professionalism* further as teachers or academic staff developers. This process of controlled action research may remind us of the control system of cybernetics in which the action is controlled by constantly measuring the achievements against the aims and by correcting the action accordingly.

However, there is a fundamental difference between cybernetics and emancipatory action research in that the objectives of the latter are not only to correct the action, but to revise or reform the original aims as well, if necessary. This critical openness extends to all boxes of Figure 16 (i.e. to all aspects in the whole process of action research in higher education). This has implications for the research methodology to be discussed in Chapter 7.

Second, the CRASP model can also be explained in terms of Leontiev's subject–action–object schema (cf Figure 5): *critical attitude*, personal constructs, aims, values, etc. refer to the subject; *research into teaching* is the action; and that which is being researched is the object. The object also includes the external constraints related to the subject's *accountability* and, as a result of the action and of the reflection upon the action, the teacher's or staff developer's *self-evaluation* leading to *professionalism*. Staff control their action research *and* they are changed by it, for they learn from their research, that is, their whole personal construct and value system is reorganised and will affect the aims and intentions of their future actions or research. On the one hand, action research has an influence on the object of improving learning, teaching, professionalism and the wider educational context in higher education; on the other hand, the complexity of this object, especially limitations in the learning–teaching conditions and the requirements of professional accountability, all have an impact on the nature, scope and significance of this action research as critical education science.

Third, with reference to critical education science, the CRASP model (Figure 16) can be explained in terms of its constructive and reconstructive nature and the four moments of action research (Figure 15). The constructive moments of *planning* and *acting* involve:

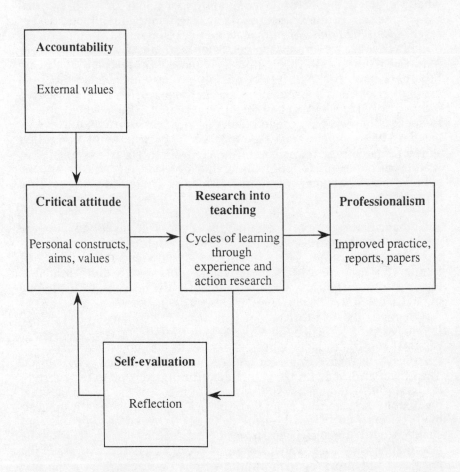

Figure 16 *The CRASP model of action research in higher education*

1. a *critical attitude* for the analysis of the problem situation by the academic staff as part of their planning, taking into consideration external values for reasons of *accountability* as well as their own values and aims; and
2. their *research into teaching* as action research activities with retrospective guidance from their critical analysis and planning.

The reconstructive moments of *observing* and *reflecting* refer not only to the staff observation of their planned activities and their reflection on the observation results, but also to a critical *self-evaluation* of the whole action research experience in relation to their own limitations and to external constraints. This evaluation and *self-evaluation* may lead to social and personal change and contribute to their *professionalism*.

The CRASP model has been explained in terms of cybernetics, Leontiev's subject–action–object schema and of critical education science with implications for academic staff development. It could be further extended by other theories. It is hoped that this tentative model might stimulate further research and development in higher education or in other fields.

Conclusion

Action research can be conducted by students as well as by academic staff. It is a process and method of learning and knowing through action and experience (cf Leontiev's model in Figure 5 and Kolb's model in Figure 12). However, the focus of this book is on action research conducted by staff. Therefore, the term 'action research' is understood mainly as research by higher education teachers into their own teaching practice, with the aim of social change and of improving higher education learning, teaching and the curriculum. This kind of learning by academic staff through action research has been based on Lewin's theory, Kolb's experiential learning theory, Kemmis' critical education theory and the CRASP model of this book.

Action research, according to Lewin, is a learning process, an ongoing spiral of cycles of enquiry consisting of systematic planning, acting, observing and reflecting. It is not a static, but a dynamic, process of experiential learning consisting of a dialectic between theory and practice, abstract generalisations and concrete experiences, observation and action (Dewey, Kolb); between accommodation and assimilation (Piaget); between apprehension and comprehension, intentional reflection and extensional action, social knowledge and personal knowledge (cf Kolb; Figure 12). In brief, experiential 'learning is the process whereby knowledge is created through the transformation of experience' (Kolb, 1984, 38).

However, knowing through experience is not enough. Action research in higher education must consist of a group process of rational reflection generating a critique of the social and educational milieu in which the members operate. For the aim of action research is not only the improvement of learning, teaching and professional development, but also the improvement of the social context in which this personal and professional development takes place. This aim can be achieved through the 'organisation of enlightenment' in critical communities (Habermas) (i.e. through participation and collaboration in rational reflection and critical discourse, strategic action orientation and a spiral of cycles of planning, acting, observing and reflecting). Strategic action, characteristic of critical education science, means 'a specific social practice', undertaken consciously and deliberately and based on the practitioners' rational reflection rather than on their uncritical perception or on custom and habit. Practical action may be informed by, but cannot be justified by reference to, theoretical principles. It must be justified by the circumstances and determinants which constrain action and by the practitioners' judgement. This judgement is based on a kind of personal knowledge and not just knowledge of principles.

Kemmis and his associates have argued for, and successfully introduced, action research in teacher training at the primary and secondary levels. This book suggests that action research in higher education is not only possible, but particularly appropriate for at least five reasons (CRASP model): it promotes a *Critical attitude, Research into teaching, Accountability, Self-evaluation,* and *Professionalism,* all of which are important goals in higher education. These goals have been stated and demanded frequently in recent years, but they have not been achieved satisfactorily, because they are difficult to put into practice. Action research may provide a practical solution to this problem. Through systematic, controlled action research, higher education teachers can become more professional, more interested in pedagogical aspects of higher education, and more motivated to integrate their research and teaching interests in a holistic way. This would in turn lead to greater job satisfaction, better academic programmes, improvement of student learning, and practitioners' insights and contributions to the advancement of knowledge in higher education.

Educational researchers may stimulate, encourage and facilitate the action research process and provide relevant advice and references for the practitioners' analysis and solution of problems. The joint findings can be disseminated in educational or professional journals, as shown in the case studies in the companion book.

The next chapter discusses the educational methodology, methods and techniques appropriate not only to action research in higher education, but also to any other interpretative, phenomenological and critical research based in the alternative paradigm as distinct from the methodology used in the traditional paradigm.

Chapter 7

Educational research methodology

Introduction

The purpose of the previous chapters was to explain the theoretical framework for action research as professional development. This chapter explains the methodological framework and the rationale for selecting certain methods of developmental research (e.g. of improving learning, teaching and staff development and of evaluating these activities) in preference to others. The following two chapters (Chapters 8 and 9) will discuss several issues in staff development and present some strategies and methods which have been usefully applied in higher education to develop the professionalism of academic staff as teachers and facilitators of student learning. To begin with, I shall make my methodological assumptions explicit and state my educational paradigm.

Paradigms of research in higher education

Educational research, like all research in the social sciences, is affected by a battle between at least two competing paradigms, reflecting the dichotomy in the fundamental debate of what philosophy should inform the educational research activities. The traditional approach draws on the empirical–analytical research methodologies used in the natural sciences. The non-traditional, alternative approach is located in the interpretive or hermeneutic tradition; one view in this tradition is based on an analogy drawn from research in social anthropology and is therefore often referred to as 'ethnographic'. The traditional paradigm is frequently referred to as 'scientific', implying that social science research is only scientific if it applies empirical–analytical methods adopted from the natural sciences. My position is that research in the human or social sciences is scientific too, but that it has to use different methods in order to research and fully understand the human or social reality under investigation.

I should mentioned that there is a third paradigm coming up on the horizon of educational research: the critical. The critical paradigm is only foreshadowed, but not explained in this book, because as yet it has been relatively unexplored in education, especially in higher education. This book is primarily exploring questions and issues within the interpretive paradigm and considers critical research as a kind of interpretive research. The following is a brief characterisation of the differences in the two dominant paradigms of research in higher education.

The natural science approach to the human sciences is also called 'experimental', because the researcher sets up an experiment, intervenes in a process and manipulates certain variables. The ethnographic approach, on the other hand, is called 'naturalistic', because the researcher observes or tries to find out what happens in natural settings.

Another pair of contrasts sometimes used in the literature for these two approaches is 'experimental' versus 'holistic'. Gilbert and Pope (1982, 19) suggest that the contrast between 'reductionist' and 'holistic' would be more appropriate. For it could be argued that social and human phenomena, if studied scientifically, cannot be reduced to a few isolated variables. The reductionist approach tends to make a deliberate attempt to isolate particular components and to study the relevant variables. Whilst this is possible in the physical sciences, it is much more difficult, if not impossible or inappropriate, in the social sciences. The holistic approach tries to describe the context and a wide range of variables. Therefore, 'reductionist' versus 'holistic' seems, indeed, to be a more appropriate contrast pair.

With regard to the researcher's aims, the contrast labels 'prescriptive' versus 'descriptive' are frequently used. While the experimental approach seeks to prescribe and predict future events on the basis of a study, the alternative approach seeks to describe a natural setting as fully (holistically) as possible, with the aim of better understanding the people/events in that setting. The researcher in the prescriptive, experimental study is an outside, objective observer with an 'external' perspective of the people/events he/she is studying, while the researcher using the descriptive approach becomes part of the group of people and participates in the events he/she is studying in order to gain an 'internal' perspective or a view through the subjects' eyes.

Finally, terms also used to label two distinct approaches to educational research are 'nomothetic' and 'ideographic' (Kemmis, 1978). The former relates to the search for general laws, the latter to the study of individuals. (*Collins English Dictionary*: nomos — law, custom; thetos — laid down; ideos — private, separate; graphain — to write). Thus, in nomothetic studies, data are collected from a number of cases in order to produce information on 'norms' or trends in a wide population. Ideographic studies are case studies focusing on the one individual or a small group of individuals. As a result, nomothetic studies tend to be reductionist (i.e. the number of aspects to be studied has to be reduced) and prescriptive (i.e. prescribing and predicting trends), whereas ideographic studies tend to be holistic, descriptive and naturalistic.

Cohen and Manion (1985) describe these two approaches as the two different perspectives in the sociology of education, namely 'normative' and 'interpretative' or positivist and anti-positivist. The normative model is based on the idea that human behaviour is essentially rule-governed and that it should be investigated by the methods of natural science. In contrast, the interpretive paradigm is characterised by a concern for the individual and describes and explains human behaviour by means of methods that are appropriate and in their own way as rigorous as the ones used in positivist research. Further differences between the two paradigms relate to the concepts of *behaviour, action* and *theory*. In the normative paradigm, *behaviour* — a key concept — refers to responses either to external stimuli (e.g. from another person or the demands of society) or to internal stimuli (e.g. hunger, motivation to achieve) and is oriented to the past. The key concept in the interpretive paradigm is *action* or behaviour-with-meaning (i.e. intentional behaviour which is future oriented). Cohen and Manion (1985, 40) succinctly identify the difference in the two paradigms with regard to *theory* (i.e. its nature, role and the aims of scientific enquiry):

> As regards *theory*, the normative researcher tries to devise general theories of human behaviour and to validate them through the use of increasingly complex research methodologies... The role of theory is to say how reality hangs together in these forms or how it might be changed so as to be more effective. The researcher's ultimate aim is to establish a comprehensive 'rational edifice', a universal theory, to account for human and social behaviour.

And in the interpretive paradigm:

Table 4 *Two paradigms of research in higher education*

Paradigm 1	Paradigm 2
Natural science	Human science
Traditional	Alternative
Experimental	Naturalistic
Prescriptive	Descriptive
Reductionist	Holistic
External	Internal
Nomothetic	Ideographic
Normative	Interpretive
Positivist	Non-positivist

Theory is emergent and must arise from particular situations; it should be 'grounded' on data generated by the research act. Theory should not precede research but follow it. The investigator works directly with experience and understanding to build his theory on them. The data thus yielded will be glossed with the meanings and purposes of those people who are their source. Further, the theory so generated must make sense *to those to whom it applies*. The aim of scientific investigation for the interpretive researcher is to understand how this glossing of reality goes on at one time and in one place and compare it with what goes on in different times and places. Thus theory becomes sets of meaning which yield insight and understanding of people's behaviour.

Table 4 is, admittedly, an over-simplified, but possibly a helpful, list of those labels which reflect the salient characteristics of the conventional and non-traditional approaches. The term 'paradigm' is used in Kuhn's (1970a, 175) definition: 'A paradigm is what the members of a scientific community share... it stands for the entire constellation of beliefs, values, techniques, and so on shared by the members of a given community'.

Gilbert and Pope (1982, 21) recognise and clarify a confusion in the literature which sometimes refers to paradigms (e.g. as quantitative or qualitative) instead of using terms such as methods, techniques or types of data. Certain methods, techniques and types of data are paradigm-dependent (e.g. experiment and tests in paradigm 1; case study and observation in paradigm 2), but others are not (e.g. survey, interview, questionnaire, quantitative or qualitative data in either paradigm).

This present book and its companion are committed to paradigm 2 (i.e. to the alternative, ethnographic, naturalistic, descriptive and holistic approach to research in higher education). They should be read within these terms, because my intention is not to develop a 'grand theory' in higher education, but to describe, explain and improve learning, teaching and staff development in one particular context. Each reader will have to decide which of the phenomena described and which of the principles developed in the books would apply to his/her own situation.

It has been repeatedly pointed out in recent years (Elton and Laurillard, 1979; Rudduck, 1985; Becher, 1980; Stenhouse, 1975) that educational research has been irrelevant to and aloof from educational practice. The practising teacher's perspective is essentially holistic, because he/she is faced with a highly complex learning–teaching situation. Therefore, if research results are to be relevant and helpful to the practitioner, they have to be presented in a holistic manner. As Elton and Laurillard (1979) point out, both the problems which research should tackle and the methodology which it should employ have to be different in the educational setting from an experimental, laboratory setting in the natural sciences. Instead of studying a complex situation through the traditional paradigm of taking the situation apart into components, studying the parts (through controlled variation of single variables) and then reassembling them again into the original whole, the authors suggest a holistic approach to educational research. They refer:

1. to Cronbach (1975) who proposes that researchers should concentrate on 'interpretation in context' as opposed to generalisations;
2. to Stake (1967) who calls for more attention to the contingencies among background conditions, learning/teaching activities, and scholastic outcomes in curriculum evaluation; and
3. to Parlett and Hamilton (1976) who propose an alternative methodology appropriate to the interaction between the student and the complex context within which he/she works.

The purpose of this methodology, known as 'illuminative evaluation', is to interpret the complex patterns which are observed in terms of underlying structures. Such interpretations are necessarily partial and lead to model building. But the models emerging from the holistic paradigm are not used as simplified descriptions of *all* relevant reality as in the physical sciences; they are used to unify limited aspects of a particular reality.

A comparison between holistic educational research and critical psychology is informative in this context. Holzkamp (1983; 1984), the main representative of critical psychology (and a disciple of Leontiev's), has shown how trivial the findings of psychological research have been, because the methodology used (i.e. the experiment) has ignored the interests and personal standards of the researchees. Critical psychology, like phenomenology and ethnomethodology, puts the individual with his/her subjective viewpoint, integrity and autonomy in the centre of interest and research. The subjective–scientific analysis is based on certain assumptions:

1. The individual has certain alternative possibilities of action within the limiting framework of social and historical conditions (cf Leontiev, Kelly, Lewin).
2. The role of science is not to show people solutions and proposals of action, but ways in which they can recognise and understand their own situations, problems, risks, possibilities of action and then decide which conclusions and forms of practice to choose in their concrete individual case (i.e. an emphasis on the process of knowing).
3. This process of knowing must be undergone by the individuals themselves and cannot be taken over by psychologists (cf experiential learning).

Even if psychological research on, and theories of, social conditions are correct, they are of little use to, and do not fully comprise, the concrete situation and the possibilities of the individual. Critical psychology has tried to find ways to develop methods of subjective science in order to take into consideration the concepts and processes of an intervention between social conditions and processes on the one hand, and the individual ability of action on the other. Thus a new paradigm has evolved in both the West and the East, and a search for new, more appropriate ways of studying the processes of knowing and learning is continuing. Burrell and Morgan (1979) and Reason and Rowan (1981) present the philosophy, methodology and examples of the new paradigm research in more detail.

Here only some of the methods and techniques which are relevant to research in higher education and especially to action research are briefly outlined.

Research method

The method used for the investigation of the central question of this book as well as of the individual case studies in the companion book can be broadly termed as 'holistic'. It has been oriented towards those features which Miller and Parlett (1974, ii iii) require of a holistic, 'illuminative' approach. The method is:

1. *problem-centred.* The problems addressed in my books arose from the real world of students, academics and staff developers in higher education.
2. *practitioner-oriented.* The books aim to yield results which are directly useful to practitioners in higher education.
3. *cross-disciplinary.* I have used models from a variety of disciplines.
4. *methodologically eclectic.* I have employed a variety of approaches, methods and techniques.
5. *heuristically organised.* The design of each action research project evolved as the nature of the phenomena became clear.

More specifically, the following is a brief statement of the aims and objectives of this book. The overall aims have been:

1. to improve learning, teaching and staff development in higher education; and
2. to demonstrate in theory and practice that the gap between educational research and practice can be bridged (e.g. through action research).

The objectives of the companion book have been:

1. to design, implement and evaluate action research projects jointly with teaching staff; and
2. to choose as a natural setting:
   (a) the place of my work (i.e. the School of Modern Asian Studies at Griffith University); and
   (b) similar settings at a German and a British university for case studies in Chapter 5 of the companion book.

The methods and techniques used for data collection and analysis were manifold and varied from project to project, as did the extent and range of information required. But what they all had in common was the case study methodology, including participant observation and illuminative evaluation, all appropriate to action research, and discussed below.

Case study methodology

Over the last three decades there has emerged a tradition of case study methodology which has made a considerable contribution to educational knowledge and practical wisdom about education, but which is often regarded with suspicion and even hostility. In 1975 an international conference was held in Cambridge, sponsored by the Nuffield Foundation (known as the Second Cambridge Conference) to consider *Methods of Case Study in Research and Evaluation*. Adelman et al. (1983) summarise the conference with regard to its views about the design, conduct, methods and techniques, and the code of practice for case study workers in education. They define case study research as 'the study of an instance in action', but the relation of the instance to the class from which it is drawn plays an important part. There are two types of case study research (Adelman et al., 1983, 141–2):

1. an issue or hypothesis is given, and a bounded system (the case) is selected as an *instance drawn from a class...*

2. a 'bounded system' (the case) is given, within which issues are indicated, discovered or studied so that a tolerably full understanding of the case is possible... e.g. an individual teacher, a single school, or perhaps an innovatory programme... In both contexts, the case study worker must treat the boundaries of the system and the issues as problematic, and attempt to define the immanent organisation of the case, i.e. its uniqueness.

The case studies in the companion book belong to the second category of case study research.

Since the Cambridge Conference, case study methods have been articulated more clearly, better understood and more generally accepted. For example, Bartlett et al. (1983) have edited the most important papers on this topic up to 1983 in eight volumes. Cohen and Manion (1985) present a typology of observation studies on the basis of six case study examples. Burgess (1984; 1985a; 1985b) deals with the process, issues and strategies of educational research focusing on case studies and qualitative methods.

Adelman et al. (1983, 143) argue that case study research and experimental research are based on different views in social science:

> ... case study might be seen in the context of an historical or interpretative tradition; experimental research in the context of a natural science tradition. In practice the two most important differences are in the way claims are made against truth and in the demands made upon the reader. Experimental research 'guarantees' the veracity of its generalisations by reference to formal theories and hands them on intact to the reader; case study research offers a surrogate experience and invites the reader to underwrite the account, by appealing to his *tacit* knowledge of human situations.

The truths contained in a successful case study report, like those in literature, are 'guaranteed' by 'the shock of recognition'.

They argue further that there are three major considerations which arise about the circumstances of the case, the conduct of the study and the consequences of the research. All three are interrelated and have to be considered across the board.

First, the circumstances in which case studies are conducted vary. For example, a case study may be sought, bought or sponsored and the evaluation may be by mandate, invitation or negotiation, funded by the institution or from outside. For example, the case studies in Chapter 4 of the companion book are somewhat different from the rest, because they arose out of my own interest and that of some postgraduate students in our university. The idea of eliciting staff and students' constructs of research effectiveness by the repertory grid technique was first supported by individual staff; then the research was financially supported by the Griffith University Research Grants Committee (for the purchase of computer programs) to extend the research to a study of the same topic at a British university; and finally, it was funded by a German research grant (Deutscher Akademischer Austauschdienst) to repeat the study at a German university. All other case studies arose from an immediate need and request by teaching staff or by formal committees at Griffith University.

Second, the means of collecting the data should be made explicit. The conduct of the study and the methods chosen determine, as well as depend upon, the scope and nature of the case being studied. The means of data collection must be explicit, and a distinction has to be made between description and interpretation, verbatim accounts and summaries. The raw data must be accessible and checkable, so that the researcher's account and interpretation can be assessed or be assessible in principle. For example, in my case, the collection of data in the series of case studies in Chapters 2 and 3 of the companion book differed from those in Chapter 4 in that the latter involved the repertory grid technique explained below. In the former case studies the following techniques of data collection were used: the 'nominal group technique'; 'questionnaire-based discussion'; structured and open-ended questionnaires; individual and group interviews recorded on audio cassette or videotape and transcribed or summarised; documentary evidence; and observation notes. The research reports were always checked and amended by the participants (i.e. I followed the principles of participant confirmation and 'triangulation' further explained below).

The third consideration discussed at the Cambridge Conference relates to the consequences of the research and the problems of ethics, anonymisation and protection of participants. The discussion of the ethics of case study evaluation and research focused largely on the SAFARI principles of procedure which allow informants the right to 'edit' the researcher's accounts of their views and actions. SAFARI is an acronym for *Success and Failure and Recent Innovations*, a Ford-sponsored research study.

All of my case studies resulted in two types of report: one internal report written for the participants and witholding nothing (or very little, if necessary for the protection of individuals) and subsequently a public report for the wider academic community. The latter was checked and approved by the participating teaching staff or the Dean before publication in order to safeguard individual anonymity. This double reporting served two different purposes. The first, inside, report written for the participants aimed at providing as much information and detail as possible to feed reflection and action within the situation itself. The purpose of the second, public, report was to distil not only the essence of the first report, but also the participants' reactions to it, their feedback on the whole exercise, their learning experience and the ensuing changes, all of which might be interesting to the reader — like a novel or short story — because it might represent a 'recognisable reality'.

The Conference saw the following possible advantages of a case study (Adelman et al., 1983, 148):

(a) A case study is strong in reality.

(b) Case studies allow generalisations either about an instance or from an instance to a class; they attend to subtle and complex relations.

(c) Case studies recognise the complexity and embeddedness of social truths.

(d) Case studies admit subsequent re-interpretation; the data can be stored for researchers and users whose purposes might be different from the original.

(e) Case studies are a step to action. They begin in a world of action and contribute to it. A case study can serve multiple audiences and may, therefore, contribute towards the democratisation of decision making. It allows the reader to judge the implications of the study for him/herself.

What makes case study work 'scientific' and acceptable to other educational researchers, according to Kemmis (1983a, 103, 109) is:

... the observer's critical presence in the context of occurrence of phenomena, observation, hypothesis-testing (by confirmation and disconfirmation), triangulation of participants' perspectives, interpretation and so on. Clearly these processes cannot be described simply as 'methods' in the sense of generalised procedures — they depend for their character on the kinds of 'cases' to which they are applied... Case study cannot claim its authority; it must demonstrate it.

There are two main activities involved in case study research which have caused a great deal of debate, namely observation and evaluation. Observation may be participant observation or non-participant observation. Although not all case studies are evaluative studies, case studies are frequently used in evaluation, especially in 'illuminative evaluation'. The main approaches to case study methodology used in this and the companion book are briefly outlined below.

Participant observation

Participant observation means that the researcher is not an objective, outside observer (with a set of pre-formed and specific hypotheses to be examined and tested), but that he/she is directly involved in the social world he/she is studying. He/she has a general set of problems in mind and his/her conception of events and actions is guided by a theoretical framework, but the research itself is open and flexible. Meanings and interpretations evolve through the views and perceptions of the people in the natural setting. Examples of participant observation are the American studies by Becker et al. (1968) and Perry (1970). They used open-ended interviews and treated the interview transcripts like a social anthropologist's field notes. This means, after reading them repeatedly, they identified emerging themes which they then used as categories for their analysis. This research approach to observation is also used in what has become known as phenomenography.

Phenomenography

Phenomenography is a research methodology within certain schools of thought, such as phenomenology, hermeneutics and Gestalt psychology. Phenomenology has already been mentioned in Chapters 3 and 6 as a tradition which focuses on the natural, experienced human world. Instead of applying their pre-conceived ideas to reality, educational researchers study how this world actually appears to people or how people experience and conceive the world around them.

For example, the authors of *The Experience of Learning* (Marton et al., 1984) investigate ways in which learning occurs in higher education from the student's point of view. The evidence presented in the book derives mainly from intensive interviews of learners, systematically collected, analysed and conceptualised. Thus the conceptual frameworks are derived directly from the data.

Similarly, in action research, teachers in higher education, together with educational researchers, can explore the phenomenography of learning. They can find out in interviews, recordings, 'learning conversations', etc. what and how students learn in a particular context; they will gain insights into the range of students' understandings and misunderstandings of the subject taught; and they will then be in a better position to facilitate improved learning. In this way, an interest in student learning can emerge from the teachers' existing enthusiasm for their disciplines.

Research designed to evaluate educational situations or innovations from within has been termed 'illuminative evaluation'. Like the techniques of interviewing and recording on audiotape, film (still photography and motion picture) or videotape, the field notes of participant observation represent the data which then have to be analysed and evaluated. Evaluation in the alternative paradigm has become known as 'illuminative evaluation'.

Illuminative evaluation

Stenhouse (1983, 1) states:

> The illuminative tradition, sometimes called 'portrayal', sometimes called 'humanistic', sometimes called 'descriptive', now seems to have got off the ground both in research and in evaluation. It no longer needs to fight to establish itself as an alternative to the 'psycho-statistical' paradigm worthy of consideration...

The basic emphasis of this approach is on understanding and interpreting educational practice by providing information that is recognisable and useful to those for whom the study is conducted. Illuminative evaluation utilises a flexible methodology in order to capitalise on available resources and opportunities. It uses different techniques to fit the total circumstances of each study.

Parlett and Dearden (1981) point out the differences between evaluation conducted in the traditional, 'agricultural botany paradigm' and evaluation carried out in the alternative 'social–anthropological paradigm'. Like Elton and Laurillard (1979), they believe that the traditional paradigm is for plants, not for people, because it does not allow for change and adjustment during the study. It is based on the assumption that everything goes according to the evaluation design and that nothing or little ever changes during the study. If it does, the researcher's task is not to adapt to the changed circumstances, but to discourage redefinition and new developments mid-stream. For these reasons, traditional, experimental studies (with experimental and control groups undergoing pre- and post-tests, compared and analysed by statistical techniques and a neutral or objective researcher) can rarely serve an effective 'formative' or cybernetic function. They may be of academic interest, but they are not of practical use and relevance to the teacher in higher education. Illuminative evaluation tries to describe, interpret, inform and illuminate, rather than to measure and predict.

Two processes are central to the understanding of illuminative evaluation: 'instructional systems' and the 'learning milieu'. An 'instructional system' is normally defined in the form of 'catalogue description' of pedagogic assumptions, the syllabus and the details of techniques and equipment. It is an ideal specification of a schema which the traditional evaluator uses as a blueprint. But in the practical teaching situation, objectives are often reordered, redefined, abandoned or forgotten. So the starting point of evaluation (i.e. the objectives against which the outcome is measured) is inaccurate.

The 'learning milieu' is the learning–teaching environment or Lewin's 'life space'. Parlett and Dearden (1981, 15) point out that there are many interacting variables:

> For instance, there are numerous constraints (legal, administrative, occupational, architectural and financial) on the organization of teaching in schools; there are pervasive operating assumptions (about the arrangement of subjects, curricula, teaching methods, and student evaluation) held by faculty; there are the individual teacher's characteristics (teaching style, experience, professional orientation, and private goals); and there are student perspectives and preoccupations.

Illuminative evaluation attempts to make a connection between the learning milieu and the intellectual experiences of students. For example, learning and teaching are influenced by the type of assessment in use, the scheduling of lectures and tutorials, class sizes, availability of resources, etc., which Snyder (1971) calls 'the hidden curriculum'. Illuminative evaluation is a general research strategy. The methods used are defined by the problem, not the reverse.

Kemmis (1983b) suggests 'a guide to evaluation design' in fieldwork. The title might be misleading if 'guide' is understood to be a cookbook with detailed instructions. But this guide is intended to be an 'ideas manual'; the 'checklist of ideas for evaluation' is a departure; and the whole planner is a list of evaluation design considerations which might be relevant to various evaluation approaches.

Stenhouse (1983) tries to establish acceptable standards within this research style. In order to judge the results of a research study as correct, one has to make a judgement as to whether the design and conduct of the research are correct. He introduces the use of the *quasi-historical method* for case studies, a method by which the researcher makes his/her data (case records) accessible to the reader, in a similar way to an historian referring the reader to sources by means of a footnote. Stenhouse suggests drawing on two research traditions which seem to be directly relevant to illuminative work: the ethnographic and the historical.

The prime method of ethnography is participant observation in which the researcher interprets his/her specific experience of participation and observation in the social setting while he/she is part of it (Burgess, 1985c). But Stenhouse's criticism of ethnographic theory is that it tends to be esoteric and inaccessible to the practitioners in the situation studied. He suggests that verification in ethnography can only be tightened up if the field workers' records are preserved and made accessible to others. Illuminative research should feed practice and therefore be accessible to practitioners and written in a language which is comprehensible to them. Stenhouse (1983, 7) says:

> ... an ethnographer could work in a quasi-historical way by preserving his sources and citing them in his case-study. In my terminology there would be reference in a case-study to a case-record which lay behind it and was accessible at least in microform.

Case records can be used as historians use their primary sources. If they are accessible to others, they provide a basis for verification and cumulation.

Verification and cumulation

Stenhouse (1978, 21) addresses the problem of verification and cumulation in case studies conducted in educational settings in analogy to, but different from, experimental studies:

> In the statistical–experimental paradigm of educational research verification is logically based upon replication of experiments, cumulation upon testing of theory. Replication assumes that the same experiment can be repeated and the results thereby tested. The cumulation of results depends upon the creation of a theoretical framework testable by experiments, and capable of yielding predictions over a wider range of situations than has been covered by experiments... (a) case study can be subject to verification and capable of cumulation, but according to quite

137

different principles from those governing verification and cumulation in experimental sciences.

In systematic study data are either treated as timeless... and hence replicable or as embedded in time... and hence not replicable.

The argument of this paper is that the basis of verification and cumulation in the study of cases is the recognition that a case is an instance, though not, like a sample, a representative, of a class and that case study is a basis for generalisation and hence cumulation of data embedded in time. It is the classic instrument of analytic as opposed to narrative history.

In history, verification depends on whether the sources on which a historical analysis is based are available and accessible in archives. The historian invented the footnote to refer to sources and their locations. Similarly, Stenhouse calls for written and audio-visual sources in educational research to be well cited and accessible so that the interpretation and theory offered can be critically examined. He suggests the lodgement of case records in a 'Contemporary Educational Records Archive' with open access for research workers, so that experience can be systematically marshalled as history and improve practice. His aim is not objectivity, but critical intersubjectivity which is controlled to allow critical scrutiny. He compares participant observation and interview, the two main approaches to data collection in case study methodology, with oral history and a kind of ethnography (respectively). The contemporary educational records archive seems to offer a solution to the problems of subjectivity, verification through, and cumulation of, case records (as edited primary sources accessible to other scholars), but it does not solve the problem of confidentiality, anonymity and agreement about access to data. Case records, such as my first internal reports mentioned above, are usually produced to provide the basis for the participants' critical reflection and discussion, leading to their greater insight, better understanding and proposed change of practice. But most of these internal reports have to be treated confidentially and could not be released to the public. Another method of verification is more practical and is used in my case studies: it is known as triangulation.

Triangulation

The purpose of triangulation is similar to that of critical intersubjectivity and participant confirmation: the researcher's analyses and interpretations are to be validated by others, particularly the participants of the research, either through confirmation or negotiation of meaning. This is also known as *respondent validation*.

Another definition of triangulation is given by Cohen and Manion (1985, 254):

> Triangulation may be defined as the use of two or more methods of data collection in the study of some human behaviour... triangulation techniques in the social sciences attempt to map out, or explain more fully, the richness and complexity of human behaviour by studying it from more than one standpoint and, in so doing, by making use of both quantitative and qualitative data.

The authors recommend the use of this *multiple method triangulation* as appropriate when a more holistic view of educational outcomes is required; when a multivaried phenomenon has to be elucidated; when different methods of teaching are to be evaluated; where a controversial aspect of education needs to be evaluated thoroughly; and where a researcher is engaged in case study (i.e. a multivaried phenomenon).

Adelman et al. (1983, 6) see the advantages of, and purpose for, triangulation for collecting witnesses' accounts of an event:

> ... to respond to the multiplicity of perspectives present in a social situation. All accounts are considered in part to be expressive of the social position of each informant. Case study needs to represent, and represent fairly, these differing and sometimes conflicting viewpoints.

Investigator triangulation refers to the use of more than one observer.

In my case studies I have made use of all three kinds of triangulation: respondent validation, multiple methods and investigator triangulation.

Case study methodology in action research

This book has argued that research in higher education needs to be action research in order to have an impact on the practice of learning and teaching. The case studies in the companion book provide support and evidence for this thesis. They have been co-authored with teachers in higher education who were the agents or participants in the studies. My role was not only that of an educational adviser or assistant and observer, as could be expected, but also that of a teacher and workshop leader, and hence of a participant.

The above methods in case study methodology (participant observation, illuminative evaluation, verification, cumulation and triangulation) have all been used in my case studies; they have in common that they seek to describe and explain a phenomenon (or phenomena) in a real-life situation as truthfully and holistically as possible, not only from the researcher's point of view, but from the participants' and other perspectives, with the aim of changing or improving that situation or aspects of it.

The researcher is not the detached, objective observer as in experimental studies, but is aware of the fact that his/her research questions and methods are influenced by his/her tacit knowledge. Therefore, he/she endeavours to share his/her meaning and interpretations of the observed phenomena with the people concerned in the research, to invite their views and criticism, and to negotiate a consensus of meaning for their own sake as well as for presentation to a wider community. These negotiations and discussions on action research in progress conducted in an institution with a critical community of equal participants have two major effects. First, they are 'learning conversations' for the people involved, leading to improved practice. Second, they generate insights and theories which might be of interest to the wider academic community, thus constituting a contribution to knowledge in the theory and practice of higher education (i.e. knowledge which might represent a recognisable reality and therefore be useful to other teachers in higher education).

A particularly effective tool to elicit personal meaning is Kelly's repertory grid technique which can be used as a basis for group discussion, learning conversations, and negotiation of meaning.

The repertory grid technique

Kelly's personal construct theory has been discussed in Chapter 4. The repertory grid technique, designed by Kelly (1955) and further developed by Shaw (1980; 1984) using computer technology, is described in detail in my published case studies (Zuber-Skerritt, 1985; 1987a; 1988; 1989; 1991c; 1992 and with Diamond, 1986). Here it should only be pointed out that the repertory grid enables the researcher to elicit from subjects constructs which they customarily use in interpreting and predicting the behaviour of those people whom they know well and who are important in their lives. Another important factor is that this technique facilitates the elicitation of constructs and responses from subjects without influencing them by means of questions, as is the case in interviews or questionnaires.

For example, in Kelly's method of eliciting personal constructs the subject nominates a certain number of people (or events) in his/her life (elements) and is required to compare them in triads and to say in which way two of the three elements — any two — differ from the third. The words or phrases resulting from this comparison form the construct pair. Thus both the elements and the constructs are nominated by the subjects themselves.

Meanwhile, many forms of repertory grid technique have been developed, some of which represent a significant departure from Kelly's individuality corollary (i.e. persons differ in their construction of events) in that they provide the constructs to the subjects, rather than eliciting them from the subjects. This means that the assumption behind the use of provided constructs is that people resemble each other in their construction of events.

The repertory grid forms used in my case studies (cf Chapter 4 and 5 of the companion book) were designed to achieve both the elicitation of personal constructs by the participants themselves *and* the commonality of one additional, provided construct pair (*Effective– Ineffective*) for the purpose of comparison. The elements were nominated by the subjects (e.g. researchers they knew well), but the researchers' roles were provided. Element 1 (E1) was *self as a researcher*, E2 *the (ideal) researcher I want to become*, E3 and E5 were *good researchers*, and E4 and E6 were *poor researchers*. This commonality inherent in the given element roles, combined with the provided construct pair, made it possible to compare individual grids and to arrive at a group (or mode) grid.

Conclusion

The purpose of this chapter was to explain the methodological framework of action research which is represented in paradigm 2 (Table 4). This means the approach I have described and adopted can be characterised as ethnographic, naturalistic, holistic, descriptive, ideographic and interpretative. This approach seems to be most appropriate for evaluating learning, teaching and staff development in higher education (because they are human phenomena involving complex relationships), with the aim of effecting change and improved practice and to bridge the gap between educational research and practice by integrating theory and practice in action research with or by the teachers themselves.

The holistic method used in this and my previous books aims to be problem oriented, practitioner centred, interdisciplinary, method-ologically eclectic and heuristically organised. It can also be characterised as case study methodology utilising participant observation, illuminative evaluation, verification, cumulation and triangulation. Techniques for data collection include the repertory grid technique, individual and group interviews, group discussions (e.g. the nominal group technique, questionnaire-based discussion), field notes, documentary data, audio and video recordings and transcriptions.

The quasi-historical approach (i.e. the use of and reference to case records) is used wherever possible. But wherever these are confidential, the principle of triangulation has been applied (i.e. by respondent validation, multiple methods and multiple investigators). A case record is often identical with an internal report to a teaching team or committee whose discussion of, and decisions based on, the report are included in the subsequent public report approved by the team/committee for publication. This double reporting involves a great deal of formative discussion and negotiation of meaning, leading to insight, theory building and improved practice.

The repertory grid technique is a powerful heuristic tool which can be used not only for eliciting personal constructs, but also as a basis for learning conversations, formative group discussions, problem-solving, negotiation of meaning and decision making.

In order to put action research into the context of professional development practice in higher education, the last three chapters will present some issues, methods and strategies of professional development.

Part 4

Professional development in higher education

This last part of the book deals with theories and practices of professional development in higher education, based on the theoretical framework and methodology developed in the previous three parts.

Chapter 8 discusses some major issues in staff development:

1. theory-of-action;
2. innovation and change;
3. bureaucratic rationality and human agency;
4. the role of the academic development staff;
5. the focus of staff development; and
6. institutional policies of staff development.

Chapter 9 presents some methods and strategies of staff development:

1. discussions in seminars and workshops;
2. the Excellence in University Teaching Programme;
3. academic staff development at a distance;
4. staff development through peer consultancy;
5. through appraisal and self-appraisal;
6. through curriculum development; and
7. through the development of academic development staff.

The final chapter (Chapter 10) sums up my views of the priorities for professional development in higher education in the 1990s; that is, assisting the institution in:

1. maintaining and constantly improving the quality of teaching;
2. providing evidence of high quality teaching through internal and external accountability;
3. developing management competencies; and
4. forging closer links with industry.

Chapter 8

Issues in professional development

Introduction

In this book, *professional development* (PD) is defined as the development, self-development and institutional management of faculty (or academic) staff at all levels (i.e. from tutor or teaching fellow to heads of departments and institutions) with reference to their activities and responsibilities as teachers and managers in higher education: for example, course design, implementation and review at the under-graduate level as well as postgraduate supervision and programme management. Thus professional development is understood in its wider meaning of *academic development*. In some countries (e.g. Australia and Britain) it is also called educational development, staff development or academic staff development.

During the last twenty years or so, most higher education institutions in North America, Europe and Australasia have established *units* or *centres* with the general aim of improving learning and teaching. While in German-speaking countries these centres are all called *Hochschuldidaktisches Zentrum*, their names vary a great deal in English-speaking countries, according to their focus on student learning, on professional development, on both of these or on research. Examples include:

- Research and Development Centre;
- Tertiary Education Institute;
- Institute for Educational Technology;

- Centre for the Advancement of Learning and Teaching;
- Higher Education Advisory and Research Unit;
- Centre for the Study of Higher Education;
- Office for Research in Academic Methods, and many more.

Where such a centre is referred to in general, the term *Academic Development Unit* or briefly, *unit*, will be used

In the light of the theories discussed so far, the process of professional development is seen as a process of learning and knowing in which the academic as a self-directed learner and problem-solver makes use of the unit staff developer as a resource person, facilitator, educational adviser or consultant. They are colleagues on equal terms, each with different kinds of expertise, which are not competing or hierarchical, but complementary. Although unit staff have a wide variety of functions and responsibilities other than academic staff development, the focus of discussion in this chapter is exclusively on professional development as defined above (i.e. through academic development).

The literature on professional development in higher education has increased enormously in the last two decades, but Elton's (1977, 2) statement after the twelfth annual conference of the Society for Research into Higher Education on this topic is still valid today: 'One is left with the impression that staff development in higher education is many faceted and that it is still looking for a sense of direction'.

As yet, there is no pre-service training for teachers in higher education. The only alternatives are in-service training, generally referred to as professional development or staff development, or no formal arrangements at all. It may be generally stated that professional development is and should be voluntary, but it can also be generally observed that the better teachers are usually actively involved in professional (self-) development, and the poorer teachers are not. Some are even hostile to the idea of improving teaching. Roe (1986) distinguishes four kinds of staff attitude towards professional development: first there are staff who do not want academic staff development, either for themselves or for others. Second, there are staff who do not want it for themselves, but tolerate its availability for others who might benefit from it. Third, there are those who in theory espouse enthusiasm for some development, but do not actually participate in it. Fourth, there are those academics who actively engage in development; they range from the once-only participants to the regulars who keep in contact with the unit staff. Development implies change for the better. It might be interesting to find out why some people resist change when they could improve their situation, and what the factors are which determine the success or failure of an innovation or change to be introduced in an institution.

This chapter highlights some of the theories of innovation and change which are pertinent to higher education generally, and to professional development particularly. However, only those theories which have a direct bearing on the improvement of learning, teaching and especially professional development are discussed in the following chapter. Other issues to be discussed are the role of unit staff called professional consultants, the focus of professional development, the relationship between institutional and interpersonal values, bureaucratic versus communal thinking, and the institutional approach to professional development in general: top-down or bottom-up? Specific examples of these approaches are then given in Chapter 9.

So far we have arrived at the position that the most appropriate mode of learning and teaching in higher education is that in the alternative paradigm which may be characterised as learner-centred, problem-oriented, interdisciplinary, process-centred, and using an open, critical approach. The inherent values of this alternative paradigm are the values of a relatively autonomous community of learners and scholars that deserves its autonomy on the basis of its substantive critical debates internally, not its acquiescence and compliance to externally imposed values (Jaspers, 1960; Habermas, 1974). It has also been suggested in this book that action research by the academics themselves (in collaboration with an educational adviser) would be one possible way for practitioners to gain insight into educational theory and to generate theory themselves through practical experience, critical reflection on this experience and discourse with others.

But how can the change of professional attitude and the shift from the traditional paradigm to the alternative mode be facilitated? The practice by the majority of academics reflects their adherence to the traditional paradigm which may be summed up as teacher-centred, subject- or discipline-oriented, knowledge-centred and using a systematic approach. Thus the difficulty of professional development becomes exacerbated by the need for a paradigmatic shift in staff attitude.

Three broad theories may throw light on the question of what factors support, and what factors hinder, change and development in higher education. These are Argyris' theory-of-action (a personal model), Berg and Östergren's theory of innovation (a social model) and MacIntyre's dialectical approach which emphasises the importance of human agency in bureaucratic organisations (an interactionist model).

Argyris' theory-of-action

Argyris and Schön (1974) and Argyris (1980, 1982) suggest that people have theories of action which they use to design and implement their values, attitudes and actions. The values and attitudes are always related to the theories that people espouse, but many of their most important actions are rarely related to their espoused theories. There may be a discrepancy between our *espoused theory*, consisting of our publicly proclaimed values and strategies, and our *theory-in-use*, consisting of our 'governing values' and unconscious strategies over which we have little or no control; there may also be inconsistencies between what we say we do (espoused theory) and what we actually do (theory-in-use).

Argyris and Schön (1974) have developed two models of theory-in-use. Model 1 includes the following commonly held values: defining goals in private with a minimum of consultation; maximising winning and minimising losing; being rational; and avoiding expressions of feelings. In order to achieve such goals, these values are translated into the following strategies: the control and manipulation of colleagues and the environment; the endeavour to seek responsibility for, and ownership of, particular goal-oriented tasks; and unilateral protection of self and others from being hurt. Although unintentional, in practice these values and strategies often lead to an escalation of existing problems and the creation of new problems.

Model 2 values are described as: producing valid information, especially with respect to goals and personal relationships; free and informed choice in decision making; commitment to decisions made; and the evaluation of their effects. Strategies to achieve these goals include: advocating personal positions and inviting others to confront and dispute these; being open and testing the validity of inferences and evaluations of the ideas and actions of colleagues; collaborating with others; and sharing power in solving common problems.

This openness and co-operation, characteristic of academics whose actions are informed by model 2, leads to their reflection on the causal role of their governing values, subsequent change (if necessary) and personal effectiveness. These academics are capable of what Argyris (1980, 17) calls 'double-loop problem-solving' or 'double-loop learning'. It is defined as 'the detection and correction of error that requires change in the governing values'. With reference to Jaspers (1960) and Habermas (1974), we may suggest that model 2 is meant to be the model of research communities (although it is frequently only the ideal), and that their views of the development of knowledge can be applied to teaching and to higher education in general. Academics are in the best position to know what constitutes good teaching, but we have to create a climate of enquiry in which they may explore these questions.

In contrast, academics whose actions are informed by model 1 and who do not question and change their governing values are only capable of 'single-loop problem-solving' of a routine nature, or as Argyris (1980, 14) says: 'Single loop learning is any detection and correction of error that does not require changes in the governing values', but such attempts at problem-solving are usually doomed to fail or to be ineffective in the long term. Rutherford and Fleming (1985, 439) summarise Argyris' theory-of-action as follows:

... the model emphasises the pervasive nature of Model 1 Theory-in-Use with the inevitable result that, for non-routine problems, there is often an insight and recognition of what should be done, but an inability to produce effective action that would secure the required change. A Model 2 Theory-in-Use provides a real possibility of being able to solve the challenging problems that confront institutions of higher education. However the difficulties involved in changing Theories-in-Use are very substantial.

Before addressing the question of whether and how personal theories of action may be changed from a model 1 theory to a model 2 theory, it might be interesting to consider the application of Argyris' theory to professional development and change in higher education, as attempted by Heller (1982), Fleming and Rutherford (1984), Rutherford and Fleming (1985) and Dick and Dalmau (1990). Tables 5.1 and 5.2 are summarised lists of academics' governing values, their behavioural strategies, examples of specific actions and analysis categories pertaining to the model 1 theory-in-use (Table 5.1) and to the model 2 theory-in-use (Table 5.2).

Fleming and Rutherford (1984) have used Argyris' theory for their analysis of Bligh's (1982) 'Recommendations for Learning' and the effect of these recommendations on academic practice. The recommendations of the National Study into the Future of Higher Education (1980–1983, funded by the Leverhulme Trust to the SRHE) on 'The Teaching Function' (published in two volumes and summarised in a final list by Bligh, 1982, 11–12) are consistent with model 2 values and strategies. However, Fleming and Rutherford (1984) argue that the majority of academics adhere to model 1 values and strategies as their theory-in-use. Academics can accept model 2 values and strategies at the espoused theory level, but not in practice, because they do not want to change their governing values and strategies which form part of their automatic behaviour. Fleming and Rutherford (1984, 21, 25) conclude:

Table 5.1 *Argyris' theory of action: model 1 (Fleming and Rutherford, 1984, 20–21)*

Model 1 — Theory-in-use

Governing values	Behavioural strategies	Examples of specific action	Analysis categories
Define your goals in private with the minimum of consultation	Design and manage the environment unilaterally	Make up your mind on each issue privately	Unilateral decision
		Act on your view	Unilateral action
		Avoid public discussion which might refute your view	Advocacy without enquiry
Maximise winning and minimise losing to achieve your goals	Own and control the task	Seek responsibility for the task	Control task
		Cajole others into agreeing with you	Control others
Minimise generating and expressing negative feelings	Unilaterally protect yourself	Withhold your own feelings and so avoid personal confrontation	Protect self
		Speak in abstractions to limit your accountability	Unillustrated attribution/ evaluation/ inference
Be rational	Unilaterally protect others from being hurt	Do not express negative feelings about others	Withhold information
		Keep others from exposure to blame without their knowledge	Protect others

Our thesis is that Bligh's recommendations could only be achieved in a 'model 2 world' but that the world of academia, despite its espoused claim to the contrary, acts predominantly according to model 1 — increasingly so during a time of recession. Resistance to the sort of

Table 5.2   *Argyris' theory of action: model 2 (Fleming and Rutherford, 1984, 20–21)*

Model 2 — Theory-in-use

Governing values	Behavioural strategies	Examples of specific action	Analysis categories
Production of valid information	Advocate your own personal ideas/opinions and invite enquiry/ dispute/ confrontation	Express your own ideas and invite reactions	Advocacy with enquiry
	Express and test your opinions of/reactions to the ideas/actions of others	Do not withhold negative feelings but explain these	Evaluation with data
		Refute incorrect statements made by others but give evidence	Confrontation with data
Free and informed choice in decision making	Work with others and share powers in order to solve common problems	Co-operate rather than compete with others	Co-operation
		Do not attempt to control/manipulate others	Openness
Commitment to decisions made and to their evaluation	Emphasise directly observable data	Refer to concrete examples to support your views	Advocacy with data
	Protect self and others jointly with an orientation towards growth	Confrontation on difficult issues	Confrontation with data

radical change suggested by Bligh can therefore be confidently predicted.   We will also argue that because Bligh's recommendations are, in the main, presented without a detailed strategy for implementation their impact, as Argyris has emphasised, will be minimal...

And:

The task of reorienting the governing values that inform academics' behaviour from model 1 to model 2 is a tremendous, perhaps an impossible, challenge. Yet this, we argue, must be the focus of professional development in the future.

Similarly, the AVCC (1981) Working Party's recommendations on professional development in Australian universities have been resisted or largely ignored by academic staff, probably for the same reasons. The question for professional development in both Britain and Australia (and elsewhere) is: how can this shift from model 1 to model 2 values and strategies be achieved? Fleming and Rutherford's (1984, 25) last sentence (quoted above) might be true, but it does not help the practising teacher or professional consultant in higher education. Model 2 needs to be built into the procedural structure of an institution. For example, Griffith University has tried to structure itself around model 2 values with its committee structure and course accreditation procedures which permit substantive academic debate at course team, divisional and institutional levels. However, the extent to which it has been successful, or to which the formal structure might be different from the informal power relationships at work, has not been thoroughly evaluated yet.

Heller's (1982) application of Argyris and Schön's theory-of-action seems more practical and helpful than Fleming and Rutherford's. He takes the position that for any change to be successful and effective, faculty members and administrators have to develop skills which they need to identify and solve their own problems without outside help. He presents Argyris and Schön's theory as a tool for identifying and changing any problems in higher education, and he advocates the use of heuristics (i.e. devices which can be learnt by staff to discover things for themselves). Old patterns of behaviour have to be unlearnt and new ones learnt. He mentions various approaches to professional development and studies in improving and evaluating teaching, but he maintains that there is little evidence of significant change and some evidence that basic problems remain untouched. Heller (1982, 5) says:

> The cost of nonproductive faculty members is tremendous in terms of money and reputation; one such person can cost an institution up to a million dollars in a ten-year period, and many such persons have twenty to thirty years until retirement.

Heller analyses the sources of ineffectiveness (in his Chapter 4) by means of a case study and highlights model 1 behaviour and single-loop learning in individuals, departments, and the administration. The result is decreased willingness to change, rigidity and ineffectiveness.

According to Heller (in his Chapter 5), increasing effectiveness is only possible by changing theories-in-use. His aim is to contribute to the development of teaching methods which facilitate learning a new theory-in-use. He describes the learning–teaching process in a ten-day seminar designed to teach model 2 skills to university administrators. They learnt how to identify and solve basic institutional problems by interrupting the ineffective problem-solving strategies they used automatically for achieving their goals, and by discovering new strategies designed to uncover important, previously withheld information and to maximise their internal commitment to policy decisions. They learnt heuristics for breaking old patterns and replacing them by more effective ones, and they learnt to design their own heuristics to solve institutional problems.

However, there is no evaluation of the seminars nor evidence of the participants' success or effectiveness after the seminars. Heller (1982, 110) admits: 'In reality Model II skills were never applied to those problems, so such a neat ending is not possible'.

A change in individuals' theories-in-use cannot be imposed by other individuals or by the institution; it relies on free choice and internal commitment. Heuristics cannot be memorised and then applied; values and strategies underlying the heuristics have to be internalised first. Yet Heller (1982, 86) presents the techniques and steps of a heuristic as:

... a mini-program that can be used to replace a segment of a current behaviour pattern. It is a brief, easily remembered tool for acting more effectively. A heuristic has three components: a 'flag' or clear specification of when it should be used; a recognition of what is going on in the situation at a correct level; and a concise, usable prescription for what to say or how to act to another person.

Even if we believe with Heller (1982, 120) that the only way to address the roots of these problems is to alter the theory-in-use producing them, and that those involved (in learning model 2 behaviour) perceive themselves as more effective (but so do the model 1 actors!), we do not really know at the end of the book how to go about changing from model 1 to model 2 behaviour, let alone how to teach it to others in seminars or at work. We are left with Heller's (1982, 120) assertion in his last two sentences:

That the technology for teaching a new model of action needs development is a challenge well worth answering. That such change might be possible is a source of optimism and a goal worth the investment of considerable energy, intellect, and effort.

Heller's case studies are illustrations of behaviours, values and strategies of action, both of models 1 and 2, but they provide no evidence that his hypothesis is correct, namely that faculty and administrative effectiveness can only be increased if the theory-of-action perspective is applied (i.e. if faculty and administrators learn to analyse and solve their problems with skills and heuristics pertaining to the values and actions of an alternative theory-in-use (model 2)). However, neither does this mean that his hypothesis is wrong. It means that more research has to be done in this area to test the hypothesis.

Dick and Dalmau (1990) provide an excellent overview of Argyris and Schön's work in a useful, practical workbook with a detailed, step-by-step description of several applications of Argyris and Schön's ideas.

In this book and in its companion, I have tried to highlight some of the procedures and processes of innovation and change which, at one university at least, have contributed to 'reorienting the governing values' of some staff and students. Apart from Argyris' personal model of change, it might be useful to consider a social/political model, since learning, teaching and professional development are social as well as individual processes and take place in a social/political organisation.

Berg and Östergren's theory of innovation

Traditionally, the development of innovations is regarded as a diffusion process occurring among individuals and accepted by them through imitation or some process of intellectual conviction. Apart from this diffusion research, there has emerged a growing research field oriented towards change, not only within a system, but also of a social system. This approach, described as a combination of a systems approach and a contingency approach, has been adopted by Berg and Östergren (1977, 1979). They have developed a general theory of innovation on the basis of Lewin's (1952) field theory and seven case studies on innovations and innovation processes in course development and teaching methods (within the framework of a larger study of educational planning for Swedish higher education).

They differentiate between system-consistent and system-divergent innovations, depending on whether the innovation process is consistent with or divergent from the main characteristics of the system. The former is a process of dissemination, the latter of a political battle. Berg and Östergren (1979, 264) describe their systems approach:

> A systems approach implies that events and behaviours can be explained by means of structures and forces across the social field as a whole. The importance of various parts of the system does

not follow from their inherent characteristics but from their position within the system. A social system (characterised by its main properties — membership, ideology, technology, organisational structure and relations to the environment), is a grouping of people around certain purposes. Such a system has a natural tendency to preserve the interests of its members, its ideology, its technology and so on — that is, to resist change affecting *any* of its main properties.

Berg and Östergren's analysis of change is based on Lewin's idea of change as a disturbance of the so-called quasi-stationary equilibrium in a force field and on Lewin's three phases in an innovation process: first, *unfreezing* (i.e. creating the motivation to change) — the change occurs in the force field as a whole caused by a disturbance (e.g. an innovation) in the equilibrium; second, *moving* or changing (i.e. developing new beliefs, attitudes, values and behaviours on the basis of new information and cognitive redefinition); and third, *refreezing* (i.e. stabilising and integrating new beliefs, attitudes, values and behaviours into the rest of the system). A new equilibrium is reached. Berg and Östergren (1979, 264-5) describe their preconditions for system-divergent change:

There may be — and this is a precondition for change — a lack of concordance, for instance in membership interests or ideology. This lack of conformity gives rise to 'cracks' or conflicts in the system, and these in turn constitute a further precondition for change. Change also presupposes that the system is open, i.e. that it has contacts with its environment. One could put it that such contacts allow impulses from the outside to flow into the 'cracks' in the system and to break the system by creating a potential for moving.

Berg and Östergren (1979, 265) identify four decisive factors which have emerged from their research and which enable them to explain when and why innovations are successful or fail. These concepts of innovation (as a political process within a dynamic force field) are: gain/loss, ownership, leadership and power. *Gain/loss* is a construct that explains the reactions of groups or individuals to an innovation, their advantages and disadvantages with regard to a whole range of needs and interests (i.e. security or stability versus insecurity or instability, ideological gain versus ideological loss, satisfaction or self-realisation versus personal dissatisfaction). *Ownership* (direct or indirect) refers to the extent to which groups or individuals have been involved in the creation and implementation of the innovation, and hence their commitment to its success. *Leadership* has been identified in various forms: innovation leaders who introduced the innovation; secondary leaders who were involved in part of the innovation; and formal leaders who were in a position of power and authority to support the innovation. *Power* is the most decisive factor influencing the success, maintenance and, in some cases, the institutionalisation of an innovation. The concept of power does not only imply control by legal authority, but especially real power by socially deserved and accepted authority. With reference to my examples of action reseach with academics at Griffith University, I can confirm that:

1. *Leadership* was an important factor in the success or failure of an innovation. Innovations were more likely to be successful when the formal leaders (the Dean and course convenors) were supporting or actively involved in the project; when the secondary leaders (teaching team and student representatives) were owning the problem and felt responsible for and committed to solving it; and when the innovation leader (CALT) used action research methodology and democratic leadership. On the other hand, the success of innovations was jeopardised when the formal leaders were committees that made the decisions to introduce innovative changes recommended by the innovative leader (as an outside expert), without the necessary participation of the secondary leaders in the research problem-solving, or in the final decisions which affected their practice. Consequently, lip service or change at the espoused level often occurred, rather than real effective change in action.

2. *Ownership* of the problem was decisive for the success of an innovation. This fact is illustrated by an example of course reviews (by an outside researcher as opposed to collaborative action research) presented in Chapter 6 of the companion book.

3. *Gain/loss* was also a factor influencing academic staff and students as to their involvement in innovative enquiry. For example, students were more likely to spend time on feedback and other evaluative activities if these had an immediate impact on the improvement of their courses and learning or teaching conditions, rather than on those of future courses and students. Academics appreciated action research for intrinsic reasons (e.g. job satisfaction, professional development) as well as for extrinsic rewards (e.g. tenure or promotion on the basis of reports, publications, teaching excellence), as shown in Chapter 5 of the companion book.

Rutherford and Fleming (1985, 444), after presenting three models of change (including the above two by Argyris/Schön and Berg/Östergren) conclude:

... if institutions of higher education are to respond effectively to the continuing challenges on their traditional autonomy and practices then radical changes in current values and behaviours are needed. Fortunately, Argyris and Schön's model clearly identifies those values which inhibit change and those which enable people to work together effectively and solve their common problems. However the difficulties involved in changing well-established value systems are very substantial... Berg and Östergren's contribution is at a more tactical level in that their four factors can provide an economic model through which the process of change can be monitored and necessary interventions can be planned and executed.

However, when it comes to helping people become aware of their values and world views, Hall (1986) offers a more practical approach by means of the 'Hall–Tonna Inventory of Values' which assesses the value priorities of individuals or groups, using a 77-point computer-scored questionnaire. This instrument has been adapted specifically for the Australian culture by Chippendale and Colins (1991) and by Hall et al. (1990). The latter indicate in their report where the individual or group is focusing their energy (value balance) and what the highest priority values are in the 'foundation', 'focus' and 'vision' areas. This inventory is particularly useful as a basis for discussion in management development and organisational change.

To sum up, Berg and Östergren's theory of innovation refers to system-divergent innovations in contents and methods of higher education. The conditions of change are determined by systems characteristics, such as membership composition, ideology, technology, organisational structure and the nature of its relations with the environment, all of which tend to be defended by systems such as institutions of higher education. The main phases of the innovation process are unfreezing, moving and refreezing. The main conditions for change are: 'cracks' in the system, caused by deviations from the main system characteristics and connected to the environment from which impulses flow into the 'cracks'. An innovation is likely to be successful if there are clear gains and few losses for the people involved, a strong feeling of ownership, effective leadership and some exercise of power to support the innovation.

A powerful heuristic tool to effect individual, group and organisational change is the Hall–Tonna Inventory of Values as a basis for identifying people's fundamental values and world views, for these constitute the underlying assumptions behind their behaviour, actions and strategies for change.

Argyris' personal model of change and Berg and Östergren's systems model of change might guide those endowed with leadership and power (i.e. administrators and professional consultants in higher education) in their role as 'agents of change'. However, this is the perspective of bureaucratic rationality, rather than human agency. What is needed in higher education is a dialectical relationship between the individual and the institution, between human agency and bureaucratic organisations, as the next sub-chapter will show.

Human agency in bureaucratic organisations

If we want to theorise about the possibilities of change in higher education, Argyris' personal model is useful when focusing on the individual; Berg and Östergren's system model is illuminative when focusing on higher education as a system or organisation. However, neither of them on its own is sufficient for higher education and practice.

The importance of the dialectical relationship between the individual and society, between the active learner and the educational context, has been pointed out earlier (Chapters 2 and 5). It has been stated that the individual is a product as well as a producer of society, that higher education is an individual as well as a social process. On the one hand, the institution has an influence on its staff and students (and society at large), but on the other hand, it is influenced and shaped by them and their actions (Chapter 5). The learner as a personal scientist (Chapter 4) needs the interaction with other scientists which is facilitated by the institution of higher education as a community of scholars engaged in critical discourse and as the state's conscience. This is Jaspers' (1960) legitimisation for the university's responsibility and autonomy which have to be guarded from political interests.

This dialectical relationship between the individual and the institution is important to understand if we want to effect change. People's interpretations of reality are developed in the social process. To change people means to create a different climate for generating different working relationships. Changed people are the results of changed climates, and changed climates are the results of changed people. Some recent publications are pertinent to this issue (e.g. Kemmis et al, 1984; Kemmis and Fitzclarence, 1986; Ferguson, 1984; Watkins, 1985; MacIntyre, 1981; Rizvi, 1986).

MacIntyre (1981) argues that our social existence has become increasingly bureaucratised in the Weberian sense; that the traditional organic, dialectical communities (as a source of developing knowledge and perceptions of self, others and of social relations) have been replaced by bureaucratic communities. Ferguson (1984, 9) speaks of bureaucracy as:

... a type of social system, one in which certain social acts are established and maintained, certain social objects are valued, certain languages are spoken, certain types of behaviour are required, and certain motivations are encouraged.

Weber's (1948) theory is that societies increasingly depend on greater rationality, efficiency and technology as they change and become modernised, and that the only appropriate organisational structure and means of improving organisational effectiveness is bureaucracy. MacIntyre (1981) criticises the bureaucratic rationality which has developed from this premise, rather than the organisational structure itself, and he shows how this kind of technical, hierarchical thinking has permeated and dehumanised our work and life, in which means are matched to ends efficiently and effectively with little consideration for moral goals and human understanding and responsibility. As MacIntyre (1981, 29) puts it:

The manager represents in his character the obliteration of the distinction between manipulative and non-manipulative social relation... The manager treats ends as given, as outside his scope; his concern is with technique, with effectiveness in transforming raw material into final products, unskilled labour into skilled labour, investment into profits.

The dangers of this kind of technical thinking have been discussed in Chapters 1 and 2 (on holistic dialectical thinking). Rizvi (1986, 4) argues that bureaucratic rationality as a way of thinking can only be overcome 'if we reassert forms of democracy and communitarian life and begin to make judgements, moral and political as well as administrative, *collectively*' and that democratic governance in education is only possible through a change in thinking about educational administration. Watkins (1985, 32) also advocates a shift from bureaucratic, managerial rationality to democratic thinking and acting:

For educational administration this implies a shift of emphasis from a managerial perspective whereby people are acted on, rewarded, coerced, motivated, or led, to a position that sees human agency in educational organisations as part of an ongoing dialectic. The recognition that organisations are made up of knowing and active human beings would facilitate the introduction of a more democratic and autonomous educational structure which would reflect human agents in concerned, responsible and creative ways.

The idea of the university as a place of the development of scholarship through communicative processes and critique of all social practices is endangered by bureaucratic, technical thinking. If universities are serious about their role and functions in society, they have to find new forms of communication (or rejuvenate old ones), which are themselves educative and allow for open and continuous debate about their own and other social practices.

MacIntyre (1981, 181) distinguishes between institutions and practices. An institution is socially necessary to sustain the practice of its members and their pursuit of 'internal goods' or intrinsic academic values. The argument for academic freedom rests on the basis that academic values can only be pursued through the generation and critical analysis of knowledge. Bureaucratic rationality may jeopardise this academic freedom by discouraging 'internal goods' or intrinsic values and by encouraging 'external goods' or extrinsic values. For example, as Kemmis et al. (1984) points out, promotion and tenure are granted to staff on account of their publications, no matter whether these are evidence of their pursuit of intrinsic values and internal excellence of knowing, or motivated by their pursuit of external goods. Thus there are advantages and disadvantages of the institutionalisation of research (and teaching) or, as Kemmis et al. (1984, 14) says:

> The institutionalisation of research in the University thus has both positive and negative aspects: positive, because the institution provides a foundation in resources and the human and social life of an academic community for the practice of research; negative, because the external goods attaching to research tend to become more visible and can dominate the criteria by which success in research is judged.

The merit of research and teaching must be judged primarily by academics committed to academic values, rather than by outsiders who have different values and different criteria for assessment. While it is true that higher education institutions are often threatened by bureaucratic rationality and the marketplace, it is also true that academics are in the privileged position to identify and articulate such threats. This sub-chapter and the researchers cited in it are an illustration of this point.

To sum up, change and innovation in higher education may occur at the individual level or at the managerial level. However, it is in the interests of academic freedom, the autonomy of the higher education institutions and all their members to integrate both approaches dialectically. This means, for professional development, a shift from model 1 to model 2 values, from bureaucratic rationality to human agency, from technical to dialectical thinking; it also means the establishment of critical forms of communication, not only for the analysis and development of knowledge in research, but also in all other social practices, such as teaching and professional development.

The role of professional consultants

It is the role of professional consultants in units, as it is of senior administrators in higher education, to encourage and facilitate this shift of thinking, attitudes and values, and to provide forums for critical debate, rather than merely to improve techniques, and thus to 'rehumanise' higher education and justify the existence of the university in its original idea as the nation's critical conscience. It has been argued that the following (model 2) attributes of people are favourable conditions for non-routine, 'double-loop' problem-solving and effective change in higher education: open, co-operative, exploring, evaluating, reflecting, able to change, inviting enquiry, dispute and necessary confrontation; and that the following (model 1) characteristics are likely to hinder effective change and to enable mere routine, 'single-loop' problem-solving: secretive, competitive, purposive, manipulative, pervasive and avoiding personal confrontations. It has also been argued that power and effective leadership are influential factors in system-divergent innovations and changes and, most importantly, that changes have to be negotiated democratically through critical debate. An institution of higher education is not a static organisation, but a dynamic community of active, knowing, socially aware and morally responsible people whose practices and critiques of practices constitute the foremost justification for the existence of the institution.

It follows from the above that it would be desirable if professional consultants aimed at helping academic staff develop skills, values and strategies of the model 2 theory-in-use; if senior administrators played an important role in professional development and were perceived by staff to support and reward developmental activities; and, most importantly, if senior academics and professional consultants themselves learnt and constantly developed their skills, democratic values and strategies of the model 2 theory-in-use.

Rutherford and Fleming (1985, 443) have portrayed the kind of people who will and will not facilitate innovation and change in higher education. Although the two 'pen portraits' are a model 1 and a model 2 head of department, their attributes would also fit senior administrators as well as professional consultants responsible for effecting change in their institution through professional development. The first is ineffective, the second will facilitate real change:

Model 1 Head

This Head regards himself [sic!] very much as the 'leader' of (his) department. He is a rather secretive person and sees it as his role and responsibility to make important decisions himself (often in private) and to ensure that these are carried out. He is something of a politician and is extremely skilled at persuading/cajoling others to his point of view. Some see him as a rather 'cold fish' because he is not given to expressing his own feelings and it often seems difficult to 'pin him down' on specific points. However, he is extremely protective and loyal to his own staff and does not tolerate 'idle gossip' from staff about their colleagues.

Model 2 Head

This Head regards himself as the 'chairman' of the department. He is open and cooperative. On important issues he readily offers his own ideas for discussion, with data to back them up, and invites comment. He dislikes 'woolly thinking' and constantly asks colleagues to substantiate their opinions. However he strives for consensus and joint decision making. Although he does not interfere in personal matters, he lets you know how you stand with him professionally and does not duck out of difficult situations. Where there are problems he always looks for ways to help rather than to assign blame and protect his own position.

It is important for institutions to select for senior administrative and academic development positions those people who are capable of effecting change through double-loop problem-solving and developing model 2 behaviours. Their role is to effect change in academics, just as the academics' role is to effect change in students. Learning at all levels — for students, teachers, professional consultants and administrators — is lifelong learning and problem-solving. It can be facilitated, but must be essentially self-directed to be effective. Lonsdale (1990) suggests:

> ... the will to change, to do things differently and better, and to do new things, comes from the individual. Management processes that build on the strengths, interests and motivations of individuals and that recognise their professionalism, are more likely to be effective.

Boud and McDonald (1981, 2–3), who use the terms 'consultancy' for professional development and 'consultants' for professional advisers, also see the role of the consultant as that of a facilitator of staff self-development:

> The aim of consultancy should be to enable teachers to become more self-sufficient and reliant on their own resources and those of their department, and act more as problem solvers for themselves and their peers. The goal of educational development should be to increase the professionalism of teachers so that they can address teaching and learning problems of all kinds and draw upon the resources of specialists when they need them.

Similarly, Bowden and Martin (1991) see the aims of academic staff development and the role of professional consultants as being to assist institutional management and academic staff in processes of nurturing the skill and expertise of academics so as to maximise the quality of their educational activities. They maintain that this is the best way to meet the new accountability requirements of the White Paper and to implement the Second Tier Agreement.

These aims of professional development are congruent with the aims of teaching students, in accordance with the alternative paradigm and theories of knowing and learning discussed in previous chapters. The focus and models of professional development are largely determined or influenced by these aims.

The focus of professional development

This section will highlight the focus and main models of professional development as reflected in the literature and as experienced at one institution (Griffith University), as well as those needed, wanted and requested by academics in two countries (Australia and Britain).

Overview

An international overview of professional development is provided by Teather (1979) and Huber (1981). Most issues in professional development (PD) in Australasia are discussed by Foster and Roe (1979), Boud and McDonald (1981), Cannon (1983), Roe (1986) and Murphy (1989).

The activities in academic staff development units in Australasia vary considerably, as the names indicate. Murphy (1989) has surveyed and analysed the functions of these units and found that units focus their activities on the central functions of improving teaching and learning. Other principal functions include audio-visual services, curriculum development, development of general staff, dissemination of research information, educational management, research and research facilities and other professional activities.

Models of professional development

Boud and McDonald (1981) differentiate four main models of professional development, depending on the type of work undertaken, its focus and the role of the unit staff. First, there is *the professional service model*, in which practitioners' specialist service (i.e. their organisational and technical expertise) can be utilised for solving an identified problem. Examples are academic service departments, such as audio-visual centres, computing centres, instructional development and evaluation centres, etc. Staff working with this model are usually limited in their effectiveness by their image in the institution. Second, *the counselling model* is adopted by staff (usually psychologists), who see their role as providing assistance to students and teachers with solving their learning/teaching problems. Examples are student counselling centres and centres for teaching methods. They are often underutilised because seeking advice to many staff and students means admitting a weakness or inability to cope. Third, *the colleagial model* is adopted by unit staff who work in close collaboration with teaching staff (e.g. on an action research project). The authors believe that this model is best appreciated by academics, but is only appropriate and effective when trying to solve new problems; and that it is ineffective when solutions can already be found in the literature or in the existing practice, and when the experience of others could be built upon. Fourth, Boud and McDonald (1981, 5) believe that *an eclectic approach*, including all three models, is needed in higher educational development to respond to the unique demand of each situation:

> The skills which need to be developed are those of each of the practitioners we have described: both technical competence and interpersonal skill are necessary, and the consultant's presentation to the rest of the educational community needs to be that of a colleague and fellow academic.

Based on the models of planned change (Lewin, 1952; Schein, 1969; 1972; and Lippit and Lippitt, 1978), Boud and McDonald (1981, 8–9) describe the stages in the consultation process as follows:

- The initial contact and exploration of the needs for change
- Establishing and defining a relationship in both the formal contractual sense and the informal or psychological sense
- Selecting and identifying the problems to be tackled

- Action in its various manifestations: collection of data, diagnosing various problem areas, setting goals for action, and working towards change
- Establishing the change: stabilization
- Reducing involvement and terminating the relationship; that is, fostering independence from the consultant.

The people involved in the consultancy process, apart from the consultant, may be an individual teacher, a group of teachers, a committee, a department or school, or the whole institution or any part of it.

My CRASP model of professional development (cf Chapter 6) is an eclectic approach based on a theoretical framework developed in the previous chapters of this book. It is also *an action research model* in higher education. At the primary and secondary school levels, action research has been an established model of professional development (Hustler et al., 1986; Oja and Smulyan, 1989; Altrichter et al., 1989). For example, Miller and Pine (1990, 56 and 60) conclude:

Action research is a staff development process which advances professional inquiry, improves education, and promotes teacher development...

Sustained educational improvement is accomplished most successfully through action research that engages teachers in advancing professional inquiry.

At the higher education level, the present book aims to make a contribution to action research as a model of professional development, especially in the light of criticisms discussed below.

A critique of professional development

On the basis of a literature survey on professional development of university teachers in Australia, Cannon (1983) concludes that past efforts to improve the quality of university teaching have not been very successful, mainly for four reasons:

1. a failure to appreciate the distinctive organisational characteristics of universities and the mechanism of innovation and change in universities;
2. the characteristics of academics and their work as teachers;
3. the 'improvement' approaches within the universities, which have been inappropriate or poorly executed; and
4. the 'forces of change' to improve teaching, which have been weak.

Cannon's analysis of statistical information, research studies and official recommendations on professional development (especially those by the AVCC Working Party, 1981) leads him to the conclusion that these have had little impact on professional development and on the improvement of university teaching since the 1960s due to the absence of an adequate general theory of professional development. This present book is an attempt to contribute to the development of theory within an emerging alternative paradigm of higher education research and development.

Ashcroft (1987) concludes, on the basis of his quantitative research into the effects of traditional and alternative modes of staff development operating in a New Zealand university for a five-year period, that traditional modes of staff development may effect change in attitudes, but not in knowledge (about student learning and teaching), nor in teaching behaviour. Or, in Argyris' words, traditional staff development may influence the academics' espoused theory of teaching, but not their theory-in-use. Their practice does not change significantly. Ashcroft (1987, 60) criticises traditional staff development in theory and practice:

> In short, assessment of staff development *practices* indicates growing frustration concerning ineffective implementation strategies.
>
> Assessment of current *attitudes* indicates a fixation on bureaucratic, other directed administrative structures, administrative desire for accountability and a lack of appreciation of the problems created by the multifaceted nature of the academic role.
>
> Assessment of current *theory* indicates inadequate conceptualization of the generic process controlling effective development in staff activity...

Ashcroft suggests that for changes in staff knowledge and teaching behaviour to occur, staff development has to be 'inner-directed' (as distinct from 'other directed'), based on individually relevant goals, effects and involvements. As suggestions for future developments, he briefly points in the direction of 'self reflection in a critical community', referring to the work of Kemmis and his associates, but he does not attempt to show how this self-reflection may be stimulated and operated in actual practice. My books (1991a, 1992 and this one) start where Ashcroft finished. He has provided the evidence for my hypothesis that traditional methods of staff development have not had the desired effect. However, there is a difference in the definition of staff development: while Ashcroft restricts it to instructional classroom performance, I consider it in its wider sense of professional development and academic course development.

Clark et al. (1986) are critical of staff development programmes because they tend to focus on voluntary individual development and on instructional skills, rather than on scholarship and improving the vitality of the institution. Clark et al. (1986, 192–3) conclude:

In summary, from an institutional perspective and for settings like Minnesota, efforts to enhance the vitality of existing faculty can be grouped in three prescriptive policy areas: (1) providing environmental support for the scholarly development of the faculty, (2) providing institutional support for faculty research and instructional development activities, and (3) providing differentiated support for individual faculty needs... We must learn more about adult development, the professional socialization of faculty members, how their careers are structured, and how the academic organization affects their vitality. Above all, we must probe into the nature of individual and organizational circumstances. The contextual, situational variables may not be as generizable from one institution to another as the rather prescriptive literature on faculty development programs has conventionally assumed.

The case studies of the companion book are examples of how the above three policies on support for academic staff research and teaching can be integrated in an approach to professional development as academic course development within the contextual, educational framework of a particular institution.

The focus of professional development at Griffith University

The process and focus of professional development at Griffith University is different from that occurring at most institutions of higher education because it is an integral part of the whole process of academic course or programme design and review. Professional development at Griffith University has always been indirect, 'consequential' and often incidental, arising mainly from curriculum development and course evaluation activities, rather than deliberately and primarily through activities focused on professional development as an end in itself.

The Griffith University course design and approval system generates formal and informal discussions between the teaching staff and professional consultants from the Centre for the Advancement of Learning and Teaching (CALT). It is through these discussions that academic staff become aware of educational principles, and of their need to develop specific teaching methods and skills. The same awareness often arises from a thorough review of a single course (usually involving teaching staff and students), or merely from a discussion with CALT on the results of a simple course evaluation questionnaire using student ratings and comments. Only those aspects of teaching which have been identified as problematic are then improved. The following advantages of this indirect approach to professional development can be observed:

1. University teachers develop only those concepts or skills which are directly relevant to their immediate needs and teaching practice at that particular time.
2. They do not waste time on topics or skills they might already have mastered or would not need (a problem often experienced in formal PD programmes).
3. This kind of indirect professional development is self-directed. Staff are motivated to improve a certain aspect or aspects of their teaching, because they can see the immediate gain.
4. The newly gained knowledge or skills can be immediately applied, tested and revised in their relevant teaching contexts.
5. The need for professional development, and for the improvement of teaching practice, is perceived as normal, natural and ongoing (and not as an indication of their shortcomings, a reason often stated by staff not wanting to attend formal PD sessions).

So far professional development has been discussed from the perspectives of educational researchers and development staff. But what are the views of the academics themselves (i.e. the recipients of and participants in professional development)?

Academics' views of professional development

Brown and Atkins (1986) offer some answers from the results of a national survey of academic staff training in British institutions of higher education which are similar to the survey results of attitudes of Australian academics to staff development conducted by Bowden and Anwyl (1982) and Moses (1985).

The main findings by Brown and Atkins (1986) indicate that academic staff training in Britain continues to be focused on teaching skills, but that there is a growing staff recognition of the importance of professional development in research and management. The respondents (from forty-one universities and twenty-five colleges, each represented by a senior academic or a committee on behalf of the institution) completed a questionnaire and provided additional suggestions for enhancing development. These may be summarised as three major recommended strategies: first, a greater institutional recognition and rewards for those involved in undertaking and conducting development activities (financial as well as psychological rewards, such as praise and recognition for training and advancement); second, departmental recognition and rewards (again material and psychological rewards, and the visible support of the Dean or head of the department); and third, ensuring that training sessions are themselves rewarding, of high quality, practical, relevant, well organised and enjoyable. Moses' (1985) results are echoed in this survey of staff training. For example, she finds:

> Most staff want practical advice, prescriptive guidance, do's and don'ts. Indeed staff, like many students in tutorials, want structure, a sense of purpose and direction and, if possible, a supportive group climate. Enjoyment of a session comes from active involvement, from a sense of achievement when one has participated and contributed but also from having learnt something new and having been stimulated to reflect upon and pursue a topic.

De Rome et al. (1985, 141) have also found that 'the overwhelming majority of staff appear to believe that teaching is undervalued in promotion decisions *vis-à-vis* research and that the status of teaching as indicated by staff advancement should be enhanced'.

The language used by academics in both countries indicates their model 1 views of staff 'training' (instead of development), their focus on extrinsic, more than intrinsic 'rewards' and 'recognition', and on a technical application of rules ('do's and don'ts', 'prescriptive guidance'). It reflects a climate in which staff are not autonomous academics. Their suggestions for staff 'training' are part of the bureaucratic pathology, not the cure.

On the contrary, following their suggestions would mean contributing to the pathology. However, like teachers who should start at the point where their students are, professional consultants must find out the developmental stages of the teachers before planning any action. Therefore, these survey studies mentioned above provide valuable information for unit staff and others interested in academic staff development. They also suggest that staff from all departments should be involved in the formulation of institutional policies on professional development. The next section will deal with this important issue.

Institutional policies on professional development

Concern for quality assurance in higher education is an issue which has been discussed since the late 1960s by both the public and the institutions themselves. As a response to this problem, most higher education institutions in Europe, North America, Canada and

Australasia have established staff development units. However, as most of these units work with academic staff on a voluntary basis, and are not fully integrated into an institutional accreditation or reward system, they cannot safeguard high quality teaching of *all* staff. Therefore, The Williams Committee (1979, 200, R 5.24), in its Report on *Education, Training and Employment* in Australia, recommended:

... that the Australian Vice-Chancellors' Committee appoint an expert Working Party to formulate programs for staff in the theory and practice of teaching, curriculum development and examining, and then later consider whether satisfactory participation in such programs should become a normal condition of tenured appointment.

The AVCC Executive set up a working party whose report (1981) was based on their terms of reference and included considerations of The Canadian Association of University Teachers' (1980) *Guide to the Teaching Dossier*; Murray's (1980) Report on a *Comprehensive Evaluation Program*; The New Zealand Association of University Teachers' (1979) *Policy for the Professional Development of Academic Staff in Universities;* FAUSA's (1977) *Statement on Higher Education Units*; and HERDSA's (1980) *Guideline Policy Statements on Professional Development.* Extracts of these documents are included in the report as appendixes. The most important recommendations are summarised in Table 6.

It is interesting to note that this AVCC report (1981) does not recommend a significant increase in funding for professional development and units, but changes in the university environment itself to encourage professional development. The working party believes that the effectiveness of units (or centres) cannot be increased by additional funds, but by a change towards a more supportive environment in which professional development is not seen to be a threat, burden or remedial work, but a regular, continuous professional activity and responsibility.

Another important recommendation is the design and implementation of an induction programme, lasting throughout the first year of service, of all faculty members on probationary appointments, as a condition of appointment and a requirement for the reward of tenure. New staff are in most need of, and most receptive to, assistance when in a new physical and social environment and having to prepare their course material and research projects.

The recommendation to establish a systematic programme evaluating the performance of *all* academic staff for both formative and

Table 6 *An institutional policy for professional development (AVCC Report, 1981, 26–7)*

A comprehensive institutional policy for staff development would:

1. require selection committees to endeavour to obtain information about *all* aspects of the academic performance of short-listed applicants for posts;
2. ensure that a well designed induction programme was conducted for all staff on probationary appointment;
3. require attendance at the induction programme as a condition of service of all such staff;
4. allocate a significantly reduced teaching and administrative load to all such staff in their first year of service;
5. ensure that all such staff are given explicit guidance and assistance to enable them to become effective staff members;
6. include specific procedures for evaluating the effectiveness of *all* staff members and use such evaluation in publicly stated ways in arriving at decisions on tenure and promotion;
7. allocate specific responsibility for staff development activities to heads of departments/chairpersons of schools;
8. actively support a staff development unit and allocate it specific responsibilities related to induction programmes and the support of senior staff members who are allocated staff development responsibilities.
9. include institutional support for a system of effective course review procedures;
10. assist staff in the development of appropriate administrative and managerial skills.

summative purposes has been the most controversial issue in all institutions. It is difficult to create and maintain a supportive environment if professional development is linked with evaluation for staff assessment (i.e. for tenure and promotion decisions) and for *all* staff (i.e. including tenured staff). However, that it is possible has been demonstrated by several academic divisions at Griffith University, and by many other institutions or departments.

Most units in Australia hold the view that they cannot be involved in judgemental decisions on academic staff performance for tenure and promotion, because an inspectorial role would be detrimental to a trusting, confidential work relationship with academic staff. This judgemental role is, therefore, undertaken by the Dean or Head of Department and the appropriate decision making staff committee. The AVCC Working Party's report also recommends that the head and a senior member of his [sic!] department (who should be an expert teacher and researcher and also knowledgeable about professional development) have a particular responsibility to initiate and conduct a programme of professional development with assistance from the academic development unit.

The role of units is seen by the AVCC Working Party as collaborating with the heads of departments; serving as information centres providing details of research findings and examples of teaching materials (e.g. Moss, 1977; Elton et al. 1986); providing workshops and short courses; and participating in the proposed induction programmes. Most units in Australia in 1981 already fulfilled these functions to a greater or lesser extent, but these PD activities were informal, unsystematic and voluntary. What was new in this AVCC report (1981, xi) was the recommendation 'That each university should develop a declared professional development policy'.

. The report can only be seen as a wider national framework for institutional PD policies and as an external reference which has to be adapted, fleshed out and specified in more detail by the individual institutions according to their staff opinions. For example, there might only be one new appointment in a department per semester or per year. So what does an induction 'programme' actually consist of? According to the report, a professional development programme should not be 'formal' (i.e. leading to a qualification), but the report does not define what 'a programme lasting throughout the first year of service' should entail, especially if only one individual is involved. This is left up to each institution.

Although the impact and effect of this report on practice in higher education have not been evaluated, we might assume that the support of the top administration (i.e. the condition of power) and the work of the units (i.e. the condition of leadership) in each institution have largely determined:

1. to what extent academic staff have been convinced of the need for a professional development policy;
2. how well and comprehensively the institutional policy has been designed; and
3. whether such a policy has been implemented and adhered to by all staff.

In any case, the report has had at least three effects: universities in Australia have been taking a fresh look at the professional development of academic staff in a time of financial, community and government pressures; the report has stimulated research into systematic, effective evaluation to enhance 'informed professional judgement' (Roe and McDonald, 1983) and to provide advice and guidance on 'reviewing academic performance' of departments as well as individuals (Roe et al., 1986); and higher education in general had been somewhat prepared for the government's Green and White Papers and the Second Tier Agreement by which higher education institutions are now committed to ensure that proper processes and procedures are followed with regard to staff appraisal and development.

Similar developments can be observed in other countries. For example, in Britain the government had released a Green and White Paper a year earlier than in Australia, and has since provided resources to implement incentives, processes and procedures for quality assurance in higher education, including the establishment of the 'Enterprise in Higher Education' initiative by the Department of Employment and the 'Higher Education for Capability' initiative by the Royal Society of Arts of Great Britain. The Committee of Vice-Chancellors and Principals (CVCP) has established a Universities' Staff Development and Training Unit (USDTU), located at the University of Sheffield, and a National Academic Audit Unit (AAU), located at the University of Birmingham.

The New Zealand Association of University Teachers (1979) adopted its policy for professional development of academic staff in universities because it wanted 'universities and its own members to accept the highest possible professional standards in academics. The Association would oppose the imposition of an externally applied registration system for university academics'. For, as Imrie and Murray (1980, 214) put it, 'self-regulation must be a better alternative than external intervention and control'.

This is also true within an institution. Self-appraisal, self-determination and self-development of academic staff are more appropriate to academic freedom than institutional appraisal forced upon them. Boud (1980) has developed one possible scheme of self-appraisal supported by peers. Other methods are described in detail in the already mentioned handbooks by Roe and McDonald (1983) and Roe et al. (1986).

It will be necessary for institutions to reorganise their structures, to reallocate their resources and to increase student numbers, with reduced numbers of courses and staff, in view of the drastic cuts in higher education. It would be disadvantageous, and in fact counter-productive, if institutions tried to review their resources without at the same time reviewing the academic viability and coherence of their programmes. Review activities are taking place everywhere now in Australian institutions. Departments or whole institutions are being reviewed by review teams who have developed criteria and procedures of review. In Britain, too, members of the AAU selected by the CVCP from senior professors of twenty-two different institutions will audit the quality control within institutions from 1991 onwards.

Conclusion

This chapter has dealt with some of the major issues in professional development: theories of innovation and change at the personal and social-political levels; the dialectical relationship between intrinsic academic values and institutional bureaucracy; the role of professional consultants; the focus of professional development; and institutional policies on professional development.

At the individual level, it was found that the radical changes recommended by the Leverhulme Study in Britain and by the AVCC Working Party in Australia could only be achieved in a world of Argyris' model 2 theory-in-use. The generality of academics may agree to the recommendations at the espoused theory level, but in practice they behave according to the model 1 theory-in-use. The task of changing one's (and others') governing values and strategies from model 1 to model 2 theory-in-use is a very difficult one, but this must be the focus of professional development, if fundamental changes (such as the above recommendations) are to be achieved. This is new ground for educational research and development: the design and testing of skills and heuristics to change theories-in-use from model 1 to 2.

At the organisational level, the four main factors influencing the success or failure of an innovation are: the extent to which the participants perceive a gain or loss; the extent of the participants' perceived ownership (i.e. their involvement in the creation and implementation of the innovation); leadership; and power behind the innovation.

Neither individual changes for merely personal achievements nor changes imposed by the authority of the institutional management are satisfactory solutions to the problem of professional development for teachers in higher education. Rather, it is the role of an institution to create a climate and forms of communication in which constant critical debate about academic and other social practices is made possible and enhanced by the intrinsic academic values of its staff. Academic freedom and institutional autonomy are endangered by technical, bureaucratic rationality, but constituted by critical, dialectical thinking.

The role of professional consultants and senior administrators responsible for professional development in their institution is first to learn, demonstrate and model the skills, values and strategies of the model 2 theory-in-use; and second, to help academic staff to do the same, in order to be able to engage in double-loop problem-solving and to effect non-routine, system-divergent change. Professional consultants are facilitators of staff self-development; they need technical, interpersonal and research skills for an eclectic approach to professional development, including aspects of the professional service model, the counselling model and the colleagual model of professional development.

Surveys of staff attitudes towards professional development in both Britain and Australia have suggested institutional and departmental recognition and reward of professional development activities and of excellence in teaching; visible support from the top administrators; and training sessions which are well conducted, practical, relevant and enjoyable. Some of these suggestions are congruent with the Leverhulme and AVCC recommendations; others imply a merely technical approach to teaching and professional development. The latter indicates a kind of bureaucratic thinking, rather than academic autonomy, a phenomenon identified and criticised in recent publications.

One of the main recommendations of the AVCC Working Party on Professional Development is that each institution develop its own professional development policy following a recommended framework summarised in Table 6. An institutional staff development policy is a so-called 'top-down' approach to professional development and has the advantage that *all* academic staff are involved and affected by it. But it is essential that it is backed up by 'bottom-up' strategies at the grass-roots level and negotiated democratically through critical debate.

As Murray (1979) has demonstrated, student evaluation of teaching may or may not lead to improved practice, depending on the availability of academic development facilities. He offers two main explanations: first, the person concerned must have the motivation to improve; second, it is not sufficient for academic staff to know where and why their teaching is ineffective; they must have the opportunity to receive advice on what the alternatives are. Thus it is not a matter of 'top-down' *or* 'bottom-up' strategies, but both the high and the low action levels (Huber, 1981) in combination (i.e. an institutional staff development policy *and* voluntary developmental opportunities). Neither action level is effective unless combined with the other. The introduction of any educational reform (e.g. a professional development policy) is threatening and resented by academic staff when they do not know how to implement it. Voluntary staff development opportunities without an institutional reward system are least utilised by ineffective teachers. However, if both action levels are in operation, staff know that they are accountable, and that their effort in professional development as teachers will be recognised and rewarded; they first become extrinsically, and then more and more intrinsically, motivated to improve their teaching. The results are better programmes for students and a more open, self-critical environment which has a positive effect on staff, students and staff–student relationships.

Professional consultants must be flexible, using an eclectic approach, and therefore be knowledgeable and familiar with a whole range of methods and strategies of professional development. Like research methods, methods and strategies of professional development can be used within a paradigm 1 approach or a paradigm 2 approach. It depends on the user (i.e. the professional consultant), whether the methods are appropriate or inappropriate and effective or ineffective in a particular situation. In the next chapter I will present the major methods and strategies used in professional development.

Chapter 9

Methods and strategies of professional development

Introduction

The purpose of this chapter is to present a number of methods and strategies designed to help academics to develop in their profession as teachers. To 'develop' means to learn and to change for the better, to move from one stage to the next; it means to change one's personal constructs (consisting of both thought and feeling), attitudes and the values underlying one's strategies and actions.

The previous chapter has indicated how difficult it is to effect fundamental or radical change in individuals and in organisations. An institutional policy, backed up by the power of persuasion and enforcement from the top and a supportive environment at the bottom of the hierarchy with the assistance and guidance of professional consultants, seems to be a necessary condition for continuous development to be undertaken by *all* academic staff.

Within this framework, and even where this desirable condition is not established (yet), there are a number of approaches to professional development which may effect change in staff and improvement of learning and teaching in higher education through a shift from model 1 to model 2 values and strategies, a shift from mere single-loop problem-solving and technically applied knowledge and skills to higher level problem-solving.

The methods discussed in this chapter are not all-inclusive, but they are considered to be potentially effective in a paradigm 2 world.

They often do not appear in isolation, but there might be considerable overlap between them. It should be stressed here that it is not sufficient to learn 'mere' techniques; it is necessary to develop an educational climate and context in which substantive academic values are of foremost concern and then determine the use of techniques, strategies and methods, which then become of secondary importance.

Discussions in seminars and workshops

An effective way of learning, developing or coming to know is through active problem-solving and discussion, especially when confronted with new problems in uncertain situations and when there is not one right answer, but several possible solutions. This same principle of learning through discussion and problem-solving applies to student learning as well as to professional development (PD). Thus the task of professional consultants in higher education is not to 'teach' academics educational knowledge and skills which they would apply to their teaching like technicians, but to facilitate discussion for personal scientists who come to insight and understanding through critical discourse with their colleagues and then design their own teaching strategies and methods. The two most common forms of discussion are in seminars and workshops.

Seminars are based on the presentation of a paper (or several papers) by an academic or a professional consultant, or jointly by both. This material is then discussed in a critical discourse by the rest of the participants. A seminar may have the advantage that the presenters in a supportive group may receive constructive criticism which they may use for developing their work further; or it may have the disadvantage in a competitive environment that they may be discouraged by destructive comments to continue or complete their work. For the rest of the participants, it might be advantageous to be presented with new ideas which they may or may not absorb, depending on the permeability of their personal construct systems.

Another advantage may be that the seminar paper(s) can be the basis of informed discussion, but there is also the possibility that it could be detrimental to a discussion unless, first, its length is such that it leaves sufficient time for group discussion and, second, the group size is small enough for everyone to participate in the discussion. From experience, leaderless groups should not exceed six members. Groups of more than six need a democratic leader to be effective.

Workshops are ideal for discussion in small, leaderless groups. Gibbs (1981) has developed a pyramid technique for larger groups: first individuals work on a topic or question on their own, then in pairs and groups of four, and finally their results are presented to, and discussed by, the whole group. This method may have the advantage that everyone is actively and creatively involved in the process of generating a solution to a problem, if the workshop leader is a skilled manager (or chairperson) in structuring the workshop programme and keeping to a time schedule. However, if the leader is unskilled, the discussion may be chaotic, frustrating and ineffective; if he/she is authoritarian, a lot of creative ideas may be blocked. Thus workshop leaders themselves need to develop democratic leadership skills.

Workshops may be one-off sessions or organised as a series in a coherent PD programme. One-off workshops may have the advantage, for example, that staff can be introduced to a topic or a problem which they are specifically interested in and which they find relevant and useful to their teaching practice, but they will normally not follow it up with evaluative discussions on the usefulness of the experience to their teaching practice. For the latter purpose, a series of workshops might be more suitable.

However, if the series consists of unrelated workshops, each of which is independent of the others and can be attended without attending the whole series, the same advantages and disadvantages apply to such a series as to one-off workshops. The disadvantage of an integrated series of workshops may be that they take up more time, but this can also be an advantage (something not recognised by most academics), for more time allows for more in-depth and individualised discussion. A discussion is only effective if it is relevant and useful to each participant. The aspect of length also applies to one-off workshops: one-day or half-day workshops can be more thorough than one- or two-hour sessions at lunchtime or after work.

One of the major aims of workshop discussions is to make academic staff aware of their behaviour and actions as teachers. Behaviour is a response to stimuli, whereas action is deliberate and controlled. Teachers' activities in lectures or tutorials are frequently not action, but behaviour (i.e. responses stimulated by students or the scientific community — that is, colleagues' expectations — rather than conscious and controlled action).

In PD workshops, academics can be made aware of the fact that they are able to control their actions. In the beginning, they might insist that they cannot do anything about certain barriers or constraints and that they merely have to respond to them. So professional consultants have to start from staff behaviour, although their ultimate goal must be to guide them to more controlled action. For example, Perlberg's (1984) and Kagan's (1984) work on video self-confrontation starts with academics' behaviour which is video recorded. The teachers then recall their behaviour (first without, then with, the aid of video replay), reflect, discuss and try it again differently in a similar situation. They then confront themselves again, until gradually, they find a way to control their action consciously and deliberately. With reference to Boud and Pascoe's model (Figure 13), staff may arrive at generalisations (i.e. abstractions or theories) after reflecting on their observed experience (inner circle). The task of professional consultants is to help them reflect (outer circle). This reflection on experience (with or without video self-confrontation), leading to generalisation and controlled action, may occur in a one-to-one consultation or in a supportive peer group or workshop discussion. Micro-teaching (Turney et al., 1973; Allen and Ryan, 1974; McAleese, 1984) is a form of this experiential staff development, but under artificial conditions (i.e. teaching to peers instead of students). According to Brown (1978), micro-teaching may be conducted with peers, students or pupils.

The process of 'unfreezing' old behaviour, trying out alternative behaviours and arriving at new, improved, deliberate and controlled action must be at the core of all PD workshops if they are to effect real change. The following sub-chapter is an example of a coherent but non-qualifying PD programme consisting of a series of four three-hour workshops.

The excellence in university teaching programme (EUT)

As is true for most methods of professional development, the Excellence in University Teaching (EUT) programme has been adapted from a secondary in-service programme called Excellence in Teaching (ET) after being successfully conducted with high school teachers in Queensland (Smith, 1985). Both programmes are based on Glasser's (1969; 1980; 1984) psychology and Hunter's (1976; 1983) pedagogy, but the programme could be based on any other educational theory in paradigm 2. The EUT programme was first trialled with academic staff in one division at Griffith University and its results are published in Adie et al. (1986). In brief, the main principles of the EUT programme are as follows:

- Teachers in higher education are able to discern and reach excellence in teaching.
- The starting point is the individual teacher's existing knowledge, skills and experiences on which to build.
- The process of professional development is a problem-solving cycle or rather a spiral of cycles.
- Theories, generalisations, insights and knowledge are generated by the participants themselves, through reflection and discussion on

their experience, and supported by theories established in the literature (e.g. Glasser, Hunter).

The knowledge thus generated by the academics themselves from their previous experience (modified through discussion with others) is immediately applied and trialled by them in their teaching, and this new experience (failures as well as successes) is reported in the subsequent workshop and discussed by the whole group. Thus the integration of theory and practice means the EUT programme is of direct relevance and usefulness to the practice of teachers in higher education. The content of the EUT programme is summarised in Table 7.

One example might suffice. The aim of the first workshop (apart from an overview of the programme) is to make staff aware of and sensitive to students' basic needs, expectations and motivations. The strategy is to ask staff to brainstorm about:

1. what motivated Sir Edmund Hillary to undertake the hardship and to achieve what he did;
2. what motivated the participants to become teachers in higher education (instead of choosing other professions with higher rewards);
3. what motivates students in higher education to study instead of choosing a job and earning money; and
4. what motivating reasons all three groups have in common.

Table 8 is an example of such a brainstorming list.

Only after this generation of ideas by the participants and of their conclusions about common motivating factors in people's decisions and actions do the workshop leaders present Glasser's theory of basic human needs consisting of feelings of:

1. success, worth;
2. respect, belonging, love;
3. fun, enjoyment; and
4. choice, freedom.

Comparing these results from educational psychology with the list generated in the workshop (cf Table 8), the participants realise that they can create educational principles themselves as 'personal scientists'. In this case, they have generated knowledge about basic human needs.

These basic needs are the same for all people. If they are not met, we feel frustrations, stress and misery. That is why we have to make a *conscious* effort to satisfy our own basic needs and those of our

Table 7   *The modules of the EUT programme*

Module 1: Progamme overview
This session describes the purposes, content and processes of the programme, and clarifies the demands that will be placed on participants.

Module 2: Success pathways; building a positive learning/teaching climate
Glasser suggests that there are four basic psychological needs for happy, successful lives. This module looks at ways of developing a positive educational climate which provides the opportunity for both academics and students to have these needs met daily.

Module 3: Designing lectures for success; prime time; catering for different learning styles
This module addresses the principles of an effective lecture design, and includes suggestions as to when, during a lecture, retention and learning is likely to be optimised, and how university teachers may cater for the preferred learning modes of their students.

Module 4: Motivating students
This module highlights techniques that have been found to be motivational, leading to more successful learning.

Module 5: X-raying behaviour; minimising conflict; assessing and building a positive and valid self-esteem in students
In this module, the links between self-esteem, behaviour and achievement are explored; characteristics that can indicate self-esteem problems are identified; and ways of building positive self-esteem, especially for students 'at risk', are suggested.

Module 6: Increasing productive behaviours; the power of reinforcement
This module explores the appropriate use of positive and negative reinforcement in the teaching and learning processes.

Module 7: Establishing effective rules for academic behaviour
The emphasis in this module is on the exploration of ways to establish and maintain proper academic behaviour (e.g. avoiding plagiarism; submitting essays and assignments on time; attendance of tutorials and participation in discussions).

Module 8: Academic improvement circles; developing critical thinking skills
This module examines questioning strategies that help students to raise their level of thinking from 'recall' to 'analysis' and 'evaluation'.

Module 9: Problem analysis; problem-solving
During this module, the principles from the previous eight modules are used to address participants' specific problems of teaching, assessment and student learning.

Module 10: Building influence with students and colleagues; Glasser's five-step approach to learning
This module addresses Glasser's approach to discipline, which emphasises 'self-discipline' and 'self-responsibility' through a process that enables students to accept the consequences of their behaviour.

Table 8   *Motivating reasons for human action*

Sir Edmund Hillary	University teachers	Students	Common features
Challenge	Money (being paid	Training,	Challenge
Excitement	to read, i.e. for	education	Excitement
Success	something we	Lifestyle, exciting	Success (money,
Recognition	enjoy)	social life	rewards, career
Satisfaction	Influence (e.g. on	Friendship, fun	achievements)
Money	students)	Expectations,	Recognition
Title	Challenge	career, etc.	(immortality,
Excellence	Lifestyle,	Respect/rewards	respect)
Danger, frostbite,	stimulating	for achievements	Status (title,
etc.	atmosphere	Frustrations,	expectations)
	Immortality (e.g.	boredom	Friendship
	through research		Satisfaction or
	publications)		frustrations
	Status		
	Friendship		
	Frustrations		

students. Therefore, the next step in this module is to ask staff in small groups (of about four) to discuss and list what strategies they might use to meet their students' four basic needs in their normal teaching situations. These suggestions are shared with the whole group, tried out in the following week in lectures, tutorials, marking, consulting, etc., and the experiences are again shared by the whole group at the beginning of the next workshop. Thus academics learn to shift from a content and lecturer-centred approach to a process and student-centred approach by trying to consider and to respond to students' psychological needs.

The trial group of staff at Griffith University showed a real change in this respect. Table 9 shows a shift from their initial approach to teaching (i.e. improving teaching skills) to a more student-oriented approach (i.e. helping students learn).

The whole EUT programme consists of alternatives (resources) from which staff can select what seems appropriate to them in their particular situation. They experiment, evaluate and decide whether to adopt, adapt or reject a certain strategy or method. Figure 17 shows this problem-solving cycle and the role of the EUT programme as a provider of alternative methods.

Table 9 *Staff needs, concerns and priorities (before EUT) compared with their assessment (after EUT) of modules of high relevance to higher education*

	Before EUT	After EUT	
Ranking order (mentions)	*Staff needs, concerns and priorities: how to*	*Modules seen as highly relevant and applicable to university education*	*Staff comments (summarised)*
13	Design lectures and tutorials	Lecture design	Making more conscious use of lecture design, especially planning the steps that focus students' attention and check their understanding
10	Develop better teaching skills	Learning styles	Increased awareness of individual differences in learning styles for both students and lecturers and the implications of teaching. 'I am going to consciously try to incorporate more learning modes (auditory/visual/kinesthetic) into my teaching preparation'
9	Motivate students to study	Student motivation	Providing students with study guidelines (e.g. student check-sheets for essay writing and oral tutorial presentations)
7	Improve students' confidence and attitudes towards learning	Self-esteem and reinforcement	Consideration of a range of emotional and psychological factors that affect teaching and learning. 'I have learned to be more positive and encouraging with students'
5	Help students develop more reponsibility for their own learning	Basic need–success pathways	Having gained more insight into student behaviour, and therefore more direction in planning

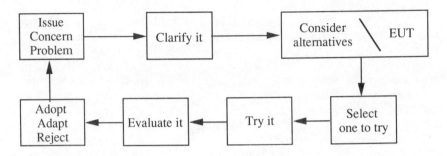

Figure 17 *The problem-solving cycle in the EUT programme*

This problem-solving cycle is used as a model for the whole programme as well as within each module. This means staff are encouraged:

- to start with some sort of issue or concern or problem;
- to take from the programme (alternatives, resources) what is going to help them with these issues or concerns;
- to select *one* idea from the general information; and
- to try it out, evaluate it and adopt, adapt or reject it.

The problem with this EUT programme — like any other voluntary professional development programme or workshop(s) — was that the best teachers attended and appreciated the learning experience, while others who would have needed it and benefited from it most did not attend. Reasons given by non-attenders were mainly pressures of teaching timetables and supervising exams. Apart from these plausible reasons, there might be other contributing factors (e.g. a lack of intrinsic motivation or a lack of extrinsic rewards), for the EUT programme is a non-qualifying programme which might be more attractive to less successful teachers if it were integrated into a diploma course, as discussed in the following sub-chapter.

Professional development at a distance

In order to overcome the problem of the timetable pressures mentioned above, Moss (1977) suggests 'staff development by post or the mountain to Mohamed'. He introduces a new system of bringing ideas, information and developments in professional development (PD) to the direct notice of teachers in higher education. After identifying staff interests and needs by means of a questionnaire (i.e. a checklist of areas of interest), the service to individual staff consists of loaning specialist books, articles, papers, etc. in the areas specified by them and of providing photocopies of articles prepared in-house.

This system is similar to the idea of a newsletter or bulletin produced by many academic development units in Australia, Britain and elsewhere, except that Moss' system caters for special individual requests. However, these requests may change over time and eventually not be fully met any more, unless the questionnaire (i.e. the checklist of areas of interest) is applied at regular intervals. The system of staff development by post fulfils staff need for information and new ideas about improving learning and teaching, but it is not sufficient by itself. Generating the academics' own theories, insights and understanding and facilitating their designing strategies which are appropriate for their particular purposes can be better achieved through on-campus discussion in seminars and particularly in workshops, as discussed above, or through a distance education course, such as the Diploma in the Practice of Higher Education (DPHE) offered by the University of Surrey and outlined below.

Elton et al. (1986) describe the origins and current practices of the DPHE (and MSc with the possibility to continue to MPhil/PhD) consisting of a project, four compulsory modules ('Teaching and Learning Methods'; 'Course Design'; 'Assessment'; and 'Students and Teachers') and of one optional module to be chosen from four offered ('Communication and Media'; 'Individualised Learning'; 'Staff Development'; and 'Research in Teaching and Learning'). The module on research has developed into two modules: 'Making Use of Research into Teaching and Learning' and 'Doing Research into Teaching and Learning' and a 'reacter'. Each module consists of five to seven units presented in two volumes: a study guide and a set of extracts from published books and articles in higher education. The difference between this course and Moss' system of staff development by post is, first, that all course members in the DPHE receive and study the same extracts from the published literature (which might be an advantage or disadvantage); second, the DPHE is a qualifying course (i.e. an incentive to study the material more closely); and third, the study guide provides questions, exercises and assignments by which members relate the course material to their own teaching experiences and conditions, and thus integrate theory and practice. They do not merely assimilate knowledge from the literature, but actively use and apply it immediately in order to be able to answer the assignment questions. The project is initiated and independently carried out by the members themselves. However, they also receive some guidance in a brief module on 'advice before starting a project'.

This Diploma in the Practice of Higher Education (DPHE) conducted and awarded by the University of Surrey has over a hundred members enrolled from all over the world. It is fully self-financing and may serve as an effective model of professional development for other institutions or organisations, for an independent, external evaluation of the DPHE (by questionnaire and selected interviews; in Elton et al., 1986) proved its success in terms of its aims:

1. Members felt they were more knowledgeable about the variety of teaching methods available, about assessment, course design and evaluation.
2. The course had made them reflect on their own teaching. Some felt they had increased their awareness about a variety of topics, their self-awareness, self-criticism and questioning their own teaching practice.
3. Members claimed that they had increased their skills in communicating with students by realising that teaching is a two-way communication with students, not merely disseminating their knowledge to students.
4. They felt that after the DPHE they were better acquainted with a variety of teaching methods. They mentioned small-group teaching most frequently, but also project work, individualised and interactive learning.

Most strikingly, Elton et al. (1986, 37) report:

Respondents (to the questionnaire) cited over 25 different ways in which *they had actually changed their teaching*. The most frequently mentioned examples included:

- introduction of and experimentation with systematic course design;
- use (or increased use) of small-group work, especially buzz groups;
- revised assessment procedures;
- greater use of student feedback and student self-assessment;
- greater consciousness of the role of the lecture, followed by more careful planning;
- generally enhanced awareness of teaching and learning possibilities in general;
- greater appreciation of both using and carrying out research;
- *a total revision of previous teaching methods.* [My emphasis]

This favourable outcome of the evaluation is proof of the viability and acceptability of this PD programme through distance education.

Moreover, it represents an example of professional development which adheres to paradigm 2/model 2 values.

Within the framework of this book, the most interesting results of the DPHE evaluation are, first, that it effected change in the course members' teaching practice and, second, that they were autonomous learners in their project work as well as in their coursework, because they had to relate course material constantly to their own conditions and experiences. For the course team's experience, it was most interesting (Elton et al., 1986, 39):

> ... that the means by which we encouraged autonomy are quite radically different from the means used in face-to-face teaching. There, they tend to be based on group interaction and negotiated curricula; we relied very largely on the interaction of members with their work and work environment. This is a good illustration of the important principle that in order to achieve similar aims under very different learning conditions it may be necessary to use very different methods.

Thus professional development at a distance might have the following advantages:

1. Academic staff need not be released for on-campus training.
2. They can integrate theory and practice.
3. They can remain in their normal environment while undergoing professional development and thus have a greater opportunity to achieve change.
4. A small group of highly qualified professional consultants can provide professional development for a large group in one country or world-wide.

The advantages given in points 2 and 3 also apply to an on-campus professional development programme, such as the EUT programme, but those given in points 1 and 4 are distinct advantages in professional development at a distance.

A disadvantage, as Elton himself recognises, is the difficulty of developing skills at a distance, because skill training requires immediate feedback. However, this debit is outweighed by the gain in attitudinal changes, which are a precondition for developing appropriate teaching skills. Another disadvantage might be the lack of opportunity for oral discussion with peers and professional consultants. DPHE members commented on this disadvantage and the difficulties of distance learning both in terms of space and time. Elton et al. (1986, 38) report:

Well over half the sample referred to the lack of face-to-face or immediate contact with tutors and the frustrations that this generated. It was not easy, for example, to hold discussions on paper: written dialogues had to be carefully planned and did not allow easily for immediate or unanticipated ideas to be pursued and debated. Two-way communication was highly structured.

However, in isolated areas or where no appropriate or acceptable professional development programme is available locally, the advantages of DPHE by far outweigh the disadvantages. Ideally, the DPHE, combined with regular seminar and workshop discussions, would constitute a comprehensive PD programme in which autonomous teachers in higher education have the opportunity to gain professional knowledge and skills which equip them for continuous change and improvement of learning, teaching and self-development.

The following sub-chapter deals with a model of professional development which emphasises not only the teachers' autonomy and ability to change, but also processes that enable them to gain insights, acquire understandings and exercise a measure of empowerment over their own teaching through critical enquiry as a way for them to generate theories about their own practice.

Professional development through peer consultancy

What is termed as 'peer consultancy' in this book is known in secondary teacher education as 'clinical supervision' (Cogan, 1973; Goldhammer, 1969; Snyder, 1981; Garman, 1982; Smyth, 1984a) or 'instructional supervision' (Smyth, 1984b) or 'partnership supervision' (Rudduck and Sigsworth, 1985). It is an alternative approach to traditional teacher education which is based on what Smyth (1984b) terms the business management canons of accountability, inspection and quality control or the technical, bureaucratic and psychological control of teaching. In contrast, as Smyth (1984b, 426) points out:

> ... the principles, practices, and philosophy of 'clinical supervision' are explored as a responsive way in which teachers might use collegial support to acquire greater personal control over knowledge gained about their own teaching, ascribing meaning to that teaching, and learning what is involved in genuinely autonomous growth as a teacher. Clinical supervision, as a form of collaborative action, is posited as a conceptualization of what it might mean for tea actively involved in the reflexive process of theorizing about their own teaching, its social possible consequences. Though struggling t reconstruct their own histories and the realities in

190

embedded, the proposal is that teachers acquire the capacity to understand, challenge, and ultimately transform their own practices.

The philosophy, rationale, and constructs of the approach are very much akin to those of action research and belong to paradigm 2. It is therefore interesting to translate 'clinical supervision' at the secondary teaching level into professional development through 'peer consultancy' at the higher education level. The prime objective of peer consultancy is the bringing about of improvement in the practice of teaching through a collaborative process of consultation, observation, analysis and feedback. However, there is a danger that the steps in this process can simply be followed mechanically (i.e. single-loop learning). It is important that this process is accompanied by a critical stance or according to Smyth (1985, 12):

... a preparedness to reflect upon one's own history and practice, to speculate about the possibility for change, and to actively follow through this commitment to change... it is an emancipatory or liberating process through which teachers assist each other to gain control over their own professional lives and destinies.

Reflection and critical awareness must then be followed by action in order to be practical and useful. Moreover, critical peer consultancy can enable teachers in higher education to examine, understand and challenge the institutional conditions and circumstances which might limit their work (cf Leontiev, 1977; Lewin, 1948; 1952; Kelly, 1955; Carr and Kemmis, 1986).

The model of (clinical supervision, partnership supervision and) peer consultancy, based on Goldhammer (1969), has the advantage that it gives a structure to the whole process of performance analysis and that this analysis is initiated and requested by the person him/herself, rather than imposed from above or outside. The autonomous academic invites a colleague to observe his/her teaching performance and jointly to examine and interpret the observation data. However, in professional development at the higher education level, the authority figure of the 'supervisor' is removed, non-existent and replaced by Habermas' (1978) 'symmetrical communication', a colleague-like dialogue grounded in the evidence of the events observed.

Goldhammer (1969) suggests that a formal contract should be made between the two colleagues (i.e. the observer and the one to be observed). This might, at the higher education level too, guarantee a more professional approach and safeguard personal difficulties. The main advantage of the suggested contract is that the focus of the observation is defined by the academic whose performance is to be analysed, not by the observer who would only see the situation from his/her own perspective. Briefly, and with reference to Rudduck and Sigsworth (1985), the contract between two academics would consist of the following agreements:

1. The one to be observed would propose a focus for observation by nominating one or more topics or problems which he/she would like to have feedback on. The focus is discussed and clarified until both academics have arrived at a shared understanding.
2. Both discuss what kind of evidence would illuminate the agreed focus and, given the constraints of the situation, agree how the evidence might best be gathered.
3. The peer consultant shapes his/her observation according to the agreed focus.
4. The peer consultant disciplines the content of his/her post-observation feedback by accepting a strict principle of relevance as defined by the focus.
5. The peer consultant agrees not to discuss the content of their discussion with anyone, unless mutually agreed that this would be helpful to the observed.

In practice, peer consultancy would fall into four stages of activity: pre-observation, observation, analysis and post-observation, as Smyth (1984a, 7) illustrates in Figure 18.

Each of the four stages is distinct and purposeful. *Pre-observation* includes the considerations under 1 and 2 above. The *observation* would consist of taking field notes (only what can be seen or heard; no

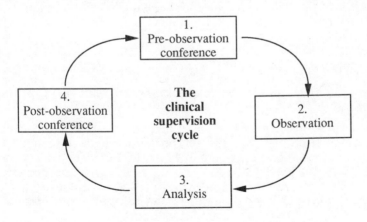

Figure 18 *The peer consultancy cycle (Smyth, 1984a, 7)*

interpretations or comments), audio or video recordings and transcripts. During the *analysis* phase, both the teacher and his/her consultant, while separately trying to discern themselves, discover patterns and interpret the teacher's behaviour represented in the raw data. The role of the peer consultant is to give his/her colleague another perspective and, thus, to contribute to a more balanced analysis. It is in the *post-observation* conference, when teacher and consultant meet to share their separate views and interpretations of the observed teaching experience, that they try to draw inferences and plan future action. A new focus might be considered for a future lecture or tutorial and a new cycle would start. Like action research, peer consultancy is likely to be more of a spiral than a cycle; teacher and consultant would start to plan future action, which would also have to be observed, analysed, interpreted and reviewed. This process is described by Smyth (1984a) in more detail.

The reader might have noticed that the description of peer consultancy as professional development for teachers in higher education has been written in the conditional tense. The reason is that so far, to my knowledge, it has not been practised at the higher education level. However, it seems a worthwhile area of research and development for the future, for it meets most of the requirements of the CRASP theory discussed in Chapters 1 and 6. The academic is autonomous, a personal scientist and enquirer into his/her own practice, involved in solving his/her own problems with the help of supportive colleagues who are partners in a critical reflection on a certain experience and towards a construction of improved future action. In addition, the model meets the institution's responsibility for constant review, change and accountability of its activities, without any extra resources.

Peer consultancy is an informal, yet structured, form of appraisal and self-appraisal, a theme to be discussed in the next sub-chapter.

Professional development through appraisal and self-appraisal of teaching

The conclusion of Chapter 8 was that institutions of higher education need both institutional policies for professional development and supportive academic development units to be effective in their responsibility to teach students in a time of rapid and significant change. A combination of top-down *and* bottom-up strategies are required, resulting in formal appraisal and informal self-appraisal of academic courses, programmes and teaching staff.

The topic of appraisal and evaluation has been discussed widely in the literature of higher education in the last 15–20 years. Why was it not of concern before? Eraut et al. (1980, 1) give a plausible explanation:

It is only in the last few years that universities... have begun to consider seriously both the systematic appraisal of their teaching function and the professional competence of their staff as teachers. During the 1960s institutions were preoccupied with recruiting appropriately qualified and experienced staff and with establishing courses to meet the needs of the growing number of students. Many curricular innovations were introduced but there was little opportunity to evaluate their effects in other than the crudest terms; and a few gave any consideration to the pattern and style of teaching. Higher education was not an established area of research, and the talents of lecturers were rarely used to develop and evaluate their own teaching.

After this period of expansion, there was first the 'steady state' of higher education. Then the emergence of students' articulate influence and impact on policy-making have had an effect on both the higher education curriculum and its teaching methods. The latter, in particular, have been under serious attack. Last but not least, more recently there have been cuts in resources, public pressures for accountability, effectiveness and efficiency in higher education.

Although this chapter intends to deal with methods and strategies of professional development, this sub-section merely points to the possibility of appraisal and self-appraisal as methods of professional development, without discussing in detail the various techniques of appraisal and self-appraisal as such. A discussion of the abundance of techniques in this area would go beyond the limits of this book. Instead, the reader is referred to what I consider the best literature on this topic.

Appraisal of teaching departments, programmes, courses and staff

As mentioned before, the two most comprehensive handbooks in this field of higher education are the guides by Roe and McDonald (1983) and Roe et al. (1986). The guide on 'Standards for Evaluations of Educational Programs, Projects, and Materials' by the Joint Committee on Standards for Educational Evaluation (1981) should also be mentioned here, as well as Elton's (1987) book linking appraisal and professional development in higher education. Elliott's (1989) study demonstrates how an appraisal scheme, which meets the government's appraisal requirements, can operate as 'a ritualistic mechanism for ideological construction' or as 'a counterhegemonic practice' in the appraisal context. For the latter he presents an action research guide outlining the process of improving performance at all levels of the hierarchy in schools which could be adapted to higher education.

However, no matter how well the conduct of an evaluation is being carried out, it is important to remember that the results will only be taken seriously by academic staff if their effort of making the suggested improvements is recognised and rewarded in some way by the institution. If it is not, time spent on curriculum development, evaluation or the improvement of teaching (at the expense of research) will be considered as a time-consuming diversion from research, and thus from advancement in their professional career. At the same time, this argument is a justification for the establishment of an institutional system of formal evaluation of teaching (including course design and evaluation, innovations as well as the performance as lecturer, tutor, marker and consultant to students) which is taken into consideration in administrative decisions on tenure and promotion of staff. Such a system provides a framework and the institution's recognition that teaching is important, but it is only formative if supported by a development system (cf Chapter 8). It is in these developmental activities and discussions that academic staff move towards intrinsic values and motivations for self-appraisal and self-development.

Self-appraisal of academic staff

Boud (1980, 225) succinctly sums up the need for self-appraisal and for a debate on the professional development of academic staff:

> If professions are to maintain their traditional autonomy and freedom from influence by governments it will become increasingly necessary for them to be able to indicate publicly that they are engaged in their own internal schemes of accountability and self-monitoring. This applies as much to the academic profession as it does to medicine, law and others. Whatever may be the current reaction of academics to demonstrate their competence in teaching and other matters it is clear that they will have to establish their own mechanisms for self-appraisal if they are not to have external appraisal thrust upon them. There are many ways of establishing schemes of self and peer appraisal.

Boud presents one such possible scheme. In a similar way to the method of peer consultancy, he concentrates on the individual staff member and his/her needs, rather than on a course, a subject, a teaching method or a problem. This approach to self-appraisal utilises the expertise and support of peers, not in pairs, as in peer consultancy, but in small groups of up to ten members. Such self-appraisal groups are conceived as working together voluntarily, in informal settings, and agreeing on a common area or topic.

In the first meeting, the three major considerations in the peer appraisal process are established:

1. producing a list of criteria for a common area of practice by
   (a) brainstorming; and
   (b) agreeing on an extracted few criteria after discussion;
2. devising methods to evaluate the quality of practice;
3. 'armchair' appraisal by each individual of his/her performance with respect to the criteria chosen in 1(b).

In the interim between the initial and the second meeting, the academics in their daily practice are engaged in self-monitoring:

1. of their own teaching or other activities using the methods defined by the peer group; and
2. of the changes they might have made as a result of the previous monitoring in 1.

In the second meeting, the experience of self-monitoring is examined by the group, with each member reporting. The disclosure of self-appraisal depends on the level of trust and co-operation within the group. Questions, comments or feedback from the group may be critical, probing or playing the devil's advocate, but a positive appreciation is essential. Criteria and methods can be revised; the cycle may be repeated, or skills and knowledge developed in other defined areas.

Another alternative method of self-appraisal should be mentioned here, because it is different from all the other proposals of improving teaching effectiveness in that it does not require a pre-specification of criteria. Keen (1981, 79) contends that the behaviourally oriented methodologies by which the teacher is assessed against certain criteria of an 'ideal profile' are inappropriate; but that:

> ... the teacher should be perceived as a professional, capable of undertaking his [sic!] task with autonomy. This is particularly valuable if a mechanism exists to assist him in identifying his strengths and weaknesses so that he can capitalise on the former whilst endeavouring to eradicate the latter (through the application of appropriate staff development).

Keen has designed such a mechanism to raise the teacher's perceptual awareness to his/her strengths and weaknesses and to become a more effective teacher. His teaching appraisal system has become known as TARGET (i.e. an acronym for Teaching Appraisal by Repertory Grid Elicitation Techniques and based on the principles of Kelly's (1955) personal construct theory). It is accompanied by an interactive computer programme providing direct feedback in terms of the teacher's strengths and weaknesses.

The TARGET system utilises the repertory grid technique. Illustrations of the use of this technique for eliciting personal constructs of research effectiveness are included in the case studies in Chapters 4 and 5 of the companion book. Similarly, teachers' constructs of teaching effectiveness can be elicited. Keen's (1981) computer programme is somewhat different from the one used in my case studies; however, the principles are the same: the criteria of effectiveness are elicited from the respondents themselves and not by 'experts' whose language and constructs are often alien to the respondents. Keen does not claim that his TARGET system produces 'better' teachers, but that the respondents to a TARGET grid may well experience heightened perceptual awareness of teachers and teaching. Like Elton et al. (1986), Keen believes that teaching skills can be acquired by perceptual enhancement.

What is important in professional development with TARGET is that the academics themselves are the 'experts', motivated to change or to modify their practices in the light of their own perception of their teaching style relative to their own perception of effective teaching. On comparing the two teaching style profiles, a teacher may conclude that there is some inadequacy or deficiency in his/her own teaching style which needs improvement. It is at this point that help and consultancy have to be available and provided. The primary aim of using the repertory grid technique is to raise perceptual awareness of teachers in higher education in order to facilitate the improvement of teaching effectiveness.

There is the danger with the use of all these methods and strategies of professional development, as Coles (1978, 7) points out, that one assumes

... that staff development is an 'entity'; 'something' that can be done 'by' someone 'for' (or worse 'to') someone else. Inevitably, if you make this assumption you find yourself in the business of deciding how best to bring it about.

It might have become clear by now, or else it must be strongly emphasised here, that the methods and strategies of staff development discussed in this book are not suggestions based on such an assumption; rather, they are seen as supportive and complementary activities to what I consider the heart and essence of professional, continuing development, namely indirect professional development through and in the context of course or programme development.

Professional development through curriculum development

As mentioned earlier, Griffith University, since its inception in 1974, has employed an approval system in which curriculum development (i.e. course and programme design, evaluation and review) is a continuing process. Each new or revised course outline has to be submitted and approved by a committee structure first at the division, then at the university level. Academic staff are assisted in their tasks at the planning as well as the approval stages by professional consultants. This system was designed primarily to safeguard the quality of academic programmes for students, but it turned out to be a system of continuing debate and development for academic staff as well. If staff are continuously involved in curriculum development and justifications for their actions, they are unconsciously, almost incidentally and indirectly engaged in professional development as teachers in the widest sense. This idea is further explored and illustrated in Chapters 2 and 3 of the companion book.

Coles (1978, 7) independently came to the same conclusion, but more radically dismissed all other methods of professional development:

> Much of my work of looking at courses seems to be suggesting that conventional efforts at staff development have only a marginal effect: the problems of teaching and learning are not being solved by 'training university teachers'. But what is the alternative? I want to suggest that it is more profitable to think of staff development as a 'spin off' from, and curiously, a prerequisite for, curriculum development. In other words, let us stop trying to be 'staff developers' and be 'course developers' instead.

Academics are both teachers and subject experts. Professional development must be related to the subject taught, rather than being based on generalisations about learning and teaching. Academics themselves can generate their own personal theories based on their experiences with teaching a subject (cf Kelly, 1955; Lewin 1948; 1952; Kolb, 1984). These generalisations about learning and teaching are subsequent to, not preceding practical experience.

The process of curriculum development needs a structure and guidelines. At Griffith University there is a format for the first submission of a course outline (i.e. the rationale for mounting the course or programme and its role, place and function in the overall academic programme of the school) and a format for the second, more detailed description of a course (the central question or problem to be addressed in the course, the aims, content, teaching and assessment methods and their rationale). The completed course submissions enable the Divisional Standing Committee and the Education Committee of the university's Academic Committee to assess whether a course is desirable, feasible, necessary, coherent and academically as well as educationally sound. The course descriptions are also useful information for students, published in the *Handbook*, but what is unnoticed by most is the fact that a lot of thinking, debating and professional development has been going on in the process of arriving at the final, approved course description.

Another form of professional development through curriculum development is action research, as discussed in Chapter 6 in this book and in Chapters 5 and 6 in the companion book. Within the framework of a common philosophy and methodology, this integrated approach to professional development through curriculum development seems to be the deepest and most effective professional development in both Coles' (1978) and my own experience, for it relates teaching and subject expertise, course improvement and the improvement of teaching; it has a snowball effect, and eventually, it will involve *all* staff (also those who would not attend staff development programmes), especially if a course design and approval system is institutionalised. If it is, the existence of an academic development unit is essential and its critical as well as guiding role vital. The AVCC in its submission to the CTEC supports this direction:

> A majority of universities have Academic Development Units which perform a wide variety of functions associated with the improvement of teaching and learning and the evaluation of courses. The effectiveness of units in improving the quality of teaching, course structures and assessment, establishing educational philosophies, confirming or changing institutional policies, and assisting in the evaluation of departments, schools and faculties is not in doubt. It is important that these units continue to receive adequate resources to carry out their task.

A decisive influencing factor in the effectiveness of such units is their staffing and funding which depend on the institutions' (and government's) short- or long-sightedness with regard to continuous change and academic development. For example, for about the first fifteen years of its existence, Griffith University's academic development unit (CALT) had the highest unit staff-to-academic staff ratio in Australia, justified by its integrated approach to curriculum development. However, even from a bureaucratic viewpoint, if one ineffective academic may cost the university up to one million dollars in a ten-year period, as quoted earlier, it might be much more cost effective to adopt an integrated approach and employ professional consultants in units to assist academic staff in developing a more professional approach to curriculum development and teaching. This assumes, of course, that unit staff themselves are efficient in their profession and involved in continuous development and self-development.

Before turning to the development of professional consultants, it is worth discussing the facilitation of professional development of academic staff through organisational development.

Professional development through organisational development

As shown in the previous section, there is evidence that curriculum development is an effective way of developing the professional competencies of academic staff in higher education. However, the problem is that *not all* academics who would benefit from collaborative curriculum work with colleagues and professional consultants are prepared to discuss and critically reflect upon their courses or programmes with others. Therefore, it has been suggested (Lucas, 1989; 1990) that a more effective way is for consultants in higher education to work with deans and heads of departments who are in the most advantageous position to improve teaching and to revitalise demoralised faculty. This work also constitutes organisation development which has been defined by Huse and Cummings (1985, 2) as 'a systemwide application of behavioral science knowledge to the planned development and reinforcement of organizational strategies, structures, and processes for improving an organization's effectiveness'.

The aim of organisation development is systemwide change. Action research has been associated with organisational change and development since the beginning in the 1940s and 1950s (Clark, 1972; Huse and Cummings, 1985; Clark, 1989; McLennan, 1989). Lucas (1989, 158) maintains that working with academic chairs to teach them faculty development skills means increasing 'the possibility of making large numbers of faculty more aware of ways improvement of teaching can be brought about'.

Lucas (1986a; 1989b;1989, 159) identifies the following key topics for faculty development workshops which chairs have found most useful:

1. power and influence: where it comes from, how it is developed (Tucker, 1984);
2. the task and relationship functions of leadership (Blake and Mouton, 1964; Hersey and Blanchard, 1977);
3. the use of structure to bring about change (Lucas, 1988):
    - sponsoring department seminars on teaching;

- using student evaluations for faculty development;
- department expectations for student performance;
- using course goals as the basis for constructing examinations;
- sponsoring department colloquia as the first in a series of steps to improve scholarship;

4. identifying the norms that affect departmental functioning (Feldman, 1985):

- confronting negative norms;

5. reinforcement and relationship building with faculty (Kouzes and Posner, 1987); and

6. creating commitment to departmental goals through participative decision-making (Tucker, 1984).

Just as academics have not been formally trained for their teaching responsibilities and duties, deans and heads have not formally been prepared for their roles as administrators, managers and supervisors of faculty staff; and professional consultants in higher education have not received any formal training as change agents. Therefore, the focus on continuing professional development for all staff and on organisation development is of paramount importance for effectiveness and efficiency in higher education.

The development of professional consultants

Both the role of professional consultants and their focus of attention have been discussed in the previous chapter. It was concluded that, ideally, unit staff should demonstrate and model the skills, values and strategies of the model 2 theory-in-use to assist academic staff in doing the same, to facilitate staff self-development and double-loop problem-solving and to effect system-divergent change by human agency and responsibility, rather than through bureaucratic rationality. Consultants need a wide variety of skills — technical, interpersonal and research skills — for an eclectic approach to professional development.

So how do they learn to develop these attitudes, strategies and skills? Like other academics, most unit staff have not been initially trained for their 'teaching' profession prior to their appointment. 'Teaching' refers here to all responsibilities and activities of unit staff (i.e. mainly curriculum and staff development). Whoever has had an insight into such units will agree that their staff come from a variety of disciplines, frequently from the physical sciences, but have a tendency towards an interdisciplinary, problem-solving approach. Some, but not all, have a higher degree in education and fewer still in higher education, the reason being that higher education is a relatively new field.

One could argue, then, that they are not any better qualified than normal teaching academics. Although this might be true in many cases when unit staff are first employed, it is also true to say that they rapidly develop their professional skills and knowledge in educational research through their special interest and motivation to develop their expertise in higher education. This development is also accelerated by the fact that they are normally freed from teaching students, and they can therefore devote their interests and activities to higher education development and research full time. But essentially they learn on the job. This means that any academic with a particular interest in this field, and the incentive and vocation to engage in retraining and professional self-development, is potentially qualified to occupy such a position. However, as the field of higher education advances and diplomas and higher degrees are being offered, more and more qualified candidates will be able to compete for vacant positions.

Basically, the possibilities of professional development for existing unit staff are very similar to those for academic staff, except that unit staff have organised themselves in professional associations, such as the staff development group within HERDSA (Higher Education Research and Development Society of Australasia) or within the SRHE (Society for Research into Higher Education). Let us briefly look at these possibilities one by one.

Conferences and workshops

HERDSA, SRHE and similar professional societies in other countries hold annual conferences where professional consultants and interested senior academic staff (in a minority) meet to share, exchange and discuss their ideas, innovations and research. More recently, special interest groups have been established who meet immediately before or after the conference; one such group is the Staff Developers' Group. These meetings are fairly informal, consisting mainly of sessions in which information and experiences are exchanged and of workshops in which a problem of mutual interest is solved or in which new strategies are tried out. The atmosphere is generally open and supportive (rather than secretive and competitive), as may be expected of a group of change agents who try to create supportive environments in their own institutions. In addition, there are one, two or several local branch meetings, formal seminars or workshops organised in each state of Australia and New Zealand. A fairly recent innovation is the outside-funded national training workshops organised by HERDSA (e.g. on the evaluation of departments).

In Britain, the newly established CVCP Universities' Staff Development and Training Unit (USDTU) co-ordinates the professional development of academics and staff developers for all institutions in all regions; it organises an annual conference as well as regional conferences and workshops, and provides a network for professional consultants with a large database of references, bibliographical materials, training packages and video programmes which are available on loan to institutions in Britain.

Specialist accredited courses for professional consultants can be organised by CVCP/USDTU in Britain or by the Centre for Action Learning and Action Research (CALAR, Division of Commerce and Administration, Griffith University) worldwide. For example, consultants need training and accreditation for conducting certain workshops, such as programmes on learning styles (Honey and Mumford, 1986), team management profiles (Margerison and McCann, 1990), decision preference analysis (Kable, 1988), values and world views (Hall et al., 1990), etc.

The development of professional consultants at a distance

The above-mentioned Diploma in the Practice of Higher Education (DPHE), described by Elton et al. (1986) and offered by the University of Surrey, is an appropriate induction programme for professional consultants without a formal qualification in higher education. Further development in higher education research by distance education can also be provided by the University of Surrey in Britain or by Deakin University in Australia.

Apart from these formal education programmes, there are library facilities at every university through which unit staff usually obtain book and journal publications. As members of professional associations (e.g. HERDSA, SRHE), they are kept informed of the latest developments in the field by newsletters, journals and other publications.

There are two further noteworthy arrangements facilitating development of professional consultants. The first is LABYRINTH, a clearing house for development and research undertaken by unit staff. Materials produced in units, consisting mainly of 'grey literature', internal reports, questionnaires, workshop materials, etc., are collected by LABYRINTH and listed (with brief descriptions) in an annually published bulletin which also lists the addresses of all units in Australasia and their research in progress. The second innovation to be mentioned is *Training Activities for Teachers in Higher Education* (Cryer, 1982; 1985; 1986), a series of volumes of training materials (games, simulations and other structured activities) suitable for professional consultants to adopt or adapt for staff development courses or workshops. The authors of these training materials are experienced staff developers who have trialled the materials themselves and presented them according to set guidelines (Cryer, 1981a); the materials have also been tried out and evaluated by external referees and changes may have been made before publication. An example of workshop materials for unit staff is a chapter on 'Developing Discussion Skills' (Zuber-Skerritt, 1986b) which has been developed from my experience as a workshop leader, first with students, then with staff, and finally with professional consultants at a HERDSA conference. Why is the production of staff development materials important? Cryer (1981b, 192) believes:

... the production of direct support staff development material is worth while, both for the staff developer who produces them and for the rest of the staff development community. The mere act of documentation requires that the author gives greater consideration to what he (sic!) is doing, and that in making them available to others, he necessarily conducts more trials and makes more modifications than he otherwise would. The rest of the staff development community benefits through the cross-fertilization of ideas which develop from contact with these materials. Yet, ... there is a dearth of those materials which support staff development directly.

Professional consultants are in need of continuous professional development themselves. It is important that they themselves engage in activities of training and development as teachers, lecturers, moderators and workshop leaders. They must constantly reflect upon their own performance and practice, in order to keep abreast or ahead of their teaching colleagues (i.e. the academics they are trying to 'teach' and to assist in learning and developing professionally).

Conclusion

This chapter has discussed the major methods and strategies of professional development which are appropriate or acceptable in a paradigm 2 world of higher education.

First, professional development was seen as the facilitation of discussion in seminars and workshops, guiding academic staff from habitual behaviour to awareness of alternatives and, finally, to consciously controlled action.

Second, the Excellence in University Teaching (EUT) programme, conducted as a series of workshops, was designed to provide the resources or alternatives from which the academics selected the appropriate strategies for solving their particular problem(s) of teaching. In all modules they followed a problem solving cycle (Figure 17) by starting with some sort of concern, selecting an appropriate strategy, trying it out, evaluating, adopting, adapting or rejecting it, and sharing this experience with their peers.

Third, if attendance at such a programme or of workshops is not possible, staff development can be arranged 'by post' (Moss, 1977) or, preferably, it can be organised as distance education (Elton et al., 1986). An evaluation of the latter proved that such a distance education course may not only disseminate information, but effect real change in staff attitudes and teaching strategies by relating the course material directly to their teaching practice.

Fourth, another method of bringing about change or improvement of practice in higher education is professional development through one-to-one peer consultancy (derived from 'clinical supervision'), following a contract and structure (Figure 18). The academic him/herself determines some sort of issue or concern as the focus of enquiry, then the peer observation concentrates on this issue; the observation data is analysed, the issue is discussed from the two different perspectives and conclusions are drawn for future action.

Fifth, professional development through appraisal (top-down) and self-appraisal (bottom-up) strategies are not only demanded by governments, students and the public, but they are more and more accepted by the academic community. One without the other strategy is ineffective. We have reached a high level of sophistication in evaluation strategies, but more structured self-appraisal techniques need to be developed and researched. One such technique has been designed by Boud (1980) utilising a supportive peer group. Keen (1981) has designed TARGET using the repertory grid technology for raising the teacher's perceptual awareness of his/her strengths and weaknesses in order to improve his/her teaching.

Sixth, all the above techniques are not mutually exclusive, but they complement each other. However, a more effective method of professional development was considered to occur through an integrated and more professional approach to curriculum development with the assistance, scrutiny and guidance of unit staff.

Seventh, helping academic chairs become faculty developers seems the most effective strategy for professional development staff, because it is a vehicle for reaching large numbers of faculty. In addition, support from deans and heads for promoting excellent teaching is important for successful change and job satisfaction in a department.

Finally, unit staff themselves have to be skilled and knowledgeable in order to assist faculty staff, heads and deans in their professional duties. They must undergo similar processes of appraisal and self-appraisal; training and development through the attendance of conferences and workshops held by their professional associations; through formal diploma and degree courses on campus or by distance education; and through reading and applying materials and adopting or adapting them to their needs. The authors' production of such materials, like that of action research papers, is in itself developmental for them and useful to other professional consultants.

Whilst this chapter and Chapter 8 have been based on theoretical principles and practical experiences in the past and present, the next chapter looks into the future by discussing priorities for professional development in higher education in the 1990s.

Chapter 10

Priorities for professional development in the 1990s

Introduction

In the last three decades there have been prognoses about the future of academic staff development in higher education at the beginning of each decade. For example, Piper and Glatter (1977) wrote about *The Changing University: A Report on Staff Development in Universities* in the 1970s on the basis of their 'Staff Development in Universities' programme 1972/4, and Rhodes and Hounsell (1980, 9) viewed their edited collection of papers on *Staff Development for the 1980s: International Perspectives*:

> not as astrology, but as something more akin to the work of meteorologists. While predicting the weather with a high degree of accuracy is a risky undertaking, forecasts based upon available evidence and extrapolations from past trends are quite useful in planning for the future.

Similarly, the essays in the volume by Ball and Eggins (1989) on *Higher Education into the 1990s: New Dimensions* consider the development of higher education generally from many different points of view and in many contrasting dimensions.

This chapter can only briefly outline the priorities for professional development in higher education in the 1990s with particular reference to the social, political and economic context of Australia. Other countries, especially Britain and New Zealand, are experiencing similar situations. The focus is on one major problem, namely that we are experiencing the most drastic changes in higher education (HE), industry and government in this country. There are no simple answers or recipes; we have to develop alternative approaches, theories and methodologies, social technologies and strategies to develop, train and prepare people for these changes, including our own staff.

Professional development of academic staff has become a most important issue in Australian higher education institutions in the last couple of years, especially since the government's White Paper, the Second Tier Agreement and the Aulich Report. Like organisations in industry and government after the award restructuring and restructuring of departments, we are all searching for new ways of staff development and training to adapt faster and more efficiently to the rapid changes in society, technology and economy of this country and worldwide.

This chapter is structured in four parts, arguing that:

1. Change and innovation in higher education can be encouraged by certain features of organisational climate and culture.
2. New managerial and teaching/training competencies are needed for the future and therefore alternative methods of professional development; and we in higher education can learn from, and contribute to, management education and development (MED) in business and government.
3. Action learning and action research have been suggested as appropriate alternative methods of professional development in situations of uncertainty and rapid change.
4. Priorities for professional development in higher education relate to assisting the university in:

   • the maintenance and constant improvement of high quality teaching and research;
   • meeting internal and external accountability;
   • management development and training; and
   • forging closer links with industry.

Change and innovation in higher education

We are undergoing an enormous and radical peacetime transformation. Change, 'reconstruction', 'restructuring' and 'profound cultural transformation' are topical constructs. We have seen drastic worldwide changes in the last year or two, in Australia and in the HE sector.

Politically, there have been great upheavals in Europe, South Africa and the Gulf; economically we are in a world recession or depression. This has led to social changes and to restructuring of organisations in industry, government departments and higher education (HE) institutions.

Dawkins' White Paper (1988) requests universities to develop more flexible graduates with generic skills. This requires changes in teaching. The main objectives of the White Paper are:

* *to raise participation in HE.* However, this might lead to higher staff–student ratios and problems of maintaining the quality of teaching with reduced resources;
* to take account of national priorities. However, these will be constantly changing; and
* to improve the effectiveness and efficiency of the resources used in higher education by better governance and management and greater performance orientation. However, apart from this economic efficiency, universities should also be concerned with academic and educational quality.

The Aulich Report (1990) calls for a greater emphasis on teaching within HE institutions. The major recommendations are that good teaching be promoted by:

* designating teaching a national priority; and
* requesting HE institutions to provide information on policies and programmes which they have adopted to achieve this aim.

The report also promotes a general programme for students to broaden the nature of their educational experience, including a sound knowledge of their society — its history, cultural traditions and social structures — as well as their competencies in the arts and sciences which underlie the professional practice they choose.

The major changes in HE have been based on the government's requirements for greater efficiency, effectiveness, accountability and high quality assurance (e.g. through award restructuring, performance indicators, appraisal systems and staff development schemes). These requirements have severe implications for the conditions of learning, teaching and research. Changes have to occur in at least three major areas: culture, learning and teaching, and research and development.

1. *Changes in the Australian culture and HE sub-culture.* From a conformist *laissez-faire* attitude of 'she'll be right, mate' to a culture in which learning, quality and excellence are highly valued; and in which acquired skills are considered as a 'valued added' component to the 'human resources' of this country. A university needs a corporate culture that has not a built-in conservatism, but that is open for change and able to overcome obstacles to performance.

2. *Changes in learning and teaching.* From a concept of knowledge transmission, acquisition and reproduction to a concept of learning for individuals and organisations as a lifelong process and the means by which to cope with continuous or radical change; and a concept of teaching as the facilitation of learning for change and of problem-solving in unknown situations. The role of staff development is not just training, but educating staff so that they develop their own models of teaching and management. Instead of looking for outside educational experts, academics should be encouraged and helped to become their own experts.

3. *Changes in HE research and development.* From an individualistic (often esoteric) to a collaborative, practice-oriented approach. The role of this new approach to HE research and development is to identify:

- what constitutes good practice in teaching, research and management in HE;
- what competencies are needed for teachers and managers in HE in the 1990s and in the twenty-first century; and
- how these competencies can be developed.

In Chapter 8, I have discussed several theories of innovation and change (e.g. Argyris and Schön's (1974) personal model of change, Berg and Östergren's (1977; 1979) social/political model of innovation and change in organisations, and MacIntyre's (1981) model of the dialectical relationship between the individual and the institution or between 'human agency and bureaucratic organisations').

In this chapter I wish to use some recent research findings in the management literature to point to some implications for higher education. For example, Strata (1989, 63) makes a strong argument that:

> industry's most serious competitive problem lies in a declining rate of innovation — and that this decline can be traced more to a lack of *management* innovation than to weak *product* or *technology* innovation.

So how can the climate of innovation, change, flexibility and creativity be improved? The Centre for Creative Leadership in the USA has developed a model for the improvement of the climate in which creativity can be stimulated, mainly by:

- *goal clarity*: long term-goals and clear shared vision, as well as short-term goals;
- *freedom*: personal autonomy within this framework;
- *resources*: money, information, co-operation; and

- *encouragement*: to take risks in forming, sharing, and trying out new ideas.

A very important condition for innovation and change is the appropriate organisational culture. The following are salient features of an organisational culture encouraging innovation and change:

- more receptivity to new ideas;
- faster approval, less red tape;
- more collaboration between departments;
- abundant praise and recognition (which is often missing or lacking in academia);
- advance warning of changes;
- open circulation of information;
- extra resources available; and
- the attitude that we are always learning.

In higher education, too, we have to create a more open environment of collaboration in research and teaching and of continuing lifelong learning. We have to be role models for the people we are educating and preparing for constant or rapid change.

Therefore, the role of professional development must first be to identify the skills and competencies of academics which are required to help students develop their skills needed in the future, and then to design appropriate strategies and methods to develop those skills. The aims of teaching and professional development will be to develop flexible, creative thinkers and problem-solvers, good communicators (orally and in writing) with a capacity for lifelong learning. This applies to students, teachers, administrators and staff developers, as well as to top managers in HE. We have to be a learning organisation in order to become a learning society.

New competencies for the future

Research in America (Peters and Waterman, 1982; Boyatzis, 1982; Margerison and Kakabadse, 1984) and in Australia (Limerick et al., 1984; Cunnington, 1985; Cunnington and Trevor-Roberts, 1986; Limerick and Cunnington, 1987) has identified the managerial skills and competencies needed by managers for the year 2000. In my recent paper entitled 'Management Development and Academic Staff Development Through Action Learning and Action Research' (Zuber-Skerrit, 1990c) I showed that the competencies required of managers as identified in the management literature are similar to those of academics needed in the future. For I see the role of the academics changing from one of content experts and lecturers to that of process managers and facilitators. This means academics have to be:

- managers of student learning as well as their own learning (both conceived as lifelong learning);
- managers of their fast-changing curricula in response to societal needs and technological change;
- effective managers of their institutions, faculties, departments;
- managers of the various committees and boards; as well as
- managers of budgets for their research projects, teaching programmes and conferences.

It is true that we have always performed these tasks in HE (although we might have used a different language), but in future we will have to be more effective and efficient managers of these tasks. It should be stressed here that 'management' is not defined in the traditional sense of control management (i.e. management for and by the managers, following corporate goals and strategies of productivity (doing more with less) and having little concern for the individual workers and their development). Rather, management is seen as managing and facilitating the process of people's work and continuing learning in a climate of trust, responsibility, enterprise and open sharing. For as the chairman of Sony, Akio Morita (1989, 20–21) testified:

> we don't really know what causes a terrific new idea to be born, but we know that it is more likely to happen in an open, free and trusting atmosphere...
>
> I feel that my essential mission and that of any other manager, is to create an atmosphere in people relate to each other easily, in which ideas and enthusiasm are shared, and in which there is a zest for making things happen.

Recent research at Griffith University has concluded that much of our current management development technology is obsolete and inadequate for today's organisations. On the basis of interviews with chief executive officers (CEOs) of fifty of the better run business and government organisations in Australia, and as a result of a survey of the key management literature since the early 1900s, Limerick and Cunnington (1987) have identified four models or blueprints in the history of management education and development in the Western world: the traditional classical model, the human relations model, the systems model and 'the fourth blueprint' or loosely coupled systems model.

In Table 10, I have summarised the characteristics of these models and the required managerial skills within each model. Of particular interest are the five categories of skills in the newly emerging model

Table 10   *Models of management education and development (after Limerick and Cunnington, 1987)*

Paradigm/ blueprint	Catalysed by	Characteristics	Required managerial skills
1. The traditional classical model	The Industrial Revolution and a class-based society	Formality, specialisation, hierarchy	Planning, scheduling, organising, motivating, controlling, disciplining, etc.
2. The human relations model	The Great Depression	Social context (especially the group) influencing the individual worker	Social motivation, democratic leadership, informal organisation, team development, discovery of self through group, etc.
3. The systems model	The increasing use and complexity of organisations	'Everything is related to everything else'	Cognitive skills of systems theory and contingency theory, operational skills of organisation development
4. The 'fourth blueprint', away from a tightly coupled systems model	The extreme rate of change in our time	Loosely coupled systems of action; decentralised organisations; collaborative individualism; a vison of how to integrate strategy, structure and culture	The ability to: • manage and relate to people • get things done • see the big picture • think clearly Personal maturity

which according to Limerick and Cunnington (1987, 59) 'has been developing as a response to the extreme rate of change in our

Table 11 *Examples of cluster competencies (Cunnington and Trevor-Roberts, 1986, 40)*

Cluster	Competencies
1. The ability to manage and relate to people	Empathetic skills; closeness to people; human qualities — strength and warmth; ability to get along with people; good communication; able to delegate; able to think in terms of people; to be a good judge of people; provide leadership; develop one's own people; ability to mould together a team; skills in managing, developing and training people; ability to get on well with subordinates; able to supervise autonomous individuals; able to mould.
2. The ability to get things done	Self-drive, self-motivation; people who are doers; tough-minded approach; bias for action; ambition; enthusiasm; good knowledge of what the business is about; common business sense; smell for the dollar; overall market orientation; awareness of bricks-and-mortar side of business; entrepreneurial flair; capacity to manage change.
3. The ability to see the big picture	Political skills; ability to read the political climate; having a feel for what the community is looking for; getting on well with people in the industry; public relations skills; able to read the economic climate; outward looking; able to run an entire business; able to see the total picture; the helicopter factor.
4. The ability to think clearly	Imaginative; innovative; creative; analytical; well endowed with brains; having raw intelligence; ability to think laterally; able to ask 'what if' questions; able to assess facts and reach correct solution; basic conceptualisation; sense of reality.
5. Personal maturity	Professionalism; adaptability; understanding oneself and one's strengths and weaknesses; continuing learning by self-evaluation; ruthlessness with oneself; being ethical in business practices; having a feeling of pride in the organisation; loyalty; commitment to the goals of the organisation; capacity to cope with stress; ability to work under pressure; maturity.

times. Tightly coupled systems cannot change and adapt fast enough... loosely coupled systems handle change and turbulence more effectively.'

The five clusters of managerial competencies identified by the CEOs are provided in Table 11.

In more recent years, 'enterprise' skills have been added to the managerial competencies needed in the future. Turner (1989, 33) defines enterprise skills as: 'Those skills essential to the design, planning, management and review of a project organised by the participants; whether the project be an economic, social or political venture'. This definition coincides with the skills needed in action research when planning, acting, observing and reflecting as a collaborative group of participants, rather than as competitive individuals.

My colleagues in management education at Griffith University have concluded that the most appropriate methods to develop managerial competencies are action learning and action research.

Action learning and action research

Action learning has been introduced in Chapter 3 as a basic concept of action research. Revans' (1982) concept of action learning is based on a five-stage model of the scientific method: observation, theory, experiment, evaluation and review. It is founded on assumptions similar to the model of 'experiential learning' developed by Lewin (1952) and Kolb (1984), as discussed in Chapter 6.

The common assumption of these models of learning and development is that knowledge can be gained from concrete experience or action through observation of, and reflection on, this experience or action, formulating abstract concepts and generalisations. These constructs have then to be tested in new situations, leading to new concrete experience and starting a new cycle of experiential learning (see Figure 9).

In contrast to action learning, the traditional view of learning has assumed that knowledge must be transmitted and received in the form of information, theories and research findings before it can be applied to practice. It is a fairly recent insight that the learner at any level can acquire knowledge through following a similar *process* of active search and research which specialist researchers undergo, rather than being taught and passively absorbing the *results* of their research.

Action learning can be used when no one knows the solution to the problem, and no one knows the way out of the complex situation. However, it is inappropriate when the answers are straightforward or already known, or can be found more simply, cheaply and quickly (e.g. by computer programs), and when the top person or top group of people are determined to go their own way regardless of the outcome.

The difference between action learning and action research is the same as between learning and research in that action research includes action learning, but is more deliberate, systematic and rigorous and is made public. I have presented my model, meaning and interpretation of action research in higher education in this and in the companion book.

The aims of *action research* are to learn and develop one's performance as well as to improve one's practice and to change those existing conditions and organisational constraints which impede practical improvements. This means, for example, that we need not accept government policies and reports uncritically and as given, but that we must constantly engage in critical enquiry and open debate to prevent erosion of the central values of teaching and research.

The benefits of action research, as I see them, are that action researchers can:

- solve a practical problem in the curriculum systematically and collaboratively;
- improve the practice of learning, teaching and professional development;
- improve the social context and conditions in which this practice takes place;
- advance knowledge in higher education by generating grounded theory, research and publications; and
- document excellent teaching.

On the other hand, action research can initially seem problematic because it requires:

- time (the long-term benefits are often not seen in the beginning);
- developing a team spirit, group collaboration and consensus;
- breaking old habits, traditions, inertia, hierarchy; and
- getting support from top management.

Future priorities

Futurists see the necessity for democratisation of our business organisations and a changing value system in which ethics and integrity play an important part. In this respect, business and industry may learn from HE institutions. On the other hand, as Nirenberg (1990, 2) reports, the German futurist Louis Antoine Dernoi predicts a 'blending' of jobs requiring the skills of the scientist, artist and craftsman:

> With personnel selected on the basis of education, social skills, and ability to work independently and creatively, large organisations will have the luxury of creating cultures that support

and reinforce individuals who can succeed at blended jobs. Managers will play a very different role. Instead of concentrating on directing and controlling, they will need to coordinate, coach, teach, motivate, facilitate, defend, and, from time to time, rejuvenate.

As competition heats up in all business areas and conern mounts for the economy's future, management and labor will of necessity need to work more closely together.

This requires the development of team building and group communication skills. In higher education, too, we need to develop these skills for the success of our own organisation, as well as for preparing our students to develop those blended and new managerial skills.

I conclude from my research, observation and reflection on my own experience that there are four main priorities for professional development in HE in the 1990s. These are to assist the institution in:

1. maintaining and constantly improving high quality teaching and research;
2. providing evidence of high quality teaching through internal and external accountability;
3. developing management and organisation effectiveness and efficiency; and
4. forging closer links with industry.

With reference to Figure 19, this can be achieved through the following devices:

1. The *maintenance of high quality teaching* can be assured through

   • a reward system and climate in which high quality teaching is valued and rewarded;
   • an institutional staff development policy as suggested by the AVCC Working Party on staff development in 1981 (see Table 6);
   • an institutional approval system of course design and review; and
   • opportunities and facilities for professional development as they have been offered in the past (see Chapter 9); however, we also have to develop new alternative approaches, such as collaborative action research into problems of curriculum and student learning (see Chapter 6), leading to publications which, among other purposes, serve the purpose of internal and external accountability.

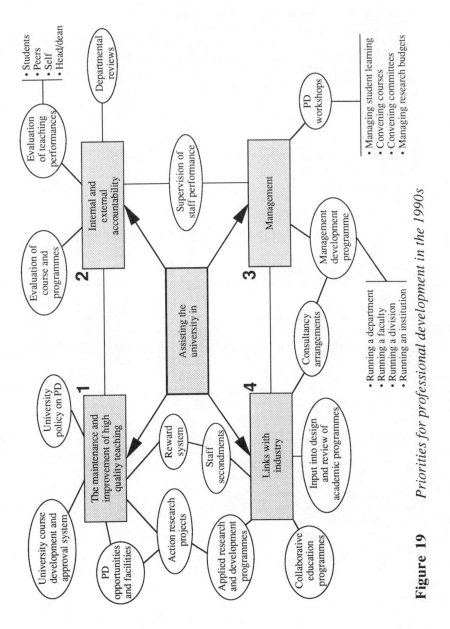

Figure 19 *Priorities for professional development in the 1990s*

2. *Internal and external accountability* can be achieved through:

- departmental reviews, using internal departmental criteria as well as institutional performance indicators;
- periodical evaluation of courses and programmes;
- a system of evaluating teaching performance, including assessment by students (e.g. the TEVAL system developed at the University of Queensland), peers, self and the head of department in his or her new supervisory role;
- supervision of staff performance which requires executive management competencies.

3. *Management development and organisation development* are fairly new concepts in higher education, both for:

- academic staff as managers of student learning, as course and committee convenors, and as managers of research budgets; and
- heads, deans, PVCs and VCs in their tasks of effectively running a department, faculty, division or an institution.

Although much has been achieved and constantly improved in higher education management, universities in 1991 are still accused of 'gross mismanagement' (Dawkins quoted in Lewis, 1991, 33).

4. *Closer links with industry* will be advantageous to organisations in both HE and industry. For example, it is important for HE institutions to produce flexible graduates with the required managerial competencies for the future. It is equally important for industry to be familiar with, and make use of, the research findings of universities, and to commission new research; to communicate their fast changing needs of graduates; and to contribute to any new curricula.

This can be achieved through, for example:

- mutual consultancy arrangements;
- staff secondments;
- co-operative education programmes;
- industry input into the design and review of academic programmes;
- applied research and development programmes; and
- joint action research projects.

In a similar way, international links will become increasingly important. For example, Lewis (1991, 35) reported three Australian initiatives:

1. Australia's hosting of a conference in September 1991 to establish an intra-regional student exchange programme within a 'trade bloc' of Asian-Pacific universities in twenty-five countries;
2. the AVCC's consideration of a model like ERASMUS (European Action Scheme for Mobility of University Students), a programme which encourages 10 per cent of university students to undertake their education in another country; and
3. an AVCC's delegation's visit to Germany (invited by the German government) to discuss links with German industry and universities. 'In particular, Australia could tap into Germany's advanced manufacturing techniques, many of which are first developed in... higher education institutions.'

Conclusion

Traditional methods of manager and academic staff training based on the model of transmitting knowledge and skills from expert to novice, using the most effective presentation techniques, have been shown to be unsatisfactory in recent times. What has been identified as necessary is continuous 'development' and 'lifelong learning', rather than a one-off 'training' course, because the nature of the work and the work situations and conditions are rapidly changing and require different competencies than in the past. In order to facilitate this new kind of learning, staff developers, heads and deans need skills in the areas of individual, group and organisational learning processes.

Recent research has shown that management development for the future has to be process-oriented, rather than merely content-oriented; and action learning has been suggested as the appropriate method to develop process managers for the year 2000. Academics are also managers (of learning, teaching, self-development, curriculum, administration, committees, budgets, etc.) and facilitators of learning processes, rather than mere transmitters of content and subject knowledge. My research has shown that action research has been considered as a more effective approach to staff development than any of the traditional methods we have used at Griffith University.

The reason for this shift from content to process is the increasing importance of responding to the fast-changing environmental forces (e.g. technological, political, economic and socio-demographic). The boundaries of disciplines are constantly extending as the content is rapidly growing or becoming out of date or obsolete. What managers, academics and graduates need in the future are not only specific knowledge and skills, but general competencies and methods to acquire new knowledge and skills to solve completely new problems.

Furthermore, entrepreneurial attitude and 'vision' are required to compete in an international context.

Since there are clearly mutual interests, common objectives and a similar approach to management development in the private and public sectors, and to staff development in higher education, it seems obvious and mutually beneficial for those responsible for human resource development to collaborate and learn from one another.

Much more research and evaluative work needs to be done in the areas of management development and academic staff development using action learning, action research and process management. We are only at the start. In this chapter I could only briefly point to reasons why an alternative approach to management education and academic staff development is necessary; how similar the requirements are; what the new appropriate methods are; how they may be applied; and what possibilities exist for learning and collaboration among the three sectors.

Conclusions

This book has aimed to contribute to the improvement and advancement of learning, teaching and professional development in higher education; to integrate educational research and teaching practice; and to contribute to the establishment of a new, epistemological paradigm in higher education. The strategy towards achieving these aims has comprised:

1. an alternative research methodology in the interpretive, non-positivist paradigm;
2. a review of the supposed dichotomy between theory and practice;
3. an integrated framework drawing on a variety of previously unrelated theories to form an alternative model of university education; and
4. an integration of educational theory and teaching practice through action research in higher education.

First, this book has used an alternative research methodology in the interpretive, non-positivist paradigm (summarised in Table 4). Since the field of higher education belongs to the human sciences, as distinct from the natural sciences, the most appropriate approach to studying and evaluating learning, teaching and staff development in higher education seemed to be a holistic approach characterised as ethnographic, naturalistic, descriptive, ideographic and interpretive. The holistic method used in this book is problem oriented, practitioner centred, interdisciplinary (but mainly quasi-historical), eclectic and heuristically organised. It may also be referred to as case study methodology utilising participant observation, illuminative evaluation and triangulation. These methods have in common that they seek to describe and explain a phenomenon (or phenomena) in a real-life situation as truthfully and holistically as possible, not only from the researcher's point of view, but from the participants' and other perspectives, with the aim of changing or improving that situation or aspects of it.   I was not a detached, objective observer as in experimental studies, but aware of the fact that my research questions and methods were influenced by my tacit knowledge.   Therefore, my meaning and interpretations of the observed phenomena had to be checked and negotiated with the participants of each study until a consensus was reached.   These negotiations were often valuable 'learning conversations', generating insights and theories which might represent a 'recognisable reality' and therefore be useful to other teachers in higher education.

Second, this book has reviewed the supposed dichotomy between theory and practice.   As a result of this review, the relationship between theory (arising from practice) and practice (being informed by theory) has been considered to be a dialectical 'praxis'.   This means that theorising need not be totally left to educational researchers, and that teaching practice is not reduced to the technical application of educational theory, but that educational theory can be formulated by practitioners as 'grounded' theory (i.e. theory generated from the reality of higher education practice and learning–teaching experiences), and thus be more relevant and 'practical' to the people at whom it is aimed: academics, professional consultants or staff developers and students.   It is my position that the value of educational research must primarily be judged by the extent to which:

1. it improves practice;
2. teachers participate and develop an understanding of their own problems and practices; and
3. it assists them in transforming situations which impede educationally desirable, rational and critical work in educational situations.

The latter requires that the interaction between human agency and the constraints of social structure and bureaucracy must be balanced by constant practical reasoning involving judgements, decisions, responsibility and 'wisdom'.   I have taken up Schwab's (1969) notion of the 'practical', suggesting gradual, not radical, change through the practitioners' own definition and solution of curricular problems, rather than through outside researchers' theories and advice.   While Schwab's requirements for the practical are merely ideational, I have shown in this and my previous books how the following requirements of his can be met in the praxis of higher education: new forms of communication, new methods of deliberation, new kinds of educational researchers and new forms of staff development.

Third, I have developed an alternative model of learning, teaching and professional development in higher education, a model based on a range of diverse theories, with the aim of drawing the mutual resonances of these otherwise conflicting theories together to a more integrated perspective: Kelly's personal construct theory, Leontiev's theory of action, Lewin's field theory, Carr and Kemmis' theory of action research as a critical education science, Argyris and Schön's theory-in-use, Berg and Östergren's theory of innovation, MacIntyre's theory of human agency and bureaucratic organisations, and holistic learning theories, such as action learning, experiential learning and dialectical thinking.

The view of the learner which has emerged is consistent with the alternative dialectical paradigm, rather than the traditional positivist paradigm (cf Table 3). He/she is a personal scientist, actively involved in the construction of knowledge through experience and a process of problem-solving. The emphasis is on action, experience and practice as sources of constantly developing knowledge, rather than on a static, analytical conception of knowledge and of the learner as a passive receiver of that knowledge. Academics and staff developers alike are moderators and facilitators of learning as well as lifelong learners themselves. They come to know and understand the problems of their praxis by actively solving the problems themselves, rather than merely by passively receiving and relying on the knowledge and advice provided by other 'experts'.

My view of a higher education institution is also consistent with the alternative, dialectical paradigm. It is an institution necessary for providing a framework and a place for its members 'to seek truth'. Its role is to create a climate and forms of communication which fulfil three main functions: it must facilitate constant critical debate about academic and other social practices; it must act as the state's 'intellectual conscience', and therefore maintain its academic freedom and be independent from the interests of political groups; and it must encourage interdisciplinary and international dialogue and co-operation in order to make scientific contributions to the safeguarding of peace in the world. However, there is also the danger of technical, bureaucratic rationality prevailing in an institution over human agency, moral responsibility and critical, dialectical thinking. The dialectical interaction (and balance) of bureaucracy and human agency is closely linked with the dialectical relationship between theory and practice and with that between society and the individual. Members of a higher education institution are not only products shaped by the institution, but they are also actively producing and shaping the institution through constant critique and changes of those constraints which impede educationally desirable goals.

The view of the learner in higher education and his/her interactions with the curriculum, with other learners (including teachers) and with the constraints of institutional bureaucracy leads to a model of higher education which is summarised in Figures 5–8. The theorem behind this model, based on Leontiev (1977), is that subjective conditions (e.g. human memory, cognitive structures and processes, etc.) and objective conditions (e.g. tasks, problems, the curriculum, etc.) do not appear in isolation, as is mostly assumed in educational research; that the relationship between subjective and objective conditions is not a static, but a dynamic one; and that this dynamic relationship is produced by *action*. Piaget (1977, 30–31) also suggests that: 'To know is to produce the object dynamically' and that action is the source of knowledge. This theoretical transformation of action in the person called 'interiorisation' has not been sufficiently researched in higher education, but is of vital importance to learning and teaching in higher education. Action may refer to mental activities (Piaget), materialistic action (Leontiev, Galperin) or to both, as assumed in experiential learning theories.

Finally, a strategy towards achieving the aims of this book has been an integration of educational theory and teaching practice through action research projects in higher education. Action research is research by the academics themselves into their teaching practice (i.e. into problems of the curriculum and student learning). In the past there has been a 'division of labour' and a separation between educational researchers studying and theorising about aspects of higher education on the one hand and academics who were expected to (but seldom did) put educational theory into practice on the other. This separation was based on an erroneous view of theory and practice as a dichotomy, instead of a dialectical unit.

This book has also tried to contribute to the integration of educational theory and practice through the development of a theoretical model of professional development as action research (the CRASP model, summarised in Tables 1 and 2 and Figure 16), through principles drawn from practical case studies of action research with teachers in higher education (included in the companion book, Chapters 3 and 4) and from case studies of meta-action research (i.e. my reflections on action research (Chapter 6) and reflections by action researchers on action research as an effective method of professional development (Chapter 5)). The CRASP model has evolved from my practice as a professional consultant; and my practice has been improved by 'grounded' theory. Similarly, the theoretical principles arrived at in each case study in the companion book book have been the result of the practitioners' reflections on their observed practice, and their and their students' practices have been improved as a result of their theorising. The circle is closed. In one school at one university at least, it has been shown that the improvement and advancement of learning, teaching and professional development in higher education can be achieved through action research. The evidence for this advancement is provided in the previously published case studies (see Figure 2).

The limitations of this book are that it relies on experience and evidence from a limited number of case studies conducted in one particular educational setting which might be different from other, more traditional institutions of higher education. As has been pointed out earlier, the context of learning is a decisive factor influencing learning, but it is not static; it may be changed by the members of an institution, if it impedes positive educational goals. On the other hand, the limitations of this book may encourage further research and development in higher education for at least five reasons.

First, other action researchers may conduct studies in developments of learning and teaching to test whether the grounded theories developed in this volume and in the companion book are valid in their own educational context. Second, other institutions might consider encouraging action research into their academic course development systems. Third, we need more action research into institutional constraints on meaningful learning, teaching and professional development in higher education. Fourth, as action research is becoming an accepted theoretical framework and methodology in postgraduate degree programmes, it is likely to be further developed. Fifth, since action learning and action research have been suggested as appropriate methods to develop managerial competencies for the future, there are promising opportunities for links and collaboration between industry and higher education, between management education or development and academic staff development.

To sum up, professional development in higher education does not only refer to individual staff training and development, but also to team, curriculum and organisation development. It can effectively be achieved within the theoretical framework and methodology of action research as experiential learning, as critical education science, and as CRASP (i.e. *Critical* collaborative enquiry by *Reflective* practitioners being *Accountable* and making the results of their enquiry public, *Self-evaluating* their practice and engaged in *Participatory* problem-solving and continuing professional development).

References

Adelman, C., Jenkins, D. and Kemmis, S. (1983) Rethinking case study: notes from the second Cambridge conference. In L. Bartlett et al. (eds) *Case Study Methods 1: An Overview.* Deakin University Press, Victoria, 1–10.

Adie, H., Fairbrother, F. and Zuber–Skerritt, O. (1986) Excellence in university teaching: a new staff development programme, *Proceedings* of the Twelfth International Conference on Improving University Teaching, Heidelberg, 603–19.

Allen, D. W. and Ryan, K. A. (1974) *Microteaching.* Beltz Verlag, Basel.

Altrichter, H. (1988) *Lehrerbildung durch Lehrerforschung. Arbeiten zur Entfaltung eines Forschungs — und Entwicklungskonzeptes "Lehrerforschung".* Habilitationsschrift. Universität Klagenfurt, Austria.

Altrichter, H., Wilhelmer, H., Sorger, H. and Morocutti, I. (eds) (1989) *Schule Gestalten: Lehrer als Forscher.* Hermagoras Verlag, Klagenfurt.

Argyris, C. (1980) *Inner Contradictions of Rigorous Research.* Academic Press, London.

Argyris, C. (1982) *Reasoning, Learning and Action: Individual and Organizational.* Jossey-Bass, San Francisco.

Argyris, C. and Schön, D. A. (1974) *Theory in Practice: Increasing Professional Effectiveness.* Jossey-Bass, San Francisco.

Argyris, C. and Schön, D. A. (1989) Participatory action research and action science compared: A commentary. *American Behavioral Scientist* 32 (5), 612–23.

Ashcroft, E. R. (1987) *An Evaluation of Traditional Staff Development Practices for Implementing Change in University Teaching.* An unpublished PhD thesis. Faculty of Education, Massey University, Palmerston North, N.Z.

Association of University Teachers of New Zealand (1979) An AUT policy for the professional development of academic staff in universities. *Bulletin* 56.

Astin, K. T. (1991) *Assessment for Excellence: The Philosophy and Practice of Assessment and Evaluation in Higher Education.* Macmillan, New York.

Aulich (see Parliament of the Commonwealth of Australia)

Australian Universities Commission (1975) *Sixth Report 1975.* Australian Government Publishing Service (AGPS), Canberra.

Australian Vice Chancellors' Committee (1981) *Academic Staff Development* (Report of the AVCC Working Party) Occasional Papers No. 4. AVCC, Canberra.

Ausubel, D. P. (1963) *The Psychology of Meaningful Verbal Learning.* Grune and Stratton, New York.

Ausubel, D. P. (1968) *Educational Psychology: A Cognitive View.* Holt, Rinehart and Winston, New York.

Ausubel, D. P. (1975) Cognitive structure and transfer. In N. Entwistle and D. Hounsell (eds) *How Students Learn.* University of Lancaster, Lancaster, 93–104.

Baird, J. R. (1988) Quality: what should make higher education 'higher'? *Higher Education Research and Development* 7 (2), 141–52.

Baird, J. R. (1989) *Intellectual and methodological imperatives for individual teacher development.* Paper presented at the Annual Meeting of the American Educational Research Association, San Francisco Ca.

Ball, Sir C. and Eggins, H. (1989) *Higher Education into the 1990s: New Dimensions.* SRHE/Open University, Milton Keynes.

Bannister, D. (1970) Science through the looking glass. In D. Bannister (ed.) *Perspectives in Personal Construct Theory.* Academic Press, London.

Bannister, D. and Fransella, F. (1986) *Inquiring Man: The Psychology of Personal Constructs.* Third edition. Croom Helm, London.

Bartlett, L., Kemmis, S. and Gillard, G. (eds) (1983) *Case Study Methods*:
1. *An Overview*
2. *Naturalistic Observation*
3. *The Quasi-Historical Approach*
4. *Story Telling*
5. *Ethnography*
6. *The Conduct of Fieldwork*
7. *Politics and Ethics of Case Study*
8. *Exemplary Case Studies*

Second edition. Deakin University Press, Victoria.

Basseches, M. (1984) *Dialectical Thinking and Adult Development*. Ablex, Norwood, NJ.

Batchler, M. and Maxwell, T. (1987) Action evaluation. *New Education* 9 (1 and 2), 70–77.

Baxter Magolda, M. (1987) A rater-training program for assessing intellectual development on the Perry scheme. *Journal of College Student Personnel* 28 (4), 356–64.

Baxter Magolda, M. and Porterfield, W. (1988) *Intellectual Development: Linking Theory and Practice*. American College Personnel Association, Washington, DC.

Beard, R. and Hartley, J. (1984) *Teaching and Learning in Higher Education*. Fourth edition. Harper and Row, London.

Becher, R. A. (1980) Research into practice. In W. B. Dockrell and D. Hamilton (eds) *Rethinking Educational Research*. Hodder and Stoughton, London, 64–71.

Becker, H. S., Geer, B., and Hughes, E. C. (1968) *Making the Grade: The Academic Side of College Life*. Wiley, New York.

Belenky, M. F., Clinchy, B. M., Goldberger, N. and Tarule, J. (1986) *Women's Ways of Knowing: The Development of Self, Voice and Mind*. Basic Books, New York.

Bennett, R. and Oliver, J. (1988) *How to Get the Best from Action Research - A Guidebook*. MCB University Press, Bradford.

Berg, B. and Östergren B. (1977) *Innovations and Innovation Processes in Higher Education*. National Board of Universities and Colleges, Stockholm.

Berg, B. and Östergren, B. (1979) Innovation processes in higher education. *Studies in Higher Education* 4 (2), 261–8.

Blake, R. and Mouton, J. (1964) *The Managerial Grid*. Gulf, Houston.

Bligh, D. (ed.) (1982) *Professionalism and Flexibility in Learning.* Society for Research into Higher Education, Guildford.

Bloom, A. (1987) *The Closing of the American Mind.* Simon and Schuster, New York.

Bloom, B. W. (1974) *Taxonomy of Educational Objectives. Handbook I: Cognitive Domain, Handbook II: Affective Domain.* Eighteenth edition. New York.

Boud, D. (1980) Self–appraisal in professional development of tertiary teachers. In A. Miller (ed.) *Research and Development in Higher Education* 3. HERDSA, Sydney, 219–25.

Boud, D. (ed.) (1981) *Developing Student Antonomy in Learning.* Kogan Page, London.

Boud, D. (1989) Some competing traditions in experiential learning. In S. W. Weil and I. McGill (eds) *Making Sense of Experiential Learning — Diversity in Theory and Practice.* SRHE/Open University Press, Milton Keynes.

Boud, D. and McDonald, R. (1981) *Educational Development Through Consultancy.* Society for Research into Higher Education, Guildford.

Boud, D. and Pascoe, J. (eds) (1978) *Experiential Learning.* Australian Consortium on Experiential Education, Sydney.

Boud, D., Keogh, R. and Walker, D. (eds) (1985) *Reflection: Turning Experience into Learning.* Kogan Page, London.

Bowden, J. (ed.) (1986) *Student Learning: Research into Practice.* Centre for the Study of Higher Education, University of Melbourne, Melbourne.

Bowden, J. and Anwyl, J. (1982) *Attitudes of Australian Academics to Staff Development.* Centre for the Study of Higher Education, University of Melbourne, Melbourne.

Bowden, J. and Martin, E. (1991) The role of an academic staff development unit after the white paper and the second tier agreement. In B. Ross (ed.) *Teaching for Effective Learning.* Research and Develoment in Higher Education 13. HERDSA, Sydney, 284–90.

Bowden, J., Ramsden, P. and Starrs, C. D. (1987) Student approaches to language learning. In A. H. Miller and G. Sachse-Akerlind (eds) *The Learner in Higher Education: A Forgotten Species?* Research and Development in Higher Education 9. HERDSA, Sydney, 105–13.

Boyatzis, R. E. (1982) *The Competent Manager.* John Wiley and Sons, New York.

Boyer, E. (1987) *College: The Undergraduate Experience in America.* Harper and Row, New York.

Brabeck, M. (1983) Critical thinking skills and reflective judgement development: Redefining the aims of higher education. *Journal of Applied Developmental Psychology* 4 (1), 23–34.

Brandt, D. (1984) Ansätze zur Strukturierung und Evaluation von Lernprozessen in der Hochschuldidaktischen Aus — und Weiterbildung. In D. Brandt and R. Sell (eds) *Angewandte Hochschuldidaktik — Konzeption, Praxis, Bewertung.* AHD, Beltz, Basel, 30–54.

Brandt, D. and Sell, R. (1986) The development of problem solving skills in engineering students in context. *European Journal of Engineering Education* 11 (1), 59–65.

Britchcin, M. (1982) Goal information and feedback information in the conscious control of human activity. In W. Hacker, W. Volpert and M. von Cranach (eds) *Cognitive and Motivational Aspects of Action.* North–Holland, Amsterdam, 122–33.

Brookfield, S. (ed.) (1985) *Self-directed learning: from theory to practice.* Jossey-Bass, San Francisco.

Brown, G. A. (1978) *Micro-teaching: A Programme of Teaching Skills.* Methuen, London.

Brown, G. A. (1989) *The CVCP Code of Practice on Academic Staff Training: The Responses of the Universities.* CVCP, London.

Brown, G. A. and Atkins, M. (1986) Academic staff training in British universities: results of a national survey. *Studies in Higher Education* 11 (1), 29–42.

Browne, N. (1986) *Asking the Right Questions: A Guide to Critical Thinking.* Prentice Hall, Inc., Englewood Cliffs, NJ.

Bruner, J. S. (1956) You are your constructs. *Contemporary Psychology* 1, 355–7.

Bruner, J. S. (1960) *The Process of Education.* Harvard University Press, Cambridge, Mass.

Bruner, J. S. (1975) Beyond the information given. In N. Entwistle and D. Hounsell (eds) *How Students Learn.* University of Lancaster, Lancaster, 105–16.

Burch, N. and Miller, K. (1977) *Teacher Effectiveness Training: Instructor Guide.* Effectiveness Training Incorporated, Sydney.

Burgess, R. G. (ed.) (1984) *The Research Process in Educational Settings: Ten Case Studies.* Falmer Press, London.

231

Burgess, R. G. (ed.) (1985a) *Issues in Educational Research: Qualitative Methods.* Falmer Press, London.

Burgess, R. G. (ed.) (1985b) *Strategies of Educational Research: Qualitative Methods.* Falmer Press, London.

Burgess, R. G. (ed.) (1985c) *Field Methods in the Study of Education.* Falmer Press, London.

Burgess, T. (1977) *Education After School.* Victor Gollancz, London.

Burgess, T. (1981) Bias is of the essence. In W. D. Piper (ed.) *Is Education Fair?* Society for Research into Higher Education, Guildford, 1–6.

Burrell, G. and Morgan, G. (1979) *Sociological Paradigms and Organisational Analysis.* Heinemann, London. Reprinted 1980, 1982, 1985, 1987, 1988, 1989 by Gower, Aldershot, Hants.

Candy, P. (1991) *Self–Direction for Lifelong Learning — A Comprehensive Guide to Theory and Practice.* Jossey-Bass, San Francisco.

Cannon, R. A. (1983) *The Professional Development of University Teachers.* The Institute of Higher Education, Armidale.

Carr, W. and Kemmis, S. (1983) *Becoming Critical: Knowing Through Action Research.* Deakin University, Victoria.

Carr, W. and Kemmis, S. (1986) *Becoming Critical: Education, Knowledge and Action Research.* Falmer Press, London.

Cartwright, D. (1952) Foreword. In K. Lewin, *Field Theory in Social Science.* Tavistock Publications, London, vii–xv.

Chalmers, A. F. (1982) *What is This Thing Called Science?* Second edition. University of Queensland Press, St Lucia.

Chippendale, P. and Colins, C. J. (1991) *Values, Caos and the Nature of Social Reality.* Zygon Publishers for the Australian Values Institute, Brisbane.

Clark, A. W. (ed.) (1989) *Experimenting with Organizational Life. The Action Reseach Approach.* Plenum Press, New York.

Clark, B. R. (1987) *The Academic Life: Small Worlds, Different Worlds.* Princeton University Press, Princeton, NJ.

Clark, P. A. (1972) *Action Research and Organizational Change.* Harper and Row, New York.

Clark, S. M., Corcoran, M. and Lewis, D. R. (1986) The case for an institutional perspective on faculty development. *Journal of Higher Education* 57 (2), 176–95.

Cogan, M. (1973) *Clinical Supervision.* Houghton Mifflin, Boston.

Cohen, L. and Manion, L. (1980, 1985), Second edition. *Research Methods in Education.* Croom Helm, London.

Coles, C. (1978) Staff development and curriculum development. *Impetus* 8, 7–13.

Collaboration for Change (1986) Special issue of *Educational Leadership* 43 (5).

Collier, K. G. (1985) Teaching methods in higher education: the changing scene, with special reference to small group work. *Higher Education Research and Development* 4 (2), 3–27.

Committee of Vice-Chancellors and Principals (1985) *Report of the Steering Committee for Efficiency Studies in Universities.* CVCP, London.

Committee of Vice-Chancellors and Principals (1987) *Academic Staff Training: Code of Practice.* CVCP, London.

Commons, M. L., Sinnot, J. D., Richard, F. A. and Armon, C. (1989) *Adult Development. Volume 1: Comparisons and Applications of Development Models.* Praeger Press, New York.

Commons, M. L., Armon, C., Kohlberg, L., Richard, F. A., Grotzer, T. A., and Sinnot, J. D. (1990) *Adult Development. Volume 2: Models and Methods in the Study of Adolescent and Adult Thought.* Praeger Press, New York.

Commonwealth Tertiary Education Commission (1981a) *Report for 1982–84 Triennium* 1 (1), February, AGPS, Canberra.

Commonwealth Tertiary Education Commission (1981b) *Progress Report on Consolidation in Advanced Education.* July, AGPS, Canberra.

Cronbach, L. J. (1975) Beyond the two disciplines of scientific psychology. *American Psychologist* 30, 116–27.

Cryer, P. (1981a) The documentation and presentation of games, simulations and other structured activities. *Simulation/Games for Learning* 11 (4), 157–61.

Cryer, P. (1981b) The production of materials to support staff development in UK universities and polytechnics. *Programmed Learning and Educational Technology* 18 (3), 190–93.

Cryer, P. (ed.) (1982) *Training Activities for Teachers in Higher Education 1.* Society for Research into Higher Education, Guildford.

Cryer, P. (ed.) (1985) *Training Activities for Teachers in Higher Education 2.* Society for Research into Higher Education and NFER Nelson, London.

Cryer, P. (ed.) (1986) *Training Activities for Teachers in Higher Education 3.* Society for Research into Higher Education, Guildford.

Cunnington, B. (1985) The process of educating and developing managers for the year 2000. *Journal of Management Development* 4 (5), 66–79.

Cunnington, B. and Trevor-Roberts, B. (1986) Developing leaders for the organisations of tomorrow. *Business Education* 7 (4), 37–47.

Danial, J. S. (1975) Learning styles and strategies: the work of Gordon Pask. In Entwistle, N. and Hounsell, D. (eds) *How Students Learn.* University of Lancaster, Lancaster.

Dawkins, J. S. (1988) *Higher Education: A Policy Statement.* Australian Government Publishing Service, Canberra.

de Rivera, J. (ed.) (1976) *Field Theory as Human-Science. Contributions of Lewin's Berlin Group.* Gardner Press, New York.

de Rome, E., Boud, D. and Genn, J. M. (1985) Changes of academic staff perceptions of the status of teaching and research. *Higher Education Research and Development* 4 (2), 131–43.

Dewey, J. (1938) *Experience and education.* Collier Macmillan, New York.

Diamond, C. P. P. (1985) Tinker, tailor, ... scientist, psychologist, student, inquirer: an introduction to personal construct theory. *The New Psychologist,* May, 46–51.

Dick, B. and Dalmau, T. (1990) *Values in Action: Applying the Ideas of Argyris and Schön.* Interchange, Brisbane.

Elliott, J. (1977) Preparing teachers for classroom accountability. *Cambridge Journal of Education* 7 (2), 49–71.

Elliott, J. (1984) Improving the quality of teaching through action research. *Forum* 26 (3), 74–77.

Elliott, J. (1985) Educational action research. In J. Nisbet et al. (eds) *World Yearbook of Education 1985: Research, Policy and Practice.* Kogan Page, London, 231–250.

Elliott, J. (1989) *Action research and the emergence of teacher appraisal in the UK.* Paper presented at the Annual Meeting of the American Educational Research Association, San Francisco Ca.

Elton, L. R. B. (1977) Introduction. In L.R.B. Elton and K. Simmonds (eds) *Staff Development in Higher Education.* Society for Research into Higher Education, Guildford, 1–2.

Elton, L. R. B. (1987) *Teaching in Higher Education: Appraisal and Training.* Kogan Page, London.

References

Elton, L. R. B. and Laurillard, D. (1979) Trends in research in student learning. *Studies in Higher Education* 4 (1), 87–102.

Elton, L. R. B., Oliver, E. and Wray, M. (1986) Academic staff training at a distance — a case study. *Programmed Learning and Educational Technology* 23 (1), 29–40.

Entwistle, N. (1981) *Styles of Learning and Teaching.* Wiley, Chichester.

Entwistle, N. (1984) Contrasting perspectives on learning. In F. Marton et al. (eds) *The Experience of Learning.* Scottish Academic Press, Edinburgh, 1–18.

Entwistle, N. and Hounsell, D. (eds) (1975) *How Students Learn.* Institute for Research and Development in Post-compulsory Education, University of Lancaster, Lancaster.

Entwistle, N. and Ramsden, P. (1983) *Understanding Student Learning.* Croom Helm, Beckenham.

Eraut, M., Connors, B. and Hewton, E. (1980) *Training in Curriculum Development and Educational Technology in Higher Education.* Society for Research into Higher Education, Guildford.

Esland, G. M. (1971) Teaching and learning as the organization of knowledge. In M. F. D. Young (ed.) *Knowledge and Control.* Collier Macmillan, London, 70–115.

Federation of Australian University Staff Associations (1981) TEC cuts — but Razer Gang slashes. *FAUSA Newsletter* 3, 22 May, 1–3.

Federation of Australian University Staff Associations (1986) FAUSA opposes private university. *FAUSA News,* 25 July, 2.

Feldman, D. C. (1985) Diagnosing and changing group norms. In L. Goodstein and J. W. Pfeiffer (eds) *The 1985 Annual Handbook: Developing Human Resources.* University Associates, San Diego, 201–8.

Fergus, E. O. and Wilson, C. D. (1989) *Advancing educational equity through social action research: a collaborative effort between universities and schools.* Paper presented at the Annual Meeting of the American Educational Research Association, San Francisco, Ca.

Ferguson, K. (1984) *The Feminist Case Against Bureaucracy.* Temple University Press, Philadelphia.

Fischer-Appelt, P. (1984) The basic functions of the modern university. *Higher Education in Europe* 9 (4), 6–10.

Flechsig, K. H. (1979) *Leitfaden zur Praxisentwickelnden Unterrichtspraxis.* Zentrum für Didaktische Studien, Göttingen.

Fleming, W. and Rutherford, D. (1984) Recommendations for learning: rhetoric and reaction. *Studies in Higher Education* 9 (1) 17–26.

Foster, G. and Roe, E. (1979) Australia: in service, lip service and unobtrusive pragmatism. In D. Teather (ed.) *Staff Development in Higher Education*. Kogan Page, London.

Fransella, F. (1980) Man-as-scientist. In A. J. Chapman and D. M. Jones (eds) *Models of Man*. British Psychological Society, Leicester, 243–60.

Freire, P. (1970) *Cultural Action for Freedom*. Centre for the Study of Development and Social Change, Cambridge, Mass.

Freire, P. (1972) *Pedagogy of the Oppressed*. Penguin, Harmondsworth.

Fullan, M. (1982) *The Meaning of Educational Change*. Teachers College Press, Columbia University.

Gagné, R. M. (1975) Domains of learning. In N. Entwistle and D. Hounsell (eds) *How Students Learn*. University of Lancaster, Lancaster.

Gagné, R. M. (1977) *Conditions of Learning*. Holt, Rinehart and Winston, New York.

Galperin, P. J. (1967) Die Entwicklung der Untersuchungen über die Bildung geistiger Operationen. In H. Hiebsch (ed.) *Ergebnisse der Sowjetischen Psychologie*. Berlin (DDR), 367–495.

Garman, N. (1982) The clinical approach to supervision. In T. Sergiovanni (ed.) *Supervision of Teaching*. Association for Supervision and Curriculum Development, Alexandria, Va, 35–52.

Gibbs, G. (1981) *Teaching Students to Learn — A Student-centred Approach*. The Open University Press, Milton Keynes.

Gibbs, G., Morgan, A. and Taylor, E. (1982) A review of the research of Ference Marton and the Göteborg Group: a phenomenological perspective on learning. *Higher Education* 11, 123–45.

Gibbs, J. C. and Widaman, K. F. (1982) *Social Intelligence: Measuring the Development of Sociomoral Reflection*. Prentice-Hall, Englewood Cliffs, NJ.

Giddens, A. (1979) *Central Problems in Social Theory: Action, Structure and Contradition in Social Analysis*. Macmillan, London.

Giddens, A. (1982) Power, the dialectic of control and class structuration. In A. Giddens and G. Mackenzie (eds) *Social Class and the Division of Labour.* Cambridge University Press, Cambridge, 29–45, 280–81.

Gilbert, J. and Pope, M. (1982) *Diploma in the Practice of Higher Education. Module J: Making Use of Research into Teaching and Learning* (Extracts and Study Guide). IED, University of Surrey, Guildford.

Glaser, B. and Strauss, A. (1967) *The Discovery of Grounded Theory.* Aldine, Chicago.

Glasser, W. (1969) *Schools Without Failure.* Harper and Row, New York.

Glasser, W. (1980) *Both Win Management.* Lippincott and Crowell, New York.

Glasser, W. (1984) *Take Effective Control of Your Life.* Harper and Row, New York.

Goldhammer, R. (1969) *Clinical Supervision: Special Methods for the Supervision of Teachers.* Holt, Rinehart and Winston, New York.

Gowin, D. B. (1981) *Education.* Cornell University Press, London.

Green, B. A. Jr. (1971) Physics teaching by the Keller Plan at MIT. *American Journal of Physics,* July 39, 764–75.

Grundy, S. and Kemmis, S. (1982) Educational action research in Australia: the state of the art (an overview). In S. Kemmis (ed.) *The Action Research Reader.* Deakin University Press, Victoria, 83–97.

Habermas, J. (1974) *Theory and Practice.* Heinemann, London.

Habermas, J. (1978) *Knowledge and Human Interest.* Second edition translated by J. J. Shapiro. Heinemann, London.

Hall, B. P. (1986) *The Genesis Effect.* Paulist Press, New York.

Hall, B. P., Chippendale, P. and Colins, C. J. (1990) *The Australasian Hall–Tonna Inventory of Values.* Zygon Publishers, Brisbane.

Harmon, M. M. (1981) *Action Theory for Public Administration.* Longman, New York.

Harri-Augstein, S. and Thomas, L. F. (1979) Self-organised learning and the relativity of knowing: towards a conversational methodology. In P. Stringer and D. Bannister (eds) *Constructs of Sociality and Individuality.* Academic Press, London, 115–32.

Harri-Augstein, S. and Thomas, L. F. (1991) Self-organised learning environments for on-the-job effectiveness. In O. Zuber-Skerritt (ed.) *Action Learning, Action Research and Process Management.* Action Learning, Action Research and Process Management Association/ÆBIS Publishing, Griffith University, Brisbane.

Harris, S.V. and Zuber-Skerritt, O. (1986) *Identifying the gap between institutional expectations and the needs of graduate professionals in continuing education.* Paper presented to the Annual Conference of the Society for Research into Higher Education, London.

Heger, M. (1986) *Ergebnisse der Evaluation Hochschuldidaktischer Aus- und Fortbildung an der RWTH Aachen* (Teil II der Untersuchungen). Arbeitsbericht Nr. 20, HDZ, RWTH, Aachen.

Heller, J. F. (1982) *Increasing Faculty and Administrative Effectiveness.* Jossey-Bass, San Francisco.

Hersey, P. and Blanchard, K. H. (1977) *Management of Organizational Behavior.* Third edition. Prentice-Hall, Englewood Cliffs, NJ.

Higher Education Research and Development Society of Australasia (1980) Statement on the professional development of academic staff. *HERDSA News* 2 (3), Supplement.

Hirsch, E. D. Jr (1987) *Cultural Literacy.* Houghton Mifflin, New York.

Holden, P. E., Pederson, C. A. and Germane, G. E. (1968) *Top Management.* McGraw-Hill, New York.

Holland, R. (1970) George Kelly: constructive, innocent and reluctant existentialist. In D. Bannister (ed.) *Perspectives in Personal Construct Theory.* Academic Press, London, 111–32.

Holly, P. and Whitehead, D. (eds) (1984) Action research in schools: getting it into perspective. *CARN Bulletin* 6, Cambridge Institute of Education, Cambridge.

Holzkamp, K. (1983) *Grundelegung der Psychologie.* Campus, Frankfurt.

Holzkamp, K. (1984) Die Menschen sitzen nicht im Kapitalismus wie in einem Käfig. *Psychologie Heute*, November, 29–36.

Honey, P. and Mumford, A. (1986) *Using Your Learning Styles.* Honey, Maidenhead (UK).

Howard, K. and Sharp, J. A. (1983) *The Management of a Research Project.* Gower, Aldershot.

Huber, L. (1981) Zur Lage der Hochschuldidaktischen Fortbildung von Hochschullehrern — und zu ihrer Bedeutung für die hochschuldidaktische Strategie. In U. Branahl (ed.) *Didaktik für Hochschullehrer.* AHD, Hamburg, 59–93.

Hunter, M. (1976) *Improved Instruction.* Eleventh printing 1982. TIP Publications, El Segundo, California.

Hunter, M. (1983) *Mastery Teaching*. TIP Publications, El Segundo, California.

Huse, E. F. and Cummings, T. G. (1985) *Organization Development and Change*. Third edition. West Publishing Company, New York.

Hustler, D., Cassidy, T. and Cuff, T. (eds) (1986) *Action Research in Classrooms*. Allen & Unwin, London.

Ibrahim, E. Z., McEvan, E. M. and Pitblado, R. (1980) Doctoral supervision at Sydney University, hindrance or help? *Vestes* 23, 18–22.

Illich, I. (1972) *Deschooling Society*. Harrow Books, New York.

Imrie, B. W. and Murray, H. G. (1980) Freedom and control in higher education — who needs a policy? In A. Miller (ed.) *Research and Development in Higher Education* 3, HERDSA, Sydney, 205–18.

The Jarratt Report (1985)—see CVCP

Jaspers, K. (1951) *Man in the Modern Age*. Routledge and Kegan Paul, London.

Jaspers, K. (1959) *Truth and Symbol*. Twayne Publishers, New York.

Jaspers, K. (1960) *The Idea of the University*. Peter Owen, London.

Job, G. (1986) *Protokoll zum Seminar Ganzheitliches Denken*. Unpublished manuscript for seminar discussions, Hochschuldidaktisches Zentrum, RWTH, Aachen.

Johnson, R. (1982) *Evaluative Studies Program: Academic Development Units in Australian Universities and Colleges of Advanced Education*. Commonwealth Tertiary Education Commission, Canberra.

The Joint Committee on Standards for Educational Evaluation (1981)*Standards for Evaluations of Educational Programs, Projects, and Materials*. McGraw-Hill, New York.

Jones, J. (1991) A (very) short recent history of higher education in New Zealand. *HERDSA News* 13 (1), 3-4, 10.

Kable, J. (1988) *People, Preferences and Performance*. John Wiley and Sons, Brisbane.

Kagan, N. (1984) Influencing human interaction: interpersonal process recall (IPR) stimulated by videotape. In O. Zuber-Skerritt (ed.) *Video in Higher Education*. Kogan Page, London, 93–108.

Keen, T. R. (1981) Raising perceptual awareness of the FE teacher: a teaching appraisal technique. *The Vocational Aspect of Education* 23 (6), 79–85.

Kelly, G. A. (1955) *The Psychology of Personal Constructs*, Volumes 1 and 2. Norton, New York.

Kelly, G. A. (1963) *A Theory of Personality*. Norton, New York.

Kelly, G. A. (1970a) Behaviour as an experiment. In D. Bannister (ed.) *Perspectives in Personal Construct Theory*. Academic Press, London.

Kelly, G. A. (1970b) A brief introduction to personal construct theory. In D. Bannister (ed.) *Perspectives in Personal Construct Theory*. Academic Press, London.

Kemmis, S. (1978) Nomothetic and ideographic approaches to the evaluation of learning. *Curriculum Studies* 10 (1), 45–59.

Kemmis, S. (ed.) (1982, 1988) *The Action Research Reader*. Third substantially revised version, 1988. Deakin University, Victoria.

Kemmis, S. (1983a) The imagination of the case and the invention of the study. In L. Bartlett et al. (eds) *Case Study Methods 1: An Overview*. Deakin University Press, Victoria, 89–113.

Kemmis, S. (1983b) A guide to evaluation design. In Bartlett et al. (eds) *Case Study Methods 6: The Conduct of Fieldwork*. Deakin University Victoria, 1–29.

Kemmis, S. and Fitzclarence, L. (1986) *Beyond Reproduction: Metatheory and Ideology in Curriculum Theorising*. School of Education, Deakin University, Victoria.

Kemmis, S. and McTaggart, R. (1982; 1988) *The Action Research Planner* Third substantially revised edition, 1988. Deakin University Press, Victoria.

Kemmis, S., Farrall, L., Baker, L. and Moodie, G. (1984) *Research Policy Review Report*. Deakin University, Victoria.

Kevill, F. M. and Shaw, M. L. G. (1980) A repertory grid study of staff–student interactions. *Psychology Teaching* 8(1), 29–36.

Kevill, F. M., Shaw, M. L. G. and Goodacre, E. (1982) In-service diploma course evaluation using repertory grids. *British Educational Research Journal* 8(1), 45–56.

King, P. M. , Wood, P. K. and Mines, R. A. (1990) Critical thinking among college and graduate students. *Review of Higher Education* 13 (3), 167–86.

Kitchener, K. S. and King, P. M. (1990) The reflective judgement model: Transforming assumptions about knowing. In J. Mezirow, (ed.) *Fostering Critical Reflection in Adulthood*. Jossey-Bass, San Francisco, 159–76.

Knight, N. and Zuber-Skerritt, O. (1986) 'Problems and Methods in Research': a course for the beginning researcher in the social sciences. Paper presented at the Annual Conference of the Higher Education Research and Development Society of Australasia. Auckland, NZ and published in *Higher Education Research and Development* 5, 49–59.

Knowles, M. S. (1975) *Self-directed Learning: A Guide for Learners and Teachers*. Association Press, New York.

Knowles, M. S. (1985) *Andragogy in Action*. Jossey-Bass, San Fransisco.

Knowles, M. S. (1986) *Using Learning Contracts*. Jossey-Bass, San Fransisco.

Knudson, R. E. (1988) Student teachers as collaborative researchers. *Teacher Education Quarterly* 15 (3), 33–8.

Kolakowski, L. (1972) *Positivist Philosophy*. Penguin, Harmondsworth, Middlesex.

Kolb, D. A. (1978) *Applications of experiential learning theory to the information sciences*. Paper delivered at the National Science Foundation Conference (on contributions of the behavioural sciences to research in information science), December.

Kolb, D. A. (1984) *Experiential Learning. Experience as the Source of Learning and Development*. Prentice-Hall, Englewood Cliffs, New Jersey.

Kouzes, J. M. and Posner, B. Z. (1987) *The Leadership Challenge*. Jossey-Bass, San Francisco.

Kuhn, Th. S. (1970a) *The Structure of Scientific Revolutions*. Second edition. The University of Chicago Press, Chicago.

Kuhn, Th. S. (1970b) Logic of discovery or psychology of research. In: I. Lakatos and A. Musgrave (eds) *Criticism and the Growth of Knowledge*. Cambridge University Press, London, 1–23.

Kulik, J. A. and Carmichael, C. L. and K. (1974) The Keller Plan in science teaching. *Science* 183, 379–83.

Kulik, J. A., Kulik, C. C. and Cohen, P. A. (1979) A meta-analysis of outcome studies of Keller's Personalised System of Instruction. *American Psychologist* 34, 307–18.

Lakatos, I. (1970) Falsification and the methodology of scientific research programmes. In J. Lakatos and A. Musgrave (eds) *Criticism and the Growth of Knowledge*. Cambridge University Press, Cambridge, 91–196.

Lakatos, I. and Musgrave, A. (1970) *Criticism and the Growth of Knowledge.* Cambridge University Press, London.

Laurillard, D. (1984) Learning from problem-solving. In F. Marton et al. (eds) *The Experience of Learning.* Scottish Academic Press, Edinburgh, 124–143.

Lenk, H. (1978) Handlung als Interpretationskonstrukt. In H. Lenk (ed.) *Handlungstheorien Interdisziplinär II, 1.* Wilhelm Fink Verlag, München, 279–350.

Leontiev, A. N. (1977) *Tätigkeit, Bewusstsein, Persönlichkeit.* Klett–Cotta, Stuttgart.

Lewin, K. (1926) *Vorsatz, Wille und Bedürfnis.* Springer, Berlin.

Lewin, K. (1948) *Resolving Social Conflicts.* Selected Papers on Group Dynamics edited by G. Weiss Lewin. Harper and Brothers, New York.

Lewin, K. (1952) *Field Theory in Social Science.* Selected Theoretical Papers edited by D. Cartwright. Tavistock Publications, London.

Lewis, S. (1991) Campus - higher education today, *Financial Review* 21 May, 33–35.

Leverhulme Report (1983) *Excellence in Diversity.* Society for Research into Higher Education, University of Surrey, Guildford.

Limerick, D. (1991) Foreword. In O. Zuber-Skerritt (ed.) *Action Research for Change and Development.* Gower-Avebury, Aldershot.

Limerick, D. and Cunnington, B. (1987) Management development: the fourth blueprint. *Journal of Management Development* 6 (1), 54–67.

Limerick, D., Cunnington, B. and Trevor-Roberts, B. (1984) *Frontiers of Excellence.* Australian Institute of Management, Queensland Division, Brisbane.

Lindsay, P. H. and Norman, D. A. (1975) Human information processing. In N. Entwistle and D. Hounsell (eds) *How Students Learn.* University of Lancaster, Lancaster, 41–51,

Lippitt, G. and Lippitt, R. (1978) *The Consulting Process in Action.* University Associates, La Jolla, Ca.

Lonsdale, A. (1990) Achieving institutional excellence through empowering staff: an approach to performance measurement in higher education. In I. Moses (ed.) *Higher Education in the Late Twentieth Century: Reflections on a Changing System. A Festschrift for Ernest Roe.* Higher Education Research and Development Society of Australasia, Sydney, 91–107.

Lucas, A. F. (1986a) Academic chair training: the why and the how of it. In M. Svinicki (ed.) *To Improve the Academy. New Forums Press for POD Network/NCSPOD*. Stillwater Ok., 111–19.

Lucas, A. F. (1986b) Effective department chair training on a low cost budget. *Journal of Staff, Program, and Organization Development* 4, 33–6.

Lucas, A. F. (1988) *Strategies for motivating faculty to create a quality department*. Proceedings of the Fifth Annual Conference for Academic Chairpersons: In Search of Academic Quality. National Issues in Higher Education, Kansas State University, Kansas City Ka.

Lucas, A. F. (1989) Maximizing impact on the organization: teach chairs faculty development skills. In E. Wadsworth (ed.) *POD: A Handbook for New Practitioners*. New Forum Press, Stillwater Ok., 157–61.

Lucas, A. F. (1990) The department chair as change agent. In P. Seldin and Associates (eds) *How Administrators Can Improve Practice*. Jossey-Bass, San Francisco, 63–88.

Luker, P. (1984) Some case studies of small group teaching in higher education. *FERN Newsletter* 12, 15–23.

MacIntyre, A. (1981) *After Virtue: A Study in Moral Theory*. University of Notre Dame Press, Indiana.

Macquarie Dictionary (1981). Macquarie Library, Sydney.

McAleese, R. (1984) Video self-confrontation as microteaching in staff development and teacher training. In O. Zuber-Skerritt (ed.) *Video in Higher Education*. Kogan Page, London, 123–35.

McGraw, B. and Lawrence, J. (1984) Developing expertise through higher education. *HERDSA News* 6 (3), 3–7.

McIntosh, J. (1979) Barriers to implementing research in higher education. *Studies in Higher Education* 4 (1), 77–85.

McKeachie, W. J. (1975) The decline and fall of the laws of learning. In N. Entwistle and D. Hounsell (eds) *How Students Learn*. University of Lancaster, Lancaster.

McKernan, J. (1989) *Varieties of curriculum action research: constraints and typologies in Anglo–Irish and American projects*. Paper presented at the Annual Meeting of the American Educational Research Association, San Francisco, Ca.

McLennan, R. (1989) *Managing Organizational Change*. Prentice-Hall, Englewood Cliffs, NJ.

McQualter, J. W. (1985a) Teacher knowledge. Part 1: Unstopping the dam. *The Australian Journal of Teacher Education* 10 (2), 5–12.

McQualter, J.W. (1985b) Teacher knowledge. Part 2: Personal construct theory as the basis of a methodology to study teaching. *The Australian Journal of Teacher Education* 10 (2), 13–20.

McQualter, J.W. and Warren, W.G. (1984) The personal construction of teaching and mathematics teacher education. *The Australian Journal of Teacher Education* 10 (2), 41–51.

Madsen, D. (1983) *Successful Dissertations and Theses*, Jossey-Bass, San Fransisco.

Margerison, C. (1989) Action learning — a short managerial guide. *Executive Development* 2 (1).

Margerison, C. and Kakabadse, A. (1984) How American Chief Executives Succeed — Implications for Developing High–Potential Employees. American Management Association, Survey Report.

Margerison, C. and McCann, D. (1990) *The Team Management Profiles Handbook*. International Management Centre, Brisbane.

Marrow, A.J. (1969) *The Practical Theorist. The Life and Work of Kurt Lewin,* Basic Books, New York.

Martin, E. and Ramsden, P. (1985) Learning skills or skill in learning? In J. Bowden (ed.) *Student Learning: Research into Practice*, Centre for the Studies of Higher Education, University of Melbourne, Melbourne.

Marton, F. (1975) What does it take to learn? In N. Entwistle and D. Hounsell (eds) *How Students Learn*, University of Lancaster, Lancaster.

Marton, F. (1981) Phenomenography — describing conceptions of the world around us. *Institutional Science* 10, 177–200.

Marton, F. (1986) Phenomenography — a research approach to investigating different understandings of reality. *Journal of Thought* 21 (3), 28–49.

Marton, F. and Ramsden, P. (1988) What does it take to improve learning? In P. Ramsden (ed.) *Improving Learning: New Perspectives*. Kogan Page, London.

Marton, F. and Säljö, R. (1984) Approaches to learning. In F. Marton et al. (eds) *The Experience of Learning*. Scottish Academic Press, Edinburgh, 36–55.

Marton, F., Hounsell, D. and Entwistle N. (eds) (1984) *The Experience of Learning*. Scottish Academic Press, Edinburgh.

References

Marx, K. and Engels, F. (1951) *Selected Works in Two Volumes,* Volume 1. Foreign Languages Publishing House, Moscow.

Matthews, M. (1980) *The Marxist Theory of Schooling: A Study of Epistemology and Education.* Harvester, Brighton.

Mezirow, J. (ed.) (1990) *Fostering Critical Reflection in Adulthood.* Jossey-Bass, San Francisco, Ca.

Miller, C. M. L. and Parlett, M. (1974, reprinted 1983) *Up to the Mark.* Society for Research into Higher Education, Guildford.

Miller, G. A., Galanter, E. and Pibram, K. H. (1960) *Plans and the Structure of Behavior.* Holt, New York.

Miller, D. M. and Pine, G. J. (1990) Advancing professional inquiry for educational improvement through action research. *Journal of Staff Development* 11 (3), 56-61.

Moore, W. S. (1988) *The Measure of Intellectual Development: An Instrument Manual.* Centre for the Study of Intellectual Development, Olympia, Wa.

Moses, I. (1985) Academic development limits and the improvement of teaching, *Higher Education* 14, 75–100.

Moses, I. (ed.) (1990) *Higher Education in the Late Twentieth Century: Reflections on a Changing System. A Festschrift for Ernest Roe.* Higher Education Research and Development Society of Australasia, Sydney.

Moss, D. (1977) Staff development by post or 'the mountain to Mohamed'. *Impetus* 7, 26–9.

Moss, G. D. and McMillen, D. (1980) A strategy for developing problem–solving skills in large undergraduate classes. *Studies in Higher Education* 5(2), 161–71.

Mumford, A. (1990) The individual and learning opportunities. *Industrial and Commercial Training* 22 (1), 17–22.

Murphy, J. (1989) An analysis of the functions of Australasian higher education research and development units. *Australian Educational Researcher* 12 (1), 34–46.

Murray, H. (1979) *Student Evaluation of University Teaching: Uses and Abuses.* Centre for the Improvement of Teaching, University of British Columbia, Vancouver.

Murray, H. (1980) *A Comprehensive Plan for the Evaluation of Teaching at the University of Queensland.* Tertiary Education Institute, University of Queensland, St Lucia.

National Institute of Education (1984) *Involvement in Learning: Realizing the Potential of American Higher Education.* Final report of the Study Group on Conditions of Excellence in American Higher Education. National Institute of Education, Washington DC.

Newman, F. (1985) *Higher Education and the American Resurgence.* Princeton University Press, Princeton, NJ.

Nixon, J. (ed.) (1981) *A Teachers' Guide to Action Research.* Grant–McIntyre, London.

Noffke, S. E. (1989) The social context of action research: a comparative and historical analysis. Paper presented at the Annual Meeting of the American Educational Research Association, San Francisco, CA.

Norman, D. A. (1976) *Memory and Attention. An Introduction to Human Information Processing.* Second edition. Wiley, New York.

Northedge, A. (1975) Learning through discussion in the Open University, *Teaching at a Distance* 2, 10–19.

Novak, J. D. and Gowin, D. B. (1984) *Learning How to Learn.* Cambridge University Press, Cambridge.

Novak, J. M. (1981) *Personal construct psychology and other perceptual pedagogies: an early educational examination and attempt at a last Deweyian critique.* Paper presented at the 4th International Congress on Personal Construct Psychology, Brook University, St Catherines, Canada.

Novak, J. M. (1988) Constructively approaching education: toward a theory of practice. *International Journal of Personal Construct Psychology 1*, 169–80.

Oja, S. N. and Smulyan L. (1989) *Collaborative Action Research: A Developmental Approach*, Falmer Press, London.

Orteza y Miranda, E. (1988) Broadening the focus of research in education. *Journal of Research and Development in Education* 22 (1), 23–38.

Parlett, M. and Dearden, G. (eds) (1981) *Introduction to Illuminative Evaluation: Studies in Higher Education.* Society for Research into Higher Education, Guildford.

Parlett, M. and Hamilton, D. (1976) Evaluation as illumination. In D. Tawney (ed.) *Curriculum Evaluation Today: Trends and Implications.* School Council.

Parliament of the Commonwealth of Australia (1990) *Priorities for Reform in Higher Education.* A report by the Senate Standing Committee on Employment, Education and Training (The Aulich Report). AGPS, Canberra.

Pask, G. (1976) Styles and strategies of learning. *British Journal of Educational Psychology* 46, 128–48.

Peabody Journal of Education (1988) 64 (1) and (2) — A double theme issue on action research.

Percy, K. and Ramsden, P. (1980) *Independent Study*. Society for Research into Higher Education, Guildford.

Perlberg, A. (1984) When professors confront themselves: the use of video self-confrontation (VSC) in improving teaching in higher education. In O. Zuber-Skerritt (ed.) *Video in Higher Education*. Kogan Page, London, 114–22.

Perry, W. G. (1970) *Forms of Intellectual and Ethical Development in the College Years: A Scheme*. Holt, Rinehart and Winston, New York.

Perry, W. G. (1981) Cognitive and ethical growth: the making of meaning. In A. Chickering (ed.) *The Modern American College*. Jossey-Bass, San Francisco.

Peters, T. J. and Waterman, R. H. (1982) *In Search of Excellence — Lessons from America's Best-Run Companies*. Harper and Row, New York.

Phillips, E. and Pugh, D. S. (1987) *How to Get A PhD*. Open University Press, Milton Keynes.

Piaget, J. (1970) *Genetic Epistemology*. Translated by E. Duckworth. Columbia University Press, New York.

Piaget, J. (1977) The role of action in the development of thinking. In W. F. Overton and J. M. Gallagher (eds) *Knowledge and Development 1. Advances in Research and Theory*. Plenum Press, New York.

Piper, D. W. and Glatter, R. (1977) *The Changing University: A Report on Staff Development in Universities*. NFER Publishing Company, Windsor, Berks.

Polanyi, M. (1962) *Personal Knowledge: Towards a Post-Critical Philosophy*. Routledge and Kegan Paul, London.

Pope, M. L. and Denicolo, P. (1986) Intuitive theories — a researcher's dilemma: some practical methodological implications. *British Educational Research Journal* 12 (2), 153–66.

Pope, M. L. and Gilbert, J. (1982) *Diploma in the Practice of Higher Education: Module L: Doing Research into Teaching and Learning* (Extracts and Study Guide). IED, University of Surrey, Guildford.

Pope, M. L. and Keen, T. R. (1981) *Personal Construct Psychology and Education*. Academic Press, London.

Popper, K. R. (1957) *The Open Society and its Enemies.* Routledge and Kegan Paul, London.

Popper, K. R. (1959) *The Logic of Scientific Discovery.* Hutchinson, London.

Popper, K. R. (1969) *Conjectures and Refutations — the Growth of Scientific Knowledge.* Routledge and Kegan Paul, London.

Popper, K. R. (1970) Normal science and its dangers. In I. Lakatos and A. Musgrave (eds) *Criticism and the Growth of Knowledge.* Cambridge University Press, London, 51–8.

Popper, K. R. (1979a) *Objective Knowledge.* Oxford University Press, London.

Popper, K. R. (1979b) Wissen und Nichtwissen, *Uni-Report.* J.W. Goethe Universität, Frankfurt, 13 June, 3–4.

Popper, K. R. (1982) *The Open Universe.* Rowman Littlefield, New York.

Powles, M. (1988) *Know Your PhD Students and How to Help Them.* Centre for the Study of Higher Education, Melbourne University, Melbourne.

Powles, M. (1989) *How's the Thesis Going?* Centre for the Study of Higher Education, Melbourne University, Melbourne.

Ramsden, P. (1984) The context of learning. In F. Marton et al. (eds) *The Experience of Learning.* Scottish Academic Press, Edinburgh, 144–64.

Ramsden, P. (1985) Student learning research: retrospect and prospect. *Higher Education Research and Development* 4 (1), 51–69.

Ramsden, P. (ed.) (1988) *Improving Learning: New Perspectives.* Kogan Page, London.

Ramsden, P. and Entwistle, N. J. (1981) Effects of academic departments on students' approaches to studying. *British Journal of Educational Psychology* 51, 368–83.

Reason, P. and Rowan, J. (eds) (1981) *Human Inquiry. A Sourcebook of New Paradigm Research.* John Wiley and Sons, New York.

Revans, R. W. (1982) *The Origins and Growth of Action Learning.* Chartwell-Bratt, Bromley.

Revans, R. W. (1984) *The Sequence of Managerial Achievement.* MCB University Press, Bradford.

Revans, R. W. (1991a) The concept, origin and growth of action learning. In O. Zuber-Skerritt (ed.) *Action Learning for Improved Performance* Action Learning, Action Research and Process Management Association/ÆBIS Publishing, Brisbane.

Revans, R. W. (1991b) *Reg Revans Speaks About Action Learning.* A videotaped interview with Denis Loaney and John Mahoney. Programme 1 in the video series *Action Learning and Action Research* produced by O. Zuber-Skerritt in the TV Centre, University of Queensland, St Lucia.

Rhodes, D. and Hounsell, D. (1980) *Staff Development for the 1980s: International Perspectives.* Illinois State University Foundation, Ill.

Rice, R. E. and Austin, A. (1987) *Community, Commitment, and Congruence: A Different Kind of Excellence.* A preliminary report on the Future of the American Workplace in Liberal Arts Colleges. Council of Independent Colleges, Washington DC.

Rizvi, F. (1986) Bureaucratic rationality and the possibility of democratic governance in education. *The Australian Administrator* 7 (1), 1–4.

Roe, E. (1986) Practical reform and utopian vision — the dialectic of development? In J. Jones and M. Horsburgh (eds) *Research and Development in Higher Education* 8. HERDSA, Sydney, 18–28.

Roe, E. and McDonald, R. (1983) *Informed Professional Judgement: A Guide to Evaluation in Post-Secondary Education.* University of Queensland Press, St Lucia.

Roe, E., McDonald, R. and Moses, I. (1986) *Reviewing Academic Performance: Approaches to the Evaluation of Departments and Individuals.* University of Queensland Press, St Lucia.

Rogers, D. R. (1982) A research network designed to promote teacher initiated enquiries relating to learning in the classroom. *FERN Discussion Paper 9.* Leicester Polytechnic, Leicester, 1–5.

Rubinstein, S. L. (1962) Das Problem der Fähigkeiten und Fragen der psychologischen Theorie. *Beiträge zum Begabungsproblem.* Berlin (DDR).

Rubinstein, S. L. (1973) *Sein und Bewusstsein.* Seventh edition. Wissenschafliche Buchgesellschaft, Darmstadt.

Rudd, E. (1975) *The Highest Education.* Routledge and Kegan Paul, London.

Rudd, E. (1984) Research into postgraduate education. *Higher Education Research and Development 3,* 109–20.

Rudd, E. (1985) *A New Look at Postgraduate Failure.* Society for Research into Higher Education, Guildford.

Rudduck, J. (1978) *Learning Through Small Group Discussion.* Society for Research into Higher Education, Guildford.

Rudduck, J. (1985) Teacher research and research-based teacher education. *Journal of Education for Teaching* 11 (3), 281–9.

Rudduck, J. (1989) *Critical thinking and practitioner research.* Paper presented at the Annual Meeting of the American Educational Research Association, San Francisco, Ca.

Rudduck, J. and Sigsworth, A. (1985) Partnership supervision (or Goldhammer revisited). In D. Hopkins and K. Reid (eds) *Rethinking Teacher Education.* Croom Helm, London, 153–71.

Rutherford, D. and Fleming, W. (1985) Strategies for change in higher education: three political models. *Higher Education* 14, 433–45.

Säljö, R. (1982) *Learning and Understanding: A Study of Differences in Constructing Meaning from a Text.* Acta Universitatis Gothoburgensis, Göteborg.

Sanford, N. (1982) Whatever happened to action research? In S. Kemmis (ed.) *The Action Research Reader.* Deakin University Press, Victoria, 72–80.

Sanger, J. (1986) *Action research and teacher improvement.* An invited address to the Canadian Association for Curriculum Studies at the University of Winnipeg, June 2.

Schein, E. H. (1969) *Process Consultation: Its Role in Organisational Development.* Addison-Wesley, New York.

Schein, E. H. (1972) *Professional Education: Some New Directions.* McGraw-Hill, New York.

Schmidt, J. A. and Davison, M. L. (1981) Does college matter? Reflective judgement: how students tackle the tough questions. *Moral Education Forum* 6, 2–14.

Schön, D. A. (1983) *The Reflective Practitioner: How Professionals Think in Action.* Temple Smith, London.

Schwab, J. J. (1969) The practical: a language for curriculum. *The School Review* 78 (1), 1–23. Cited from the Deakin University Course Guide for 1986 on 'Action Research in Curriculum', ECT 432/732, Deakin University, Victoria, 98–115.

Science and Engineering Research Council (1983) *Research Student and Supervisor. An Approach to Good Supervisory Practice.* SERC, London.

Seeger, F. and Bromme, R. (1979) Zur Untersuchung der Lehrertätigkeit im Rahmen der kognitiven Psychologie. In H. Ueckert and D. Rhenius (eds) *Komplexe Menschliche Informationsverarbeitung.* Hans Huber Verlag, Bern, 459–525.

Seldin, P. (1985) *Evaluating Faculty Performance*. Jossey-Bass, San Francisco Ca.

Shaw, M. L. G. (1980) *On Becoming a Personal Scientist*. Academic Press, London.

Shaw, M. L. G. (1984) PLANET — personal learning, analysis, negotiation and elicitation techniques. *Possible Worlds* 1 (3), 1–57.

Skinner, B. F. (1953) *Science and Human Behaviour*. MacMillan, New York.

Skinner, B. F. (1975) The science of learning and the art of teaching. In N. Entwistle and D. Hounsell (eds) *How Students Learn*. University of Lancaster, Lancaster.

Smith, L. (1985) *Aspects of the Excellence in Teaching Program in Queensland*. Research Services Branch, Department of Education, Queensland.

Smyth, W. J. (1984a) *Clinical Supervision — Collaborative Learning about Teaching. A Handbook*. Deakin University Press, Victoria.

Smyth, W. J. (1984b) Observation — towards a 'critical consciousness' in the instructional supervision of experienced teachers. *Curriculum Inquiry* 14 (4), 425–36.

Smyth, W. J. (1985) Developing a critical practice of clinical supervision. *Journal of Curriculum Studies* 17 (1), 1–15.

Smyth, W. J. (1987) *A Rationale For Teachers' Critical Pedagogy: A Handbook*. Deakin University Press, Victoria.

Snyder, B. R. (1971) *The Hidden Curriculum*. Knopf, New York.

Snyder, K. (1981) Clinical supervision in the 1980s. *Educational Leadership* 28 (7), 521–4.

Social Science Research Council (1980) *Report: April 1979 – March 1980*. SSRC, London.

Sockett, H. (1989) *The challenge to action research*. Paper presented at the Annual Meeting of the American Educational Research Association, San Francisco, Ca.

SooHoo, S. (1989) *Teacher researcher: emergent change agent*. Paper presented at the Annual Meeting of the American Educational Research Association, San Francisco, Ca.

Stadler, M. and Seeger, F. (1981) Psychologische Handlungstheorie auf der Grundlage des materialistischen Tätigkeitsbegriffs. In Lenk, H. (ed.) *Handlungstheorien Interdisziplinär III, 1*, Wilhelm Fink Verlag, München, 191–233.

Stake, R. E. (1967) The countenance of educational evaluation. *Teachers College Record* 68, 523–40.

Stenhouse, L. (1975) *An Introduction to Curriculum Research and Development.* Heinemann, London.

Stenhouse, L. (1978) Case study and case records: towards a contemporary history of education. *British Journal of Educational Research* 4 (2), 21–39.

Stenhouse, L. (1983) The problems of standards in illuminative research. *Case Study Methods 3: The Quasi-Historical Approach,* 1–9.

Svensson, L. (1984) Skill in learning. In F. Marton et al. (eds) *The Experience of Learning.* Scottish Academic Press, Edinburgh, 56–79.

Taylor, M. (1986) Learning for self-direction in the classroom: the pattern of a transition process. *Studies in Higher Education* 11 (1), 55–72.

Teather, D. (1979) *Staff Development in Higher Education,* Kogan Page, London.

Thomas, L. F. and Harri-Augstein S. (1982) *The development of self-organised learners: the C.S.H.L.'s conversational technology for reflecting on behaviour and experience.* Paper published by the Centre for the Study of Human Learning, Brunel University, Uxbridge.

Tompkins, C. and McGraw, M. J. (1988) The negotiated learning contract. In D. Boud (ed.) *Developing Student Autonomy in Learning.* Kogan Page, London, 172–91.

Topley, J. and Willet, F. J. (1976) The organization of a new university. *The Journal of Educational Administration* 14 (1), 54–69.

Trow, M.A. (1970) Methodological problems in the evaluation of innovation. In M. C. Wittrock and D. E. Wiley (eds) *The Evaluation of Instruction.* Holt, New York, 289–305.

Tucker, A. (1984) *Chairing the Academic Department.* Second edition. Macmillan, New York.

Turner, D. (1989) Enterprise Skills, New Meaning for a Broader Purpose. *In Future* 13, 33–4.

Turney, C., Clift, J. C., Dunkin, M. J. and Traill, R. D. (1973) *Microteaching: Research, Theory and Practice.* Sydney University Press, Sydney.

Turney, J. (1985) ESRC cracks down on PhD rates. *Higher Education Supplement,* November 1–2, 1.

Verma, G.K. and Beard, R. (1981) *What is Educational Research? Perspectives on Techniques of Research.* Gower, Aldershot.

Walton, R. E. and Gaffney, M. E. (1989) Reseach, action and participation: the merchant shipping case. *American Behavioral Scientist* 32 (5), 582–611.

Ward, K. and Forrester, K. (1989) Adult education, trade unions and unemployment: What about unwaged? *Convergence: An International Journal of Adult Education* 22 (2–3), 54–63.

Wasley, P. A. and McElliott, K. S. (1989) Becoming colleagues: teachers as researchers. Paper presented at the Annual Meeting of the American Educational Research Association, San Francisco, Ca.

Watkins, P. (1985) *Agency and Structure: Dialectics in the Administration of Education,* Deakin University Press, Victoria.

Weber, M. (1948) *From Max Weber.* Edited by G. Gerth and C. Wright Mills. Routledge and Kegan Paul, London.

Welsh, J. M. (1979) *The First Year of Postgraduate Research Study.* Society for Research into Higher Education Monograph, University of Surrey, Guildford.

Weltner, K. (1978) *Autonomes Lernen.* Klett-Cotta, Stuttgart.

Whitehead, J. (1989) How do we improve research-based professionalism in education? A question which includes action research, educational theory and the politics of educational knowledge. *British Educational Research Journal* 15 (1), 3–17.

Willet, F. J. (1977) Quality control of university teaching: the responsibility of a Vice-Chancellor. *The South Pacific Journal of Teacher Education* 5 (1), 28–33.

Williams Report (1979) — see Committee of Inquiry into Education and Training.

Winter, R. (1989) *Learning from Experience: Principles and Practice in Action Research.* Falmer Press, London.

Wood, P. (1988) Action research: a field perspective. *Journal of Education for Teaching* 14 (2), 135–50.

Wyatt, J.F. (1982) Karl Jaspers's *The Idea of the University* — an existentialist argument for an institution concerned with freedom. *Studies in Higher Education* 7 (1), 21–34.

Zuber, O. and Marwick, M. (1976) Group-centred instead of lecturer–centred methods of tertiary learning and teaching — an experiment in teaching sociology. *The Australian Journal of Advanced Education* (June), 10–18.

Zuber-Skerritt, O. (1985) The use of the repertory grid technique in a study of postgraduate students' and supervisors' personal constructs of research. Proceedings of the Sixth Australasian Tertiary Study Skills Conference, Adelaide.

Zuber-Skerritt, O. (1986a) The integration of university student learning skills in undergraduate programmes. *Educational Training and Technology International* 24 (1), 62–70. Also published in J. Bowden (ed.) *Student Learning: Research into Practice*. CSHE, University of Melbourne, Melbourne, 115–30.

Zuber-Skerritt, O. (1986b) Developing discussion skills. In P. Cryer (ed.) *Training Activities for Teachers in Higher Education* 3. Society for Research into Higher Education, Guildford, 77–98.

Zuber-Skerritt, O. (1987a) A repertory grid study of staff and students' personal constructs of educational research. *Higher Education* 16 (5–6), 603–23.

Zuber-Skerritt, O. (1987b) Helping postgraduate students learn. *Higher Education* 16 (1), 75–94.

Zuber-Skerritt, O. (1988) What constitutes effective research? A case study. *Higher Education in Europe* 13 (4), 64–76.

Zuber-Skerritt, O. (1989) Case study: personal constructs of second language teaching. *Educational and Training Technology International* 26 (1), 60–67.

Zuber-Skerritt, O. (1990a) The dialectical relationship between theory and practice in higher education. In C. Gellert, E. Leitner and J. Schramm (eds) *Research and Teaching at Universities – International and Comparative Perspectives*. Peter Lang, Frankfurt, 165–192.

Zuber-Skerritt, O. (1990b) Reflections of action researchers. In I. Moses (ed.) *Higher Education in the Late Twentieth Century: Reflections on a Changing System*. Higher Education Research and Development Society of Australasia, Sydney, 295–313.

Zuber-Skerritt, O. (1990c) Management development and academic staff development through action learning and action research. *Educational and Training Technology International* 27 (4), 437–47.

Zuber-Skerritt, O. (1991a) *Action Research for Change and Development*. Gower-Avebury, Aldershot.

Zuber-Skerritt, O. (1991b) Eliciting personal constructs of research, teaching and professional development. *Qualitative Studies in Education*, 4 (4), 333–40.

Zuber-Skerritt, O. (1991c) *Action Learning for Improved Performance* Action Learning, Action Research and Process Management Association/ÆBIS Publishing, Brisbane.

Zuber-Skerritt, O. (1992) *Action Research in Higher Education — Examples and Reflections.* Kogan Page, London.

Zuber-Skerritt, O. and Cunningham, D. (eds) (1986) *Student Learning Skills Guidelines.* CALT, Griffith University, Brisbane.

Zuber-Skerritt, O. and Knight, N. (1985) Helping students overcome barriers to dissertation writing. *HERDSA News* 7 (3), 8–10.

Zuber-Skerritt, O. and Knight, N. (1986) Problem definition and thesis writing: workshops for the postgraduate student. *Higher Education* 15, 89–103.

Zuber-Skerritt, O. and Rix, A. (1986) *Developing skills in dissertation research and writing for postgraduate coursework programmes.* Paper presented to the Annual Conference of the Society for Research into Higher Education, London and published in *Zeitschrift für Hochschuldidaktik* 10, 363–80.

Author index

257

Subject index